When Mississippi Schooled America in Baseball

June 2021 – June 2022

MISSISSIPPI STATE UNIVERSITY
*2021 NCAA D1 Men's
College World Series Champions*

OLE MISS
*2022 NCAA D1 Men's
College World Series Champions*

PEARL RIVER COMMUNITY COLLEGE
*2022 NJCAA Division II
College World Series Champions*

MADISON CENTRAL HIGH SCHOOL
*2021 Baseball America
High School Team of the Year*

James R. Crockett

THE NAUTILUS PUBLISHING COMPANY

Copyright © 2024, by James R. Crockett.

All rights reserved. No part of this book may be reproduced in any form without permission in writing from the publisher, except by reviewer, who may quote brief passages in a review. Inquiries should be sent to: Nautilus Publishing at info@nautiluspublishing.com. Or by mail to: 155 CR 418, Oxford, MS 38655.

Printed in the United States of America

ISBN: 978-1-949455-55-7

Nautilus Publishing
155 CR 418
Oxford, Mississippi 38655
nautiluspublishing.com

Contents

5	DEDICATION
7	A NOTE TO THE READER
14	INTRODUCTION – SOME HISTORICAL INFORMATION ABOUT THE NCAA D1 MEN'S COLLEGE WORLD SERIES
21	CHAPTER 1 – MISSISSIPPI STATE BASEBALL, A BRIEF HISTORY
43	CHAPTER 2 – MISSISSIPPI STATE UNIVERSITY'S 2021 NCAA D1 BASEBALL NATIONAL CHAMPIONSHIP
91	CHAPTER 3 – OLE MISS'S LONG JOURNEY TO A NATIONAL BASEBALL CHAMPIONSHIP
107	CHAPTER 4 – OLE MISS'S 2022 NCAA D1 BASEBALL NATIONAL CHAMPIONSHIP
163	CHAPTER 5 – PEARL RIVER COMMUNITY COLLEGE THE 2022 NATIONAL JUNIOR COLLEGE ATHLETIC ASSOCIATION DIVISION II NATIONAL BASEBALL CHAMPIONS
202	CHAPTER 6 – THE MADISON CENTRAL HIGH SCHOOL JAGUARS BASEBALL AMERICA'S 2021 HIGH SCHOOL TEAM OF THE YEAR
219	APPENDIX
225	ACKNOWLEDGEMENTS
226	SOURCES
228	ABOUT THE AUTHOR

Dedication

This book is dedicated to
the four Mississippi head baseball coaches
whose teams won national laurels over the 13-month period
June 2021 through June 2022.

Chris Lemonis – Mississippi State University
Mike Bianco – Ole Miss
Michael Avalon – Pearl River Community College
Patrick Robey – Madison Central High School

Note to the Reader

Baseball – A Family Tradition

Baseball is not like other American sports. There is no time limit. The losing team always has as many or more stops (outs) as the winning team. The catcher's defensive position is outside the field of play. A ball hit in one-fourth of the world lands in fair territory. The right and left field lines come together in a right angle that extends past the outfield wall to infinity any ball hit within those lines is fair.. Although the diamond is of standard size, the outfield can take many shapes. For example, 310' down one line and 330' down the other and 400' or 390' to the center-field wall. Unlike football and basketball, the boundary lines are in fair territory. A foul ball caught outside the playing field in the air results in an out. There is nothing comparable in any other sport. The strike zone changes with the height and stance of the batter – again, there is nothing comparable in any other sport. Substitutions can be made at any time, but once a player leaves the game, he can't return. A batter can gain first base or make an out simply by standing in the batter's box and doing nothing: – He could walk, get hit by a pitch, or strike out. A batter can also get to first base if the ball gets away from the catcher on the third strike and the catcher is unable to retrieve the ball and throw the runner out at first base.

An infinite number of scenarios can occur in a baseball game. I have seen a major-league shortstop make an unassisted putout at first base. I saw a center fielder tag a runner out between second and third base. My son Clint was involved in a play in which the ball seemed to disappear when an outfielder tried to throw him out at home plate. Dust flew everywhere when Clint slid across the plate, and when the umpire tried to determine whether the catcher had caught and held the ball, the ball could not be located. After much confusion, it was determined that the ball had lodged in the umpire's ball bag attached to his belt, and Clint was safe. At Candlestick Park, I saw San Francisco Giant lefty Atlee Hammaker pitch a one-hitter against the Cincinnati Reds in a game where he faced only 27 batters. The Reds' Hall-of-Fame catcher, Johnny Bench, hit a single, but he was rubbed out on a ground ball double play. Nearly every year Clint and I talk about seeing a play we have never seen before.

My first baseball memory is of an incident that happened when I was 5 years old. My dad, Gaylen Crockett, was a Jackson city fireman. He and I would often listen to the Jackson Senators' minor league games on the radio. The great Bill Goodrich announced those games. Dad supplemented his fireman's salary by working other part-time jobs including taking up tickets at the old ballpark located in the fairgrounds. Dad would not let me go with him to the games when he was taking up tickets. That was strange to me because he usually took me everywhere he went on his days off. Now I realize that he could not watch a small boy while he did his job, and he would get home late because the games were at night. I took matters into my own hands one day and hid in the back seat of our 1937 Ford when he left for the ballpark. When we got there, I was afraid to let my dad know what I had done. I stayed frightened and hidden until he came to the car looking for me. My mom had called the ballpark, saying I was missing and asked if I was with my dad. Dad was so glad to see me that I never suffered any punishment. I got to watch the game and learned that you didn't have to swing the bat to strike out!

When I was about 8, we lived next door to the Sandifer family, whose youngest son, Julian, became my first hero. Julian was eight years ahead of me in school, and he was a football, basketball, and baseball star at Jackson Central High School. He also played American Legion Baseball and a lot of softball. Julian took me under his wing, and I became somewhat of a caddie for him, carrying and watching after his gear. In the summer he would let me tag along with him to American Legion Baseball practices and games at Battlefield Park and to many softball games. I got to watch Julian; Bobby Matthews, who later played professional baseball; and Billy Kinard, who later played football and coached football for Ole Miss. These guys were from the same Doodleville neighborhood I grew up in, and their performance on the diamond sparked in me a love for baseball. During my school years, 1948-1960, there were a lot of good players in south Jackson, and there was plenty of baseball – Boys Club, Little League, Babe Ruth, park league, pickup, high school, and American Legion.

I never was a very good player. But I played Little League and made the

All-Star team when I was 12. I was unable to play with the All-Stars because I was sick (one of the few times in my life). I later played Boys Club, park league, and pickup baseball, and I could always hit and catch the ball. But, when I hit the ball, it didn't go very far, and when I fielded the ball, I couldn't throw it very far or straight. Nevertheless, I came to love baseball early in life, and at age 82, I still claim it as my favorite sport.

In junior high I got interested in Major League baseball and kept up with it daily with the aid of the "Clarion-Ledger" and several baseball magazines. Ted Williams was my favorite player.

In the 1950s, contestants on the TV quiz show "The $64,000 Question" could choose baseball as a subject. The show ran from 1955-58 on CBS and was later caught up in a scandal because some contestants were given answers to the questions. As I watched the show one time, a $32,000 question went something like this: "In 1953 the Brooklyn Dodgers had five regular starters who batted .300 or better; who were they? I knew enough about big-league baseball to immediately say, Roy Campanella, Gill Hodges, Duke Snider, Jackie Robinson, and Carl Furillo. That was the correct answer.

During my teen years I got to watch Jerry Alford and Claude Reeder (Central) and Guy Parker and Frank Montgomery (Murrah) perform their magic on the mound in both high school and American Legion Baseball. I also saw outstanding position players and batters Larry Smith (Central), George Keith (Murrah) and one of my best friends, Billy Ray Lea, drive baseballs all over Battlefield Park. In college I watched Jake Gibbs and Donnie Kessinger win multiple All-American honors. Kessinger played on the 1964 team that went to the College World Series. When I was in the Air Force in the late 1960s, I was stationed at Sembach Air Base, Germany. Sembach had an outstanding baseball team that played in the United States Air Force Europe (USAFE) League. One summer Sembach won the USAFE title. Slugger Dave (Stump) Jennings, who played football and baseball for Ole Miss in the early 1960s, was the third baseman on the Sembach championship team. I went to several of their games, which were played at night without lights. It doesn't get dark until past 10 p.m. in the summer in Germany!

My friend Frank Montgomery, an All-American pitcher at Mississippi State in the 1960s, recently recommended three baseball books. They were biographies of Sandy Koufax and Tom Seaver, and "Summer of '68: The

Season That Changed Baseball and America Forever." I read all three books, and they brought back great memories of a time I followed Major League baseball extensively. I like to say that I really like football and basketball, but I love baseball.

Like my dad's interest in baseball affected me, my love of the game rubbed off on my two sons, Clint and Craig. Clint played baseball through his freshman year in high school. As a 10-year-old in Pensacola, Florida, he was privileged to play on one of the best 10-12 championship teams these eyes have ever seen. Clint gave up baseball after his freshman year in high school to concentrate on football. Although he did well in football, to this day he regrets giving up baseball. He later played adult baseball when he lived in Birmingham. Had he stayed with baseball, Clint would have been on the 1984 Tate High School team that went 38-1, won the Florida 5A Championship, and was named National Champions by "USA Today." That team included Jay Bell, who played shortstop in the majors for 17 years.

When I was writing this section, I asked Clint to share some of his baseball memories. The following are some of the things he wrote:

- I've been a baseball fan as long as I can remember and recall you telling me stories at a young age about Ted Williams and Stan Musial and listening to Cardinals games on the radio (KMOX?).

- My first baseball memories are of you taking me to an Ole Miss-State game in Starkville when I was in first grade, and a Rookie League game in Odgen, Utah, when I was in the second or third grade. The first World Series I recall was the 1973 one between the A's and Mets. That great A's team was in the middle year of winning three in a row and had Reggie Jackson, Vida Blue, Joe Rudi, Bert Campaneris, and Sal Bando, among others. But I really became a big baseball fan in 1975. The Red Sox had Fred Lynn and Jim Rice as rookies. I loved them and became a lifelong fan. They broke my heart many times, but it has paid off four times since 2004. My boys [Will and Wes] are both big fans, so we have three generations of Sox fans in the family. We are a little more rabid than you.

- You wrote about the 10-12-year-old team I was on. I was the lone 10-year-old, so I usually got one at-bat and to play one inning in the field, but I was so proud to be on that team, and my Mohawk windbreaker was one of the most-prized possessions I've ever had.

- The first Major League game I ever attended was in Fulton County Stadium around 1977. It was between the Braves and Phillies. I know the Phillies won; Bob Tolan hit a home run, and I got lost at some point.

- I made baseball road trips while I was in college to St. Louis, Dallas, and Houston. The day after I graduated, David Blount, William Foushee, and I drove toward New York and saw games at Yankee Stadium and Shea Stadium before heading up to Boston to visit Fenway Park.

- When I got the very first bonus in my professional career, I used part of it for Janna [his wife] and me to fly up for the final two games of the 1991 World Series between the Twins and the Braves. They both proved to be historic in what is considered by many to be the best World Series ever. Kirby Puckett hit a walk-off home run in the 11th inning of game six. In game seven Jack Morris and John Smoltz both threw nine shutout innings. Morris went on to throw another shutout inning in the 10th, and the Twins won it in the bottom of the 10th against Braves relievers.

- I've been to over 30 major league ballparks in my life. In many cities, I've been to both the older and newer ones. In Atlanta I've been to three.

- Almost every quarter I got my hands on as a kid was spent on baseball cards. I accumulated thousands and spent countless hours going through them in my room and creating games with them. My boys now have them.

My second son, Craig, was born with two heart defects. One was fixed when he was 10 months old by surgery, and the other one was fixed by surgery when he was 7 years old. As you can understand, he had a limited baseball career as a youngster. Our family moved from Pensacola, where I was an accounting professor at the University of West Florida (UWF), to Oxford in 1977 when I joined the accounting faculty at Ole Miss. Craig became friends with Tim Mullins, whose father, Leroy Mullins, was Ole Miss's head athletic trainer. Leroy would let Tim and Craig go to football practice and help out. Craig loved it and ended up becoming an athletic trainer. When I accepted the position of chairman of the Department of Finance and Accounting at UWF in 1979, we moved back to Pensacola.

Craig worked as a student trainer with the Tate High School football team in the fall of 1983, and future Major League shortstop Jay Bell asked him to work with the 1984 baseball team. Craig was a student trainer with the 1984 state and national champions. He has a ring to prove the state championship. Craig also served as student trainer on Tate's 1985 and 1986 baseball teams. The 1986 team, featuring Travis Fryman, won another 5A state championship, and Craig got another ring. Over a 12-year major league career, Travis Fryman played shortstop for Tate and third base for both the Detroit Tigers and the Cleveland Indians. He now serves as a hitting instructor for the Cleveland Guardians farm system. (Both Jay Bell and Travis Fryman gave numerous free major league baseball game tickets to the Crockett family.)

Craig's interest in baseball and athletic training didn't stop with high school. In 1987 I left UWF to become director of the University of Southern Mississippi's (USM) School of Professional Accountancy. We moved to Hattiesburg, which was great for Craig. USM has an outstanding athletic training program. Craig soon had himself an athletic training scholarship to USM. In addition to football and track, Craig worked with USM's baseball program during his college career. Upon graduation he passed the rigorous Board of Certification (BOC) exam, which is offered by the National Athletic Trainers' Association. He went on to practice in Louisiana as a certified athletic trainer for a few years before transitioning to the business world.

Clint's sons, Will and Wes Crockett, both played travel ball at Jackson Academy. Will was the catcher on the JA team that won the 2011 Mississippi Association of Independent Schools (MAIS) 3A state championship. He has a ring to prove it. This past summer Will and Wes played adult baseball in Nashville. Craig's son, Brandon, turned an unassisted triple play in T-ball, and the lefty pitched a perfect game when he was about 12. Brandon went on to play baseball for Northwest Rankin High School and a travel team that won a state championship tournament.

I have taken my sons and/or grandsons to major league baseball games in Tampa, Atlanta, Baltimore, Philadelphia, Washington, Boston, Toronto, St. Louis, Milwaukee, Chicago, Kansas City, and Denver. Without them I have been to Major League games in New York; Houston and Arlington, Texas; and in San Franciso and Anaheim, California. My grandsons and I also visited the Baseball Hall of Fame in Cooperstown, New York, and the Negro Leagues Baseball Museum in Kansas City. The Crockett family loves baseball.

Why This Book

The Mississippi State Bulldogs won the NCAA D1 Men's College World Series (CWS) and the National Collegiate Baseball Championship in June 2021. When Ole Miss won the 2022 NCAA Coral Gables Regional, and Southern Mississippi won the Hattiesburg Regional, it became a certainty that Mississippi would have a team in the Men's College World Series in 2022. The two teams would play each other in the Hattiesburg Super Regional, and the winner would advance to the Men's College World Series.

Southern Miss finished the regular season with a 43-16 record and ranked #10 in the country in the coaches' poll. During the season Southern Miss had ranked as high as #5. Ole Miss started the season ranked #3 and rose to #1 on March 14. But the Rebels suffered a bad mid-season slump and finished the regular season with a 32-22 record. Ole Miss was nowhere to be found in the rankings at the close of the regular season. The Rebels barely made it to the NCAA D1 Baseball Tournament. They were the 33rd and the last at-large team to be invited to the tournament.

Ole Miss swept the Coral Gables Regional, defeating Arizona 7-4, Miami 2-1, and Arizona 22-6. Southern Miss won the Hattiesburg Regional, defeating Army 2-0, losing to LSU 7-6, and then coming out of the losers' bracket by beating Kennesaw State 4-3 in 10 innings. The Golden Eagles went on to defeat LSU twice, 8-4 and 8-7, to take the title. The NCAA matched the winners of the Coral Gables Regional and the Hattiesburg Regional in the Hattiesburg Super Regional. Ole Miss swept the Super Regional and earned the right to compete in the CWS.

My sons and I love baseball. We are especially interested in Mississippi college baseball. I graduated from Ole Miss and Mississippi State, and I have taught at Ole Miss and Southern Miss. Clint graduated from Ole Miss, and Craig graduated from Southern Miss. Craig majored in athletic training at Southern Miss, and during his senior year he served as a student trainer for the baseball team. Although I had attended hundreds of Ole Miss, Mississippi State, and Southern Miss baseball games, and all three schools had previously played in the CWS, I had never been to the CWS, usually because I was working. I wanted to see a Mississippi team play in the CWS, and at 80 years of age, I felt my time was running out. Because the winner of the Hattiesburg Super Regional would automatically qualify for the CWS, Clint and Craig conspired to make sure I was there. If Southern Miss won the Super Regional, Craig would take me. If Ole Miss won, Clint would take me. What a deal for this lifelong baseball fan!

When Ole Miss won the Super Regional, Clint and I set out for Omaha on Friday, June 17, 2022. While driving to the CWS, we discussed how amazing it was that the unranked Rebels were even in the field. We knew they were hot and that they had great talent and excellent coaching. (There were good reasons they were ranked #1 early in the season.) We decided that the Rebels could win the CWS and the national championship. I told Clint that if the Rebels actually won, I was going to write a book about Mississippi State and Ole Miss winning back-to-back college baseball national championships.

We planned to see each of the Rebels' games no matter how long it took. Clint's job allowed him to perform his work via phone and the internet, and I had retired completely the past December. Clint had a lot of hotel points we could use for lodging, and as a retired Air Force Reserve officer, I could get cheap lodging at nearby Offutt AFB. It's a good thing our lodging wasn't too expensive because we stayed eight nights in Omaha and two on the road.

Ole Miss played six games in the CWS and won all but one on their way to the national championship. The final tally for the season was 42-23 and the Rebels were ranked #1 in the final coaches', Baseball America, Collegiate America, National Collegiate Baseball Writers Association, and D1 baseball polls. This was amazing because Ole Miss was unranked in all of these polls after the regular season!

But there is more to celebrate about Mississippi and baseball during the 2021 and 2022 seasons. In June 2022 Pearl River Community College won the National Junior College Athletic Association (NJCAA) Division II National Championship, and in 2021 Madison Central High School was named Baseball America's High School Team of the Year.

During the 13 months between June 2021 through June 2022, two Mississippi public universities and a Mississippi public community college won national baseball championships. In addition, a Mississippi public high school's baseball team was named the High School Team of the Year by Baseball America. Nothing like this had ever happened before in the history of college and high school baseball. It is highly improbable that one state's schools will ever experience such success in the future. I had to write this book!

Some Historical Information about the
NCAA College Baseball World Series (CWS)

The term "Baseball World Series" is trademarked by Major League Baseball, and it is licensed to the NCAA.

The NCAA College World Series was first played in 1947 at Hyames Field on the campus of Western Michigan University in Kalamazoo, Michigan. Eight teams were selected to participate in the NCAA tournament, four from the eastern part of the country and four from the west. Committees from eight regions selected their representatives. Some teams were chosen based on playoffs; some committees chose conference champions, and some simply selected their representatives. The eight teams were placed in east and west brackets, and the brackets played single-elimination tournaments. The Eastern bracket, which was played at Yale Field in New Haven, Connecticut, included NYU, Yale, Clemson, and Illinois. The Western bracket, played in Denver, was made up of California, Colorado, Oklahoma, and Texas. Yale and California won their brackets and faced each other in the finals, which had a best-of-three format. California won 17-8 and 8-7. Future President George Bush played first base for the runner-up Yale team.

The 1948 CWS was also played in Kalamazoo, and the 1949 series was played at Lawrence Stadium in Wichita, Kansas. In 1950 the CWS was moved to Omaha, Nebraska, and it has been there ever since. The tournament was played in Rosenblatt Stadium from 1950 until 2010. Since 2011 it has been played in Charles Schwab Field Omaha, which was originally TD Ameritrade Field Omaha. The stadium seats 24,000.

The format of the NCAA Baseball Tournament and the CWS has been changed several times. In 1948 the two, four-team east and west playoffs were changed to double-elimination tournaments. In 1949 the finals included the four remaining teams from eight NCAA district tournaments. A double-elimination format was employed. From 1950 through 1953 there were no preliminary rounds. The eight-team double-elimination CWS was the entire NCAA tournament. The teams came from the eight existing NCAA districts. Selection committees in each of the districts chose their representatives based on their own criteria. In 1954 NCAA Division 1 baseball began having preliminary rounds to qualify eight teams for the CWS. From 1954 until 1987, the number of teams in the preliminary rounds changed frequently and went from a low of 21 to a high of 48.

From 1988-1998 the CWS had two four-team, double-elimination brackets. The winners of the brackets played each other in a single championship game. This flawed format was designed to accommodate television. Because there was no double-elimination championship series, two teams, say A & B, could play through CWS, each having lost only one game, and one team would go home the champion. The other would go home the runner-up. This would occur if A went undefeated in its bracket, and B came out of the losers' bracket to win its bracket, and then B beat A in the one-game championship round. In 1987 and 1988 there were 48 teams in the field. Eight, six-team regional tournaments were played, with the winners advancing to the CWS.

In 1999 the field was expanded to 64 teams. The top 16 seeds now host four-team, double-elimination regional tournaments. The winners of the regionals advance to eight Super Regionals and play a best two-of-three series to determine which team advances to the CWS. The CWS teams are placed in two, four-team brackets that play a double-elimination format, and since 2003, the winners have played a best two-of-three championship series.

The 2022 CWS marked the 75th year the NCAA has crowned a national college baseball champion. Mississippi State University is one of 13 schools that have appeared in the CWS 12 times or more. Ole Miss is one of 29 schools that have appeared in the CWS six times or more.

Surprisingly, the CWS had been played 43 years before the first SEC school won the championship. Georgia defeated Oklahoma State in 1990. But since 1990 SEC schools have dominated the CWS, winning 15 of the 34 championships. Now seven SEC schools have won CWS championships. LSU has won seven, while both South Carolina and Vanderbilt have won two each. Georgia, Florida, Mississippi State, and Ole Miss have won one each. Other conferences whose teams have won CWS since 1990 are the Golden Coast Conference, the Big 12, the Big West, the PAC 12, the Big East, the WAC, the ACC, and the Big South. The PAC 12 comes in second to the SEC. Since 1990 five PAC 12 schools have won the CWS.

Since 1982 the NCAA has conducted a championship tournament for Division 1 Women's Softball, which is called the Women's College World Series (WCWS). In 2008 the NCAA Division 1 Baseball College World Series was renamed the Men's College World Series. Whenever the terms College World Series and CWS are used in this book, both terms will refer to the NCAA Men's College World Series.

Mississippi State University

CHAPTER 1
Mississippi State Baseball, a Brief History

The Agricultural and Mechanical College of the State of Mississippi was established as a land-grant college in 1878. Classes began in the fall of 1880. Originally called Mississippi A&M, the school changed its name to Mississippi State College in 1932 and to Mississippi State University in 1958. Mississippi A&M fielded its first baseball team in 1885. Coached by W.J. (Will) Jennings, the team posted a perfect 3-0 record. Except for the years 1894, 1898, 1900, 1901, 1944 and 1945, the institution has fielded a baseball team ever since. Mississippi A&M was a member of the Southern Intercollegiate Athletic Association from 1904 to 1920, and the Aggies finished first in the association three times: 1909, 1911, and 1918. From 1921 to 1932 the school played in the Southern Conference and finished first in the conference three times: 1921, 1922, and 1924.

Since 1933 State has been a member of the Southeastern Conference and has won 11 SEC baseball championships: 1948, 1949, 1965, 1966, 1970, 1971, 1979, 1985, 1987, 1989, and 2016. The first six of these championships were won in playoffs. Since the SEC Baseball Tournament was introduced in 1977, MSU has won seven tournament championships: 1979, 1985, 1987, 1990, 2001, 2005, and 2102. The six championships won in playoffs and the seven won in the SEC Tournaments, 13 in total, are more postseason SEC Baseball Championships than any other conference school has won.

This book deals primarily with how MSU fared when there was an opportunity to win an official NCAA baseball championship. That opportunity began in 1947 when the first NCAA Baseball Tournament and the College World Series were played.

In 1949 Coach R.P. (Doc) Patty took his SEC champions to the NCAA District III Baseball Tournament. They failed to advance in the double-elimination tournament, where they won a game and lost two. In 1953 Petty took State back to the NCAA District III Tournament, where they suffered the same fate.

Paul Gregory

Paul Gregory became head baseball coach at Mississippi State in 1957. He posted a 328-200-1 record over a 17-year career. Gregory's teams won SEC Championships in 1965, 1966, 1970, and 1971. His 1970 team won the SEC Championship and played in the NCAA District III Tournament, where they went 2-2. Coach Gregory's 1971 team was 32-12 overall and 13-5 in the SEC. They won the SEC title and the NCAA District III Championship and were the first MSU team to advance to the College World Series, where they lost to Tulsa 5-2 and BYU 3-1. Coach Gregory retired after the 1974 season, and his record landed him in the American Baseball Coaches Association Hall of Fame and the Mississippi Sports Hall of Fame.

Paul (Pop) Gregory was born in Tomnolen, Mississippi, in June 1908, and died in Southaven, Mississippi, in September 1999. His 91-year life centered around sports, and he saw many successes. Gregory lettered in baseball, basketball, and football at Mississippi State from 1926-1930. In 1931 he pitched for the Class A Minor League Atlanta Crackers and in 1931 and 1932, he pitched for the Chicago White Sox. Over his major league career, he compiled a 9-14 record and a 4.74 earned run average. The highlight of his brief time in the majors was a 1933 victory over Red Ruffing and the New York Yankees. In that game Gregory gave up only one run in seven-plus innings and retired Babe Ruth five consecutive times. In 1934 he was back in the minors, where he spent nine years before joining the Navy in 1943. Discharged from the Navy at the end of World War II, he returned to Minor League Baseball for the 1946 and 1947 seasons.

Mississippi State Athletic Director Dudy Noble hired Gregory to coach the university's basketball team in 1947. Coaching basketball turned out not to be Gregory's strong suit. Over nine seasons his basketball teams won only 58 games and lost 100. He had only two winning seasons: 1951-52 (12-11) and 1953-54 (11-10). His best record against SEC competition was 6-10, which were marks posted by both his 1947-48 and 1949-50 squads. Dudy Noble made a brilliant move in 1955 when he hired Babe McCarthy as head basketball coach and named Paul Gregory head baseball coach. Gregory's accomplishments as a baseball coach and McCarthy's as a basketball coach would put both men in the Mississippi Sports Hall of Fame.

There is no template for how one should approach the job of being a head coach in any college sport. Some successful coaches are screamers, and they appear to be trying to intimidate their players into performing at the height of their potential. Others never raise their voice. Some are encouragers and like to praise good performances while pointing out and demonstrating in non-intimidating ways how a player's performance can be improved. Some successful coaches are hyper, and some are laid back. Some stress technical proficiency while others are more motivational.

How did Paul Gregory become such a successful baseball coach when he had been, to put it politely, an unsuccessful basketball coach? I suspect that it was the Jimmies and Joes, not the X's and O's. That is, he coached good baseball players but not-so-good basketball players. Interviews with Frank Montgomery and Doug Hutton, who pitched for Gregory during the 1960-1964 time period, confirmed what I had suspected. The players nicknamed Gregory "Square Deal," often shortened to "Deal." As he would recruit a player to come to MSU to play baseball, he would always say something like this: "If you come to Mississippi State, I promise you a square deal."

Starting with good athletes who had usually been well-coached in high school, Gregory did very little in the way of teaching fundamentals. His practices were informal, as he would often ask his pitchers, "Who wants to pitch batting practice today?" Gregory would also say to his pitchers, "Tell me when you are ready to pitch or start," and he would put them in games when they said they were ready. This style worked for Paul Gregory when he coached baseball.

Coach Gregory's 1970 SEC Champion team posted a 32-8 overall record, the best in MSU history at the time. They were led by two outstanding senior pitchers, Brantley Jones and Dennis Hall. In 57 innings pitched, Hall allowed four earned runs to produce an 0.63 earned run average. Jones won nine games and lost none. The Dogs made it to the NCAA District III Tournament, where they lost to Maryland 3-2, beat East Carolina 12-6, beat Maryland 8-4, and lost to Florida State 5-4. This was an amazing performance, considering the circumstances. The NCAA ruled four senior MSU players (Brantley Jones, Dennis Hall, first baseman Jocko Potts, and third baseman Bill Robie) ineligible for the tournament.. All four had played varsity baseball as freshmen, and the NCAA allowed only three years of eligibility at the time. Had these four mainstays been able to play, MSU would have been a good bet to make it to the CWS.

Then came 1971 and Coach Gregory's SEC Champion team was not to be denied. The Bulldogs tied the school record of 32 wins. Among those wins were 13 SEC victories. The team was stacked with outstanding athletes, and they led the Bulldogs to MSU's first CWS. All-American Phil Still dominated the SEC offensively, leading the league in home runs with 11, RBIs 37, and runs scored 42. Still also fielded .972, which remains an MSU record for third basemen. Still had a lot of help, as the 1971 lineup was populated by three other All-Americans, infielder Bobby Croswell, catcher Dave Phares, and outfielder Ted Milton. Senior Mike Proffitt, one of the best pitchers in MSU history, was the team's ace. Proffitt completed his career having pitched 36 complete games including 11 shutouts.

The eight teams in the 1971 College World Series were Brigham Young University, Harvard, Mississippi State, Pan American, Seton Hall, Southern Illinois, Tulsa, and Southern California. MSU lost to Tulsa 5-2 and to BYU 3-1. Southern California won the title by defeating Southern Illinois 7-2. Although the Bullies were two and out in their CWS, they showed they belonged.

Against Tulsa's starting pitcher, Steve Rogers, a future 13-year major leaguer with the Montreal Expos, MSU batters stroked nine hits including a double, a triple, and an inside-the-park home run by All-American third baseman Phil Still. Still's homer snapped an almost unbelievable streak of 35 shutout innings pitched by Tulsa's great righthander, Steve Rogers. Interestingly, after the game, MSU hitters still rated Southern Miss's Ray Guy (yes, that Ray Guy) as the toughest pitcher they faced all year.

MSU then faced the Cougars of Brigham Young University, who had lost to Harvard in the losers' bracket. MSU's Mike Proffitt pitched eight innings and gave up six hits and three runs. The Bulldogs scored a run in the fifth inning and led 1-0 going into the bottom of the eighth. Proffitt retired the first two batters and then gave up a single, a walk, and a home run. MSU had 10 hits to BYU's six, but the Dawgs left nine runners on base while BYU left only four. MSU failed to score in the ninth, and the 3-1 defeat sent them back to Starkville. BYU was sent home when they lost to Southern California 8-6. Southern California won the title by defeating Southern Illinois in the final game.

In MSU's first appearance in the CWS, Paul Gregory's Bulldogs collected 19 hits over two games, scored only three runs, and left 19 runners on base. It was a story of what might have been. The Bulldogs gave up only eight runs, and they showed that they belonged among the elite of college baseball. Over the next 50 years MSU would send 11 more teams to the CWS before finally winning the title in 2021.

Ron Polk – The Godfather of SEC Baseball

Ron Polk is the winningest coach in Mississippi State University and the winningest coach in any sport in the history of the Southeastern Conference. Over five decades he reached the CWS nine times with four schools, once as an assistant coach at the University of Arizona, once as head coach at Georgia Southern University, once as head coach at the University of Georgia, and six times as head coach at MSU. Polk is one of only three coaches who have taken three different schools to the CWS. He is a former president of the American Baseball Coaches Association (ABCA) and served in the Marine Corps Reserve during the Vietnam War. He was named the National Coach of the Year in 1973 and 1985 and SEC Coach of the Year five times. Coach Polk has been inducted into the American Baseball Coaches Hall of Fame, the College Baseball Hall of Fame, the Mississippi State Sports Hall of Fame, and the Mississippi Sports Hall of Fame. He served seven times as a coach for the USA National Team, twice as head coach. Two of the national teams he coached represented the United States in the Olympic Games. Today he serves as special assistant to the athletic director at MSU.

Born in Boston, Massachusetts, on January 12, 1944, Ron Polk played baseball at Grand Canyon University and went to the University of Arizona on a graduate assistantship. While at Arizona he asked Coach Frank Sancet if he could help and ended up as the Wildcats' third-base coach. As they say, the rest is history. He earned a master's degree from Arizona and went to the University of New Mexico to work on a doctorate. Baseball intervened, and he left New Mexico after one year to accept a position as assistant baseball coach at Miami Dade Community College under Head Coach Charlie Greene. Polk moved up to hold the position of assistant coach at the University of Miami for one season.

From Miami, Polk went to Georgia Southern for his first head coaching job. From 1972-1975 Georgia Southern had themselves a gem of a coach. During Coach Polk's four seasons as the Eagles' coach, his teams posted a 155-64 record. They won 30-plus games two seasons and 40-plus games two seasons. In his second year, the Eagles went 43-12 and earned a trip to the CWS. In his third year, GSU went 47-14 and earned a spot in an NCAA Regional Tournament.

In 1975 Polk accepted the head coaching position at MSU. Polk's first year as head coach was 1976. The man who has been justly labeled the Father of Southeastern Conference Baseball would soon change MSU and SEC baseball forever. He resigned from MSU in 1997 after taking his team to the College World Series. He was disgusted by the way the NCAA treated college baseball and was determined to take on the ruling body of big-time college sports.

Under Coach Polk, MSU was the first school in the SEC to have a baseball radio network, and Coach Polk was the first to have his own TV show. Early wins brought bigger and better crowds. Polk told players he would put them in the best uniforms, have them play in the best venues, and that he wanted them to look like first-class American men in the way they handled themselves. He was going to provide them with opportunities. It was up to them to take advantage of those opportunities. At MSU he was able to out recruit others and make good decisions on players. He never set goals for players, but he made sure they knew what their responsibilities were on and off the field. He never had any motivational signs in the locker room or dugout. His plan was to help players get an education and to play pro ball if they wanted to. He used that to motivate players.

By 1978 the MSU Bulldogs were 38-18 and ended the season playing in an NCAA Regional Baseball Tournament. The very next year MSU reached the mecca of college baseball, the College World Series. During his 27 years as MSU's head coach, Ron Polk led the Bulldogs to five SEC Championships, five SEC Baseball Tournament Championships, 21 NCAA Baseball Tournaments and seven CWS appearances.

Coach Polk has never been one to mince words. The following comes from an article written by Bob Howdeshell that appeared on the High School

Baseball website:

> At a high school baseball information seminar sponsored by Encore Sports and Perfect Game ID Camps, held in Decatur, Alabama, those in attendance were treated to the insight of college baseball coaching legend Ron Polk of Mississippi State University.
>
> As Coach Polk started his discussion, which was to be on the role of high school coaches and parents in recruiting, he announced, **"The NCAA is the enemy of college baseball!"**
>
> Coach Polk further went on to explain that at this point in his career he has made it his goal to berate the NCAA leadership and its unfair treatment of college baseball programs, at every opportunity.
>
> Coach Polk explained that several years ago it was decided that all NCAA D1 men's sports scholarship totals would be reduced by 10% across the board. This in the face of Title IX compliance. If you look at total allowable scholarships for men's sports, you will see the unusual amounts, like 11.7 for baseball. This came as a result of reducing the previous number (13) by 10%.
>
> Did you know that the NCAA Division 1 men's baseball College World Series is the second (2nd) largest championship series sponsored by the NCAA? Coach Polk made this point ... the baseball Regionals, Super Regionals, and CWS are surpassed in revenue generated for the NCAA only by the men's basketball tournament. What about football? Those bowl games are not revenue shared by the NCAA, only the participating schools and in some cases, their conferences. And as Coach Polk asked ... "Does any of that baseball tournament money come back to college baseball programs in terms of increased scholarship amounts?" **NO!**
>
> ....
>
> As a footnote, Coach Polk added that when crew was added as a women's sport at Iowa, they did not even have a venue to hold home matches. They had to build a lake!

Coach Polk also mentioned that several of the NCAA Division 1 women's basketball programs do not use all of their allotted 15 full scholarships. (I know this was true at Tennessee until recently). His point was that women's basketball has 15 scholarships, while the men's programs are limited to 13, and baseball with 35-man rosters is limited to 11.7!

Coach Polk stated that in his next life he would like to come back as a women's golf coach, with six full scholarships.

Between 1997 and 2000 Coach Polk was the assistant athletics director for special projects at MSU. In that position he spearheaded the successful campaign to expand the university's Polk-DeMent Stadium in Starkville.

In 2000, Ron Polk was back in college baseball and the SEC as head baseball coach at the University of Georgia. The year before Polk arrived, UGA went 25-30-1 overall and 8-20-1 in the SEC. It didn't take the coach long to get the Bulldogs rolling. It took only two years for him to win the 2001 SEC Tournament championship and take the Georgia Bulldogs to the CWS. During the 2000 season the Dogs improved their overall record to 32-26 and their SEC mark to 14-15. The wise decision to hire Coach Polk paid off handsomely in the 2001 season when he led his team to a 49-19 overall record. That record included a 20-10 SEC regular season mark, an SEC championship, an NCAA Regional championship, an NCAA Super Regional championship, and a CWS appearance.

In 2002, when Pat McMahon resigned as head coach at MSU, Coach Polk could not turn down the opportunity to return as Mississippi State's head baseball coach. Vince Dooley, Georgia's athletic director, understood, and Polk was back in the MSU dugout for another successful run in 2002. Over the next seven seasons he led the Bulldogs to four NCAA Regional Tournaments and to the 2007 CWS. Coach Polk spent a total of 29 years as head coach at Mississippi State. His overall record during this stint at MSU was 249-168-2. Coach Polk finished his NCAA Division 1 coaching career with a 1373-702-2 (.662) record, which includes his MSU record of 1139-590-2 (.659).

In 2008 Polk became a volunteer assistant baseball coach at the University of Alabama Birmingham. He served in that position for 12 years and helped the Blazers win the Conference USA Championship and advance to the NCAA Tallahassee Tournament in 2012. UAB head baseball coach Brian Shoop served on Polk's MSU staff from 1983-1989. During that period, MSU won three SEC Championships and made a trip to the CWS. Coach Shoop said of Polk:

> It has been a personal highlight in life for me to be able to learn under Coach Polk in the '80s at Mississippi State and now to work with him again. I have more respect for Coach Polk than any other coach in college baseball. No one has had more of an influence on our game and on countless young coaches, including myself. Our players love him and appreciate the sacrifices he makes to be involved with the UAB baseball program. We are better in so many ways because of Coach's decision to donate his time to Blazer baseball.

Coach Polk also made a mark as an author. He didn't leave much out of his "Baseball Playbook," which has sold more than 125,000 copies. The book addresses just about any situation that can occur in baseball. Here are few topics he covered: baseball policies and regulations, player meetings and information sheets, baseball offensive/defensive sign structure for game situations, structured baseball practice sessions, outfield/ infield drills, fundamental drill series 1 and 2, bunt defenses, pick-off plays, fly-ball communication, bunting drills and fundamentals, 1B + 3B coaching guidelines, hitting mechanics, fundamentals and strategy, production rating system, common mental and physical faults and corrections, sacrifice, drag and push bunting, and pitching mechanics.

After finishing the "Baseball Playbook," Coach Polk sent a free copy to everyone coaching college baseball or teaching a course on baseball theory. Coach Polk continues to be a featured speaker at many baseball-coaching clinics across the country.

There is a saying in baseball that goes something like this: If the competition is anywhere near equal, you will win a third of your games and lose a third; it's the other third that counts. Major League Baseball champions usually lose about a third of their games. Coach Polk's college career produced an overall record of 1373-702-2 (.662), which means he won nearly all of the third in the middle.

I interviewed Coach Polk by telephone on December 6, 2022. He was on his way to Louisiana for a speaking engagement. He had more than 50 speaking engagements lined up, and I appreciated his working me into his very busy schedule. I needed to talk to a knowledgeable person about some of the history of college baseball and some recent developments. Coach Polk was the right man. He is a walking encyclopedia of college baseball.

I asked him about the evolution of bats and balls in college baseball. Aluminum bats were first used in the 1970s. The switch from wood was a cost-saving measure, as metal bats last much longer than wood. By the late 1990s metal bats had improved, and their use had changed college baseball tremendously. The velocity of a baseball coming off a metal bat is much higher than it is off a wooden bat. Extra base hits, especially home runs, ruled the day, and that seemed to attract more fans. The safety of players, especially pitchers, was affected as they attempted to field balls coming off metal bats. Football-like scores appeared on college baseball scoreboards, and batting averages soared. Colleges were said to be playing "gorilla ball." Over time, the NCAA made several specification changes for both bats and balls in an attempt to restore longball hitting and scoring to something close to what they were in the wood-bat era. At one time, a ball was used that was very difficult to hit out of a college baseball park. Today college baseball uses composite bats and flat-seamed balls. I asked Coach Polk what he thought about the departure from wooden bats. He explained the evolution that has taken place and said he thinks the NCAA has finally gotten it about right.

We discussed the recently developed transfer portal and players being allowed to profit from their name image and likeness (NIL). Coach Polk believes that a lot of college presidents simply tolerate athletics and that the NCAA, which is controlled by college presidents, did nothing to prevent the chaos that the new environment is going to produce. He indicated that a coach now will have very limited time to develop players. If newcomers, because of their need to develop, don't get to play as much as they think they should, they will transfer. And some players will transfer because they think they have a higher NIL value. Coach Polk said the transfer portal and NIL were not good for college baseball and that what is happening is not sustainable. He thought the NIL payments should be capped at $10,000. Coach Polk noted that the NCAA discriminates against baseball by limiting the number of players who can be on the roster. Although the number of scholarships is limited for each sport, only baseball has a roster limit—35. Because of COVID 19, the number was increased to 40 for 2021 and 2022. It returned to 35 in 2023. That means if the roster is at that limit and a player wants to walk-on, the head coach must tell him he can't. When I asked how important facilities and a winning tradition were in recruiting, he said they have been important, but with the NIL they will become less important because players will look for the best NIL deals.

I asked how important team leadership was, i.e., leadership exercised by experienced players who have earned the right to lead and are respected by their teammates. He said such leadership is important but that the coaches must be the real leaders. Then he made an interesting observation, saying when a team is doing well and winning big, observers often attribute it to good team leadership. When the opposite is true, observers often attribute it to a lack of team leadership, which is more than likely not the case.

The NCAA limited Division 1 baseball programs to three paid coaches, and it makes provisions for one "volunteer" coach who cannot be paid anything by the college or an affiliated organization. I asked Coach Polk if he thought volunteer coaches were exploited, and he said he did not think so. As noted, Polk spent 12 years as a volunteer coach at UAB, but he was retired from MSU at the time. Volunteers do earn money for doing such things as running summer baseball camps for young baseball players. They also gain valuable experience that helps prepare them to move up in the coaching world. No doubt being a volunteer under Coach Polk was a good thing to have on your resume. But being a volunteer coach was a full-time job. They did just about everything paid coaches do and often had specifically assigned duties. I thought that if the no-pay provision were challenged in court, the NCAA would lose. In 1989 the NCAA, in an effort to control costs, established a "restricted earnings coach rule" for basketball coaches. Division 1 schools were allowed a head coach, two assistant coaches, and one restricted-earnings coach. Restricted-earnings coaches could be paid $12,000 for an academic year (nine months) and $4,000 in the summer. That silly rule soon spawned a class-action lawsuit, which the NCAA lost. I thought the same thing would happen if the volunteer baseball coach rule were ever challenged in court. In researching the volunteer coach rule, I discovered that on November 29, 2022, two former volunteer baseball coaches filed a claim in the U.S. District Court of the Eastern Division of California, challenging the volunteer rule and asking for class-action status. They were also asking for treble (triple) damages! I have done a lot of research on legal matters, and I had little doubt that the volunteer coaches would win their suit, but maybe not treble damages. The two coaches won $60 million in a jury trial. Then the NCAA settled for $54-plus million and agreed not to appeal. The NCAA in early 2023 eliminated the volunteer coach restrictions for all sports. Beginning July 1, 2023, all NCAA Division 1 schools can have three paid full-time assistant baseball coaches.

When writing about Coach Polk's remarkable career, I think it's necessary to include a brief discussion of MSU's 1985 season. In my opinion, the 1985 Bulldog team is the best team to have ever played in the College World Series and not win it. That team put Mississippi State University in the galaxy of great college baseball teams.

The heartbreaking 1985 CWS experience might have been on the minds of Mississippi State Baseball fans when the Bulldogs opened the 2021 season, playing Texas in the State Farm College Baseball Showdown in Arlington, Texas, on February 20, 2021. The 1985 MSU baseball team was perhaps the best in the annals of SEC baseball. Sporting four future outstanding major leaguers, Will Clark, Rafael Palmeiro (Thunder and Lightning), Jeff Brantley, and Bobby Thigpen, the Bulldogs posted a 50-15 overall record. They finished with a 16-8 SEC mark and won the SEC Tournament Championship. By defeating Michigan in the finals of the NCAA South I Regional in Starkville, MSU qualified for the College World Series. This was the third time Ron Polk had taken MSU to the mecca of college baseball. Mississippi State joined Arizona, Arkansas, Miami, Oklahoma State, South Carolina, Stanford, and Texas in the eight-team national championship tournament. In the Dogs' first two games they dispatched Oklahoma State 12-3 and Arkansas 5-4 and then faced the Longhorns from Texas.

With MSU leading Texas 5-2 in the fifth inning, the game turned sour. State's pitcher Gene Morgan seemed to be in a groove when he was hit on the leg by a line drive off a Texas bat. Bad luck was about to raise its ugly head.

Rick Cleveland wrote an article that appeared in the June 13, 2019, edition of "Mississippi Today" entitled College World Series: skill is a must, but luck counts too – witness Mississippi State in '85. The article presented a convincing argument that MSU was better than the other seven teams about to compete in the 2019 CWS. But Cleveland reminded his readers of what happened to the Bulldogs in the 1985 CWS.

Cleveland wrote that MSU's 1985 Bulldogs were the best college baseball team he had ever seen. Coach Ron Polk's first two starting pitchers, Jeff Brantley and Gene Morgan, combined to win 32 games and lose four. Palmeiro, Clark, and Polk are now members of the College Baseball Hall of Fame. Will Clark still owns the highest career batting average in program history at .391. Rafael Palmeiro is still the program's home run king with 67. Clark is second with 61. They are the only two Bulldogs to hit more than 60 career home runs. Cleveland's article included the following:

> Those Bulldogs were ridiculously good. They won their first 15 games and were ranked No. 1 for several weeks. And, they played like world-beaters when they first reached Omaha. They swamped 57-game winner Oklahoma State 12-3 in their first game. They beat Arkansas 5-4 in the second round, and then they faced a showdown with Texas with Morgan, 14-2, on the mound. State scored two in the first, and Morgan was pitching lights out. He was cruising in the fifth inning, having shut out the Longhorns on one hit.
>
> And then it happened. Doug Johnson led off the fifth for Texas. Morgan threw him a fast ball that started out over the outside corner but tailed back into the middle of the plate. "It was a bad, bad pitch," Morgan said Wednesday, 34 years and three days after the pitch. Johnson drilled a line drive off Morgan's left ankle. Morgan didn't have a chance to get his glove down in time. The ball caromed all the way into left field. Morgan went down in a heap. The pain, at first, was excruciating. "I thought I was out of the game for sure," he said. Players crowded around him. Polk came out. The trainer came out and sprayed Morgan's ankle with

a numbing agent. After a pregnant pause, Morgan tried a few warm-up pitches – and stayed in the game.

In the 34 years since, Palmeiro, Clark, Brantley, and Polk have all told me that was the sequence that kept State from winning a national baseball championship, something no Division I Mississippi team has ever accomplished. Morgan won't go that far. "Texas was really good; Miami was really good," he said. "But I thought we had something special; we all did. Besides all those great players, we had a special chemistry as well." Morgan got through that inning and still led 5-2 going into the bottom of the seventh. Morgan's ankle? "I couldn't feel anything," he said. "I might have felt nervous about planting that left foot on my delivery. I can't say for sure. I thought I still pitched OK. They hit some good pitches."

That 5-2 lead became a 12-7 defeat. A double-play ball took a bad hop and that opened the Texas floodgates. "Who knows what would have happened had the ball not hit me in the ankle," Morgan said. "I don't know. I can't say." But many have speculated. And Morgan allowed this: "Without question, it changed the momentum of the game."

On June 8, 1985, the Mississippi State Bulldogs played the Miami Hurricanes in a CWS classic. With two outs in the top of the sixth inning, outfielder/pitcher Bobby Thigpen hit a grand slam home run, giving MSU a 4-3 lead. Rafael Palmeiro singled in the top of the eighth, driving in a run. The Canes countered in the bottom of the inning by scoring a run on a triple and a throwing error. The Bulldogs carried a 5-4 lead into the bottom of the ninth. Coach Polk called Bobby Thigpen in from right field to replace starter Jeff Brantley after Brantley walked the leadoff hitter. Brantley had thrown 136 pitches when the temperature was 98 degrees, and Thigpen was MSU's most reliable relief pitcher. The Canes' designated hitter, Greg Ellena, a walk-on, hit a walk-off two-run home run off Thigpen. A CWS championship had slipped away, and the greatest season in MSU baseball history to that point was over.

The 1985 appearance in the CWS was one the MSU fans could take pride in along with the school's first 50-win season. They could also look forward to Coach Polk continuing to put high quality teams on the field.

Like the 1985 team, the great 2019 Mississippi State team didn't win the national championship. The very talented 2019 Diamond Dawgs won only one game in the 2019 CWS. But, the sweetness of the 2021 championship lay ahead.

Pat McMahon

A former assistant coach under Ron Polk, Pat McMahon was MSU's head baseball coach from 1998-2001. He had a sterling four-year run. McMahon's 1998 squad went to the SEC Tournament, won an NCAA Regional and played in the CWS, going 1-2. His 1999 team went to an NCAA Regional. The 2000 Bulldogs won an NCAA Regional, going 3-1, and lost a Super Regional, going 0-2. McMahon left MSU to become Florida's head coach after the 2001 season in which the Bulldogs went 39-24; won the SEC Tournament, going 4-0; won an NCAA regional, going 3-1; and lost a Super Regional, going 0-2.

As has been noted, Ron Polk returned to MSU to begin what turned out to be an eight-year run. His 2002 team made the SEC Tournament, where they won a game and lost two. Polk's Dawgs went 4-0 while winning the 2005 SEC Tournament, advanced to an NCAA Regional and went 2-2 there. In 2007 Coach Polk took his team all the way to the CWS. They went 3-0 in an NCAA Regional, 2-0 in a Super Regional, and 0-2 in the CWS. Polk's last year as MSU's head baseball coach was 2008.

John Cohen

Kentucky head baseball coach John Cohen, who had played for Polk at MSU from 1988-90, became MSU's head coach in 2008. Cohen's 2009 and 2010 teams posted losing records and did not make it to any post-season tournaments. In 2011 things changed. The Bulldogs finished 38-25, went to an NCAA Regional, which they won 3-0, and moved on to a Super Regional, where they lost two games to one. Coach Cohen's 2012 team won the SEC Tournament, winning five of six games, and lost in an NCAA Regional in three games. By 2013 Cohen had all the pieces in place to make it to the CWS. The 2013 Bullies went 51-20 overall including a 16-14 conference mark. MSU went 3-1 in the SEC Tournament, defeating Missouri 2-1, South Carolina 5-3, and Texas A&M 6-4 before losing the title game to Vanderbilt 16-8. Moving on to the Starkville NCAA Regional, MSU defeated Central Arkansas three times and South Alabama once to earn a berth in the Charlottesville NCAA Super Regional. MSU defeated host Virginia 11-6 and 6-5 to advance to the CWS. In the CWS the Bulldogs defeated Oregon State 5-4 and 4-1 and Indiana 5-4 before losing to UCLA in the championship series 3-1 and 8-0. The 2013 team was led by two All-Americans, outfielder Hunter Renfroe and pitcher Ross Mitchell. Renfroe hit .345 with 16 home runs and 65 RBIs. Mitchell went 13-0 on the mound while posting a 1.36 ERA.

Andy Cannizaro

John Cohen became MSU's athletic director after the 2016 season, and he quickly hired Andy Cannizaro as his successor as head baseball coach. In 2017 Cannizaro had a very good one-year run as head coach, going 47-27 overall and 17-13 in the SEC. The Dawgs went 2-2 in the SEC Tournament. MSU won an NCAA Hattiesburg Regional, going 4-1. In the regional MSU lost a game to South Alabama, defeated Illinois-Chicago, defeated South Alabama, and defeated Southern Mississippi twice. The Dawgs advanced to the NCAA Baton Rouge Super Regional, where they lost two games to LSU.

Because of a moral failure, Cannizaro was fired from his head coaching position three games into the 2018 season. Pitching coach Gary Henderson became acting head coach, and he had a good one-year record. State went 39-29 overall and 15-15 in the SEC. Henderson's Dawgs won the NCAA Tallahassee Regional, where they lost a game to Oklahoma, beat Florida State, beat Samford, and then defeated Oklahoma twice. The SEC's all-time hits leader, Jake Mangum; Rowdey Jordan; Tanner Allen; and Ethan Small led this MSU team that was loaded with talent. In the Nashville Super Regional, MSU defeated home-standing Vanderbilt two games to one to move on to the CWS.

In Omaha the Dawgs won their first game against Washington 1-0. Ethan Small threw seven innings, giving up four hits and no runs while striking out five batters. J.P. France, Cole Gordon, and Zach Neff followed

Small to the mound and gave up a combined two hits and no runs. Neff, who threw the last 2/3 of the ninth inning, was the winner when the Dawgs' Luke Alexander singled to drive in the winning run. MSU registered 10 hits off two Huskie pitchers but left six runners on base as Washington turned two double plays.

In their next game, the Bullies blew out North Carolina 12-2. MSU scored four runs in the second inning and eight in the eighth. Jordan Westburg went 3 for 4 at the plate, hit a double and a home run and drove in seven runs. Winning pitcher, Konner Pinkington, threw six innings and gave up six hits and two runs. Cole Gordon, who threw three innings and gave up one hit while striking out two batters, registered a save.

Oregon State then turned the table on State, defeating the Dawgs 12-2. The Dawgs managed only five hits, three of which were doubles. Oregon State banged out 15 hits including three doubles and a triple against four MSU pitchers. The Dawgs' Jacob Billingsley, who was chased after 1 1/3 innings after giving up five hits and six runs, was charged with the loss. Oregon State's winning pitcher, Brandon Eisert, threw 5 1/3 innings and gave up a hit and no runs.

Ethan Small started the next game against the Beavers and allowed seven hits and five runs over 4 2/3 innings. Two Oregon State pitchers held the Dawgs to four hits and two runs, and the Beavers won the game 5-2. Oregon State went on to beat Arkansas two out of three games in the championship series to win the 2018 College World Series.

Chris Lemonis

On June 25, 2018, at Dudy Noble Stadium, MSU's Athletic Director John Cohen introduced Chris Lemonis as MSU's 18th head baseball coach. It was not the first time Lemonis had been to Starkville. His dad was a 1973 electrical engineering graduate of MSU, and the Lemonis family lived on campus for a brief time when Chris was very small. Although Lemonis had been involved with college baseball for more than 20 years, he had never played, coached, or attended a baseball game at Dudy Noble Field.

Lemonis was well qualified to take over one of the most prestigious college baseball programs in the nation. He was a two-time All-Southern Conference player at The Citadel. During his senior year he led the Bulldogs in batting average, doubles, runs, RBIs, and home runs and led the team to the College World Series. Upon graduating he began teaching school and serving as an unpaid volunteer coach at The Citadel. He moved up from a volunteer to an assistant coach under Fred Jordan and then to associate head coach. Along the way he also earned a master's degree. He is a member of the Citadel Athletics Hall of Fame. During Coach Lemonis's 12-year coaching tenure at the Citadel, the Bulldogs made six appearances in the NCAA Baseball Tournaments and established 35 school records. Lemonis moved on to Louisville as an assistant to head coach Dan McDonnell. During his time at Louisville, the Cardinals became one of the premier teams in college baseball. In Lemonis's eight-year tenure as assistant coach, the Cardinals won more games than any other team in D1 baseball, going 359-159 (.693), and they appeared in three CWS. While at Louisville, Lemonis developed a reputation as an outstanding recruiter, and he was named ABCA/Baseball America Assistant Coach of the Year. Cardinal players won 43 different All-American honors, and 40 players were drafted by Major League teams during Lemonis's time at Louisville. The University of Indiana came calling, and Lemonis was named head coach of Indiana Baseball on July 24, 2014. During his four seasons at the helm, the Hoosiers posted a 141-91-2 overall record including a 55-37-1 Big Ten Conference mark, and they advanced to three NCAA D1 College Baseball Tournaments. Those three NCAA Tournament appearances put Lemonis in a tie for first all-time at Indiana. His Indiana teams excelled defensively. They hold three out of the four highest single-season fielding percentages in the school's history. The Hoosiers shattered the school record in fielding percentage in back-to-back seasons, including a mark of .979 in 2017. Mississippi State came calling in July 2018.

Lemonis's 2019 MSU squad posted one of the best records in MSU history, going 52-10 overall and 20-10 in the SEC. The Dawgs won one game and lost two in the SEC Tournament and were selected to host an NCAA Regional Tournament in Starkville. The Dawgs swept the regional, defeating Southern University, Central Michigan, and Miami. MSU earned the right to host an NCAA Super Regional in Starkville, and they swept it, too, defeating Stanford twice to earn a trip to the CWS. In Omaha the Bullies defeated Auburn 5-4, lost to Vanderbilt 6-3, and to Louisville 4-3. Failure to win the CWS had to be a bitter experience for some very talented Dawgs including

Jake Mangum, who played for very good teams and four head coaches over four years but never won a CWS title.

During the 2019, 2020, and 2021 seasons Coach Lemonis's MSU teams went 114-37, a .750 winning clip, and they won the 2021 national championship at the College World Series. MSU also occupied the Taj Mahal of college baseball, Dudy Noble Stadium, and they played before huge crowds. Lemonis had proved to be very successful everywhere he had been in college baseball. But few if any coaches have ever experienced anything like his first three years at MSU.

On Monday, December 19, 2022, my friend Frank Montgomery and I drove to Starkville to interview Coach Chris Lemonis. Frank was an All-American pitcher at MSU in 1962, and he still has strong connections with the university. He had graciously arranged for the interview with Coach Lemonis.

When asked if there was a particular game or series in the 2021 season that he considered especially important on the road to the national championship, Coach Lemonis quickly answered, the Tulane series. Surprisingly, that was an early season series played February 26, 27, and 28 in Starkville. MSU committed four errors in the first game and lost 7-3. After the game, Lemonis told the "Clarion-Ledger":

> A big part is the energy and focus that we bring and being able to play the game every day. That was our message on Wednesday night. I wasn't really happy with the energy we brought to come and play the game [on Wednesday]. We kind of came with the same thing today. Our kids think 'It's Mississippi State. We can just roll out the ball.' There are just too many great teams. That's a really good team in the other dugout. You have to show up, and you have to be ready to go every night in this game. We have to learn to do that. Practice that way; play that way. And we do. We have some really good pieces here. We have some inexperienced pieces. We have to get going in that way. You have to be able to show up every night and be able to put out a good effort.

The real MSU team showed up for the next game. Tulane led 5-3 in the bottom of the ninth when MSU exploded for six runs to win 9-5. Logan Tanner stroked a two-RBI single to tie the score, and then Luke Hancock hit a grand slam home run, the Dawgs' third homer of the game, to supply a four-run margin and give MSU a walk-off win. MSU fielders did not commit an error.

Coach Lemonis told the "Clarion-Ledger":

> I told them before the game that we'd learn a lot about our team this weekend. After you lose the opening night [game], we brought nowhere near the intensity that we brought today. That was disappointing yesterday. We're figuring out things as a young ball club. The thing you're seeing in college baseball is that the level is so high right now. I know that Tulane isn't in the SEC, but that's a really good ball club. We're facing some really good arms. I think figuring out our team and taking that momentum into tomorrow is huge. It makes you feel a lot better when you win.

The Dawgs proceeded to take the third game 5-4 to win the series. For the second consecutive game the Diamond Dawgs scored in the bottom of the ninth inning to secure the win. With MSU trailing 4-3, Tanner Allen hit a two-run single to give the Dawgs their second walk-off win of the series.

Coach Lemonis said he thought that the biggest changes in college baseball since the early 2000s have been the NCAA transfer portal; the U.S. Supreme Court ruling that college athletes can profit from use of their name, image, and likeness (NIL); the growth in the number of fans attending games; and the growth of TV exposure. The NIL situation allows players to go to the highest bidder. The transfer portal makes it more difficult to keep players who are not satisfied with their playing time. The portal and the NIL ruling endanger competitive balance. Lemonis is not sure the present conditions are sustainable. Some realistic guidelines are needed. While the portal and NIL situation have affected recruiting, winning traditions and facilities will still have an impact on recruiting and retaining players, and MSU has both in spades.

Lemonis indicated that it is uncertain how the limitations imposed by the 11.7 scholarship rule for college baseball will be affected by the recent change that allows schools to stack other university-provided financial support on top of the baseball scholarships. The average baseball scholarship now is about 40% of a full scholarship. He said about half of his roster is made up of walk-ons with no baseball scholarship. The NIL may alleviate this somewhat in that non-scholarship players may receive NIL money. Most schools that field D1 baseball teams lose money on the sport because it is not emphasized, especially in the North. Some schools do not even use all of the 11.7 scholarships available.

When asked how important player leadership was to his 2021 team, Coach Lemonis said it was "huge." Lemonis noted that team leaders spend much more time with players than coaches, and they have more opportunities to influence their teammates. He named Rowdey Jordan, Tanner Allen, Will Bednar, and Landon Sims as excellent leaders.

Coach Lemonis said injuries have a tremendous effect on college baseball. He noted that his 2021 team did not suffer many injuries and that injuries devastated the 2022 MSU team. He also noted that the 35-player roster limitation the NCAA places on baseball is unjust because no such limit is imposed on other sports. Scholarship limits are imposed on all sports, but only baseball has a roster limit.

Polk-Dement Stadium at Dudy Noble Field

No review of MSU baseball's history would be complete without discussion of the remarkable evolution of the university's baseball facilities. When the first NCAA College World Series was played in 1947, Mississippi State's home baseball games were played at Hardy Field, an on-campus facility constructed in 1929. The facility was renamed Dudy Noble Field in 1949. As Mississippi State's baseball coach from 1920-1947, Noble compiled a 267-201-9 record.

Mississippi State's baseball facilities have come a long way since 1964 when the old ballpark was dismantled to make room for Dorman Hall. The old grandstand and bleachers were moved to the site of the present Dudy Noble Field at Polk-Dement Stadium. The move took two seasons to complete. During the 1965 and 1966 seasons, Coach Paul Gregory's teams played all of their home games at Redbird Park in Columbus, Mississippi. It seem quizzical hat the Bulldogs won the SEC Championship both of those years! The new stadium was opened April 3, 1967, with MSU defeating Illinois Wesleyan 5-3. The Bulldogs have been playing their home games at the present site ever since.

There have been several improvements to MSU's playing facilities since 1967. The Dude has been upgraded several times and was demolished and rebuilt in 1987 and 2018. In 1998 the facility was renamed Dudy Noble Field at Polk-Dement Stadium in honor of Coach Ron Polk and the late Gordan Dement, a long-time Bulldog supporter. The 2018 rebuild cost $68 million, and today Dudy Noble Field at **Polk-Dement Stadium** is the Carnegie Hall or Taj Mahal of college baseball. It seats about 15,000 fans. The famous Left Field Lounge was upgraded, and the facility now includes several luxury sky boxes and apartments just outside the park.

The two best-attended on-campus NCAA baseball games of all-time took place at The Dude. On April 12, 2014, Mississippi State played Ole Miss before 15,589 fans. That record held until April 15, 2023, when the Bulldogs and Rebels played at Dudy Noble Field before 16,423 fans to establish a new record. All 20 of the most-attended on-campus baseball games in NCAA history were played at the Dude.

From 1979-1988 MSU hosted four SEC Tournaments, and in 1995 the Bulldogs hosted an SEC Western Division Tournament on their home field. The NCAA District Tournament III was played at Dudy Noble in 1973 and 1974. Since 1979, 15 NCAA Regional Tournaments and four NCAA Super Regional Tournaments have been played at Dudy Noble.

CHAPTER 2
Mississippi State University's 2021 National Baseball Championship Season

The Season in a Nutshell

MSU finished the 2021 regular season with a 40-13 record and a 20-10 SEC mark. Although they went 0-2 in the SEC Baseball Tournament, they were named the #7 national seed and hosted an NCAA Regional in Starkville. They swept the regional, beating Samford 8-4, VCU 16-4, and Campbell 6-5.

Because they were a national seed and had won their regional, the Dawgs hosted a Super Regional match, which pitted them against hard-hitting and 10th- seeded Notre Dame at Dudy Noble Field. This would be MSU's fourth time to host a Super Regional and the 10th time to play in a Super Regional. The Fighting Irish lived up to their nickname in the Saturday, June 12, game, slugging four doubles and three home runs and scoring eight runs. But MSU claimed the victory by scoring nine runs while hitting two doubles and three homers. It was a different story on Sunday as Notre Dame controlled the game from the get-go. MSU scored its only run in the top of the first inning, and the Fighting Irish scored two runs in the bottom of the inning. Notre Dame added seven more runs over the next six innings and pulled away with a 9-1 win. The final game was played on Monday. MSU struck 12 hits including four doubles and two home runs, and Notre Dame responded with 10 hits including two doubles and two home runs. The Dogs got the timely hits and won the Super Regional 11-7. The victory squared MSU's Super Regional record at 5-5 and sent the Dawgs to Omaha for the College World Series.

All eight teams in the 2021 CWS had been there before. In order of their number of appearances in the CWS including 2021 the teams were University of Texas Longhorns (36), University of Arizona Wildcats (18), Stanford University Cardinals (17), Mississippi State University Bulldogs (12), Vanderbilt University Commodores (5), University of Virginia Cavaliers (5),

University of Tennessee Volunteers (5), and North Carolina State University Wolfpack (4). These teams had a total of 102 appearances in the CWS.

Mississippi State University won the 2021 NCAA College World Series, going 5-2 in the tournament. They defeated Texas 2-1 and 4-3 and lost to the Longhorns once, 8-5. They defeated Virginia 6-5, lost to Vanderbilt 8-2, and defeated the Commodores 13-2. Notice that three of the Dawgs' victories were by one run, and the last one was a blowout. That says a lot about the team.

MSU's 2021 National College Baseball Championship Season – The Details

In 2019, Chis Lemonis's first year as head coach, the Mississippi State Bulldogs posted a 47-11 regular season record that included a 20-10 SEC mark. The SEC performance tied the Bulldogs with Arkansas for the SEC West title. After going 1-2 in the SEC tournament, MSU hosted an NCAA Regional Tournament, which the Bulldogs won 3-0, earning them the right to host a Super Regional, which they won 2-0. It was on to the College World Series, where they won one game and lost two. Expectations were high for the 2020 season.

In March 2020 COVID stopped the young college baseball season cold. On March 11 the Mississippi State Bulldogs played their last game of the season against Texas Tech at MGM Park in Biloxi. MSU won that game 3-2 to finish the season 12-4. In Coach Lemonis's second year, his Bulldogs had not played a single SEC game. It was a disappointing ending for a club that had ranked #6 in the country and 2nd in the SEC West in the preseason polls.

COVID still raged in 2021, and the entire season would be played under restrictive protocols imposed by the NCAA and the SEC. Because the 2020 season had been truncated early, the NCAA granted players an extra year of eligibility. Normally, schools were limited to a 35-man roster, but MSU began the 2021 season with a 46-man roster. That roster was loaded with talent, and MSU was ranked #7 in the nation in the preseason "ESPN/USA Today" coaches' poll.

Preconference play

The season began February 20 when three teams from the SEC (Mississippi State, Arkansas, and Ole Miss) squared off against three teams from the Big 12 (Texas Christian University, Texas, and Texas Tech) in the State Farm College Baseball Showdown played at Globe Life Field in Arlington, Texas. The format called for each SEC team to play each Big 12 team. The bad February weather in Mississippi caused archrivals Mississippi State and Ole Miss to bus together to Birmingham and then catch the same flight to Texas. The Bulldogs won their first game 8-3 against Texas, ranked #10 in the coaches poll,; lost their second game 3-2 to #11-ranked TCU; and won their final game 11-5 against #4-ranked Texas Tech.

The Dogs did this without the services of two of their top-three starting pitchers, junior Eric Cerantola and sophomore Will Bednar. Budding superstar reliever Landon Sims was the winning pitcher against Texas. He pitched four innings, faced only 12 batters, and struck out 10. MSU hitters excelled during the showdown. Junior designated hitter Luke Hancock went seven for 12 at the plate with two homers and five RBIs. Senior first baseman Josh Hatcher managed five hits in 13 plate appearances, while senior center fielder Rowdey Jordan went four-for-14 with two home runs, a triple, and six RBIs. Ninth-place hitter Landon Jordan topped it off by batting .300 over the three games. In the loss to TCU, the Dawgs left the bases loaded in the bottom of the ninth inning. The absence of two starters allowed Houston Harding, Jackson Fristoe, Cameron Tullar, Kole Alford, and Xavier Lovett to show their stuff on the mound. The scoring differential for the showdown was 21-11 in favor of MSU. The trip to Texas got the Bulldogs' season off on the right foot. After three games against stout competition, they were 2-1.

In a game delayed one day by weather, MSU was matched against in-state rival Jackson State at Dudy Noble Field on February 24. Led by shortstop Kamren James's four hits, a home run and three RBIs, MSU won the contest 7-4. Winning pitcher Brandon Smith threw two innings, giving up no hits and no runs while striking out two batters.

The Bulldogs were ranked #8 in the coaches' poll when Tulane showed up at Starkville for a weekend series beginning Friday, February 26. The Green Wave took the first game 7-3. Tulane's starting pitcher, Braden Olthoff, gave up two runs while scattering six hits over eight innings. Tanner Allen went two-for-four at the plate, drove in a run, and stole a base for the Dawgs. Four errors didn't help State's cause. Losing pitcher, lefthander Christian MacLeod, went four innings and gave up three runs, all of which were unearned.

The Dawgs rebounded in the next game, posting a 9-5 come-from-behind victory. MSU trailed 5-3 in the bottom of the ninth but rallied to win in dramatic fashion. Rowdey Jordan got the inning off to a good start by sending a single to right center field. He advanced to third on Scotty Dubrule's single. Tanner Allen walked before Logan Tanner hit a single that scored Jordan and Dubrule, tying the score from second base. Then Tulane intentionally walked Josh Hatcher to load the bases. Catcher/designated hitter Luke Hancock made the Dude a happy place by stroking a walk-off grand slam home run. In addition to Hancock's slam, Tanner Allen and Kamren James hit homers. The Dawgs' defense tightened up and committed no errors. Both teams mustered 10 hits. All three of MSU's extra-base hits were home runs. Left-handed pitcher Houston Harding picked up the win by throwing one inning in relief and giving up a hit and no runs. Tulane's reliever, Trent Johnson, who gave up six runs in two innings, was the loser. Landon Sims pitched 3 2/3 innings and gave up three hits, one run and two bases on balls. He also struck out 10 batters.

State won the rubber game on Sunday 5-4. With four players having multiple hits, Tulane outhit State 12 to seven. But the Tulane pitchers walked seven batters, while State's pitchers walked only two. Luke Hancock hit a double and drove in a run. Tanner Allen drove in two runs with a single, while Kamren James hit a home run with a man on base. Reliever Spencer Price was the winning pitcher, despite giving up two hits and two runs in the ninth inning, the only inning he pitched. Tulane committed no errors, but the Bulldogs were again shaky in the field, committing three. Over the three-game series, State had seven errors. In the first seven games of the season, the Dawgs committed 12 errors. After the Tulane series, MSU was #7 in the coaches' poll.

On March 3, 2021, MSU faced Southern Mississippi at Dudy Noble. State got an extremely well-pitched game from Houston Harding, Preston Johnson, Cameran Tullar, and Stone Simmons. The winning pitcher, Harding, went five innings, gave up two hits and the Golden Eagles' only run.

USM's starter, Drew Boyd, threw 4 1/3 innings and gave up seven hits and MSU's four runs. MSU's Scotty Dubrule, Tanner Allen, and Logan Tanner each collected two hits. MSU center fielder and team leader, Rowdey Jordan, went 0-3 and ended the game batting .167 for the season. That had to change. USM committed four errors and MSU two.

The Kent State Golden Flashes provided the next competition in State's long home stand. The March 5 -7 series began with MSU winning 8-3. The visitors scored all three of their runs in the first two innings. In the first inning the Flashes' leadoff man, Cam Touchette, stroked a single, and with the help of a sacrifice bunt, a throwing error, and a single by Justin Miknis, Touchette scored the game's first run. In the second inning Mack Timbrook hit a home run, and Kevin Dobos walked. Thanks to a walk and a couple of wild pitches scored the last run, the Flashes would manage. Meanwhile, State scored once in the first inning and put the game away with six runs in the fifth and one in the eighth. State's starting pitcher, Christian MacLeod, lasted only 1 2/3 innings. He gave up all of Kent State's four hits and three runs. Winning pitcher reliever, Brandon Smith, struck out five batters in 4 1/3 innings and gave up no hits, runs, or walks. In his first appearance of the year, sophomore Will Bednar struck out two batters while pitching a scoreless inning. MSU pitchers struck out a total of 15 batters. The Golden Flashes' pitchers walked nine batters, helping MSU's cause. Rowdey Jordan got two hits and scored two runs while raising his batting average to .195.

Kent State got a measure of revenge in the next game by banging out 13 hits and scoring nine runs to MSU's 10 hits and five runs. Five of the Flames had two hits each, and the Flames had a home run and two doubles. In quite a change, Kent State walked only four batters, and their winning pitcher, Luke Albright went 6 2/3 innings and gave up only one run and five hits. Losing pitcher, Eric Cerantola, went three innings and gave up five hits and four runs while walking four batters and striking out four. Bulldog batters Scotty Dubrule and Kamren James had two hits each, and the Dawgs slugged three doubles. Rowdey Jordan went one-for-five at the plate, but that hit drove in a run. Jordan's average climbed to .196.

Faced with another rubber game, MSU blew out Kent State 13-0 to win their second straight weekend series. Four MSU pitchers combined to pitch a no-hitter. Starter and winner, Jackson Fristoe, went six innings, faced only

18 batters, and struck out eight. Landon Sims pitched one inning, walked a batter, and struck out two. Mikey Tepper threw 1 2/3 innings, facing five hitters and striking out three. Cameron Tullar pitched 1/3 of an inning and faced two batters and walked one. Third baseman Kamren James's two doubles and a home run produced five RBIs. With four players registering two hits each, MSU generated 16 hits and 12 RBIs. In his first four plate appearances, freshman shortstop Lane Forsythe went two-for-four and scored two runs. Moved from the number-one slot in the batting order to number three, Rowdey Jordan went two-for-three at the plate and raised his average to .227. Jordan also scored two runs and walked twice; he was becoming the big contributor he was expected to be.

MSU faced Grambling on March 9 in a mid-week game at the Dude. Coach Lemonis decided to go with a pitcher by committee strategy. In his first start of the season, Will Bednar pitched only two innings, giving up a hit and no runs while striking out five hitters. None of the other seven pitchers used by MSU threw more than an inning. MSU pitchers struck out 13 batters and gave up only two hits and two walks. Meanwhile, State's position players were at work banging out 11 hits, scoring 10 runs, and fielding flawlessly. A total of 25 Bulldogs saw action in the game. Enough said about MSU's 10-0 victory against the overmatched Tigers.

MSU rarely plays two mid-week games, but after defeating Grambling they squared off at home the next day against the University of Louisiana Lafayette (ULL) Ragin' Cajuns. Three pitchers combined to throw MSU's third straight shutout. Winning pitcher, Houston Harding, started and went five innings, giving up three hits, striking out eight and walking one. Preston Johnson took over and pitched two innings, giving up a hit and striking out four. Landon Sims finished, going two innings, giving up three hits, one walk, and striking out five of the nine batters he faced. Again, MSU played flawlessly in the field.

Meanwhile, Bulldog bats were cold. The Cajuns threw eight pitchers at the Dawgs, and the home team responded with a total of only four hits. MSU scored two runs in the first inning, thanks to an error and two wild pitches. State scored its other two runs in the sixth inning. Rowdey Jordan led off the inning with a walk and eventually scored on a wild pitch. Tanner Allen singled and subsequently scored on a sacrifice fly. Final score, MSU 4,

ULL 0.

The Eastern Michigan University (EMU) Eagles visited Starkville the weekend of March 12-14. EMU is located in Ypsilanti, where the average high March temperature is 45 degrees. It is understandable that EMU would come to Starkville, where the average March high is 66 degrees to play baseball.

The Friday game had to be discouraging for the visitors because MSU pounded the Eagles 14-0. Five MSU pitchers gave up a total of three hits and struck out 18 batters. The winning pitcher, Christian MacLeod, started and gave up one hit in five innings while striking out 11 batters. Four relievers each pitched an inning, giving up a total of two hits and striking out seven batters. This made four consecutive games that Bulldog pitchers had shut out their opponents. Once again, MSU was faultless in the field. State hitters collected 14 hits and 14 RBIs while producing 14 runs. Seven of the hits were doubles. Freshman Lane Forsythe, who had settled in at shortstop, had three hits and a walk. He also scored a run and batted in a run. Rowdey Jordan went one-for-three at the plate, walked, and scored two runs. He was now hitting a productive .246.

On Saturday, MSU pitching proved to be mortal. Well, somewhat mortal... in the fourth inning, starter Eric Cerantola gave up a home run to the Eagles shortstop, Taylor Hopkins. Bulldog pitchers gave up only one more hit in the game. But the home run put the Eagles up 1-0, a lead that they held until the ninth inning. The Eagles' starter, Justin Meis, cruised through eight innings without giving up a hit. But in the ninth inning, Meis couldn't get an out. Allen singled, and James was hit by a pitch, forcing Allen to second. Hancock singled, driving in Allen to tie the score and sending James to third. Cameron Wagoner came in to pitch for the Eagles. Logan Tanner hit Wagoner's first pitch over the left center field wall for a three-run, walk-off home run. The Dawgs scored four runs in the bottom of the ninth and dispatched the Yankee visitors 4-1. Once again MSU was flawless in the field. Tanner's home run had produced the Dawgs' fourth walk-off victory of the season.

The final game of the series resulted in a 4-1 win for State. In the second inning, Scotty Dubrule's three-run double scored Tanner, who had singled; Josh Hatcher, who had singled; and Forsythe, who had reached base on a fielder's choice. In the top of the third inning, EMU's Mark Kattula hit a solo home run. In the bottom of the third, MSU countered as Tanner hit a solo home run to left field. That ended the scoring. The Dawgs had eight hits on the day while the Flames mustered only four. Bulldog pitching excelled again. Starter Jackson Fristoe pitched four innings, struck out three, walked two, and gave up three hits and one run. Will Bednar relieved Fristoe and pitched four innings, giving up a hit and striking out seven batters. Landon Sims pitched the ninth inning and struck out all three hitters he faced.

Bulldog pitchers had given up a total of two runs in their last six games. After his team completed its first three-game sweep of the season, Coach Lemonis emphasized the importance of not walking people. He said to a news reporter:

> This group, we threw some balls week one, and so it threw me off because we had been so good pounding the zone throughout practices. In the last couple weeks, they're pitching the way they normally do, and they've been really good ... The two solo homers were the only runs we gave up all weekend, so making sure nobody is on base for that is probably the key.

MSU hosted Samford on March 16 in a game that matched Bulldog against Bulldog. The Mississippi Bullies won. Seven pitchers marched to the mound for MSU. Apparently, Coach Lemonis wanted his pitching staff to be well rested for the upcoming series against LSU. Houston Harding started and went 3 1/3 innings and allowed no runs. He gave up four hits, struck out two and issued no walks. Winning pitcher Brandon Smith faced only five hitters while throwing 1 2/3 innings and giving up nothing. The Samford Bulldogs sent eight pitchers to the mound. They combined to give up 10 hits and 10 runs while walking eight and striking out seven batters. Catcher Luke Hancock hit two home runs and drove in three runs. Josh Hatcher also homered for the Mississippi Bulldogs.

MSU's record was 14-3, and they were about to begin SEC play. The Diamond Dogs were ranked 4th nationally in the coaches' poll. But the hard part was about to begin. The Dawgs were scheduled to play 30 SEC games over the next 10 weekends and nine mid-week games against non-conference opponents.

Over the first 17 games, MSU had averaged scoring 7.2 runs per game and allowing 2.8 runs. In the first three games against top-flight competition in The State Farm College Baseball Showdown, MSU had averaged scoring 7 runs and allowing 3.67 runs per game. After the March 6 game against Kent State, Coach Lemonis made changes in the field and in the batting order. Kamren James moved from shortstop to third base, and freshman Lane Forsythe took over at shortstop and batted ninth. Rowdey Jordan, who was hitting .196, was dropped from first to second in the batting order, and Scotty Dubrule was moved up from second to the leadoff spot.

In the first seven games the Bulldogs committed 12 errors, but in the next 10 games they committed only seven. Thirty-eight walks were issued by State pitchers during the first seven games. Walks dropped to 20 over the next 10 games. The Diamond Dogs struck out 46 times in the first seven games and 47 times in the next 10 games. Rowdey Jordan was hitting .182 after seven games, but he had improved his average to .239 after 17 games. Tanner Allen was hitting .346 after seven games and .308 after 17. The two team leaders were going in different directions after 17 games. Both needed to make major contributions if MSU were to thrive against SEC foes.

The Southeastern Conference Plus

After playing their last 14 games at the Dude and going 12-2, the Dawgs hit the road to Baton Rouge to take on the Tigers of LSU. Going into the weekend series, MSU was ranked second nationally while LSU, with a 14-3 record, was ranked 10th. MSU won the March 19 game 6-1 against one of their biggest rivals. Winning pitcher Christian MacLeod started for the Diamond Dawgs and threw six innings, giving up six hits and one run while registering 12 strikeouts. Brandon Smith finished the game, facing only 10 batters, giving up a hit and fanning three. Neither team scored in the first four innings. State broke the stalemate in the fifth when Josh Hatcher led off with a double, and Brayland Skinner homered. The Tigers scored their only run in the sixth when Gavin Douglas doubled, driving home Cade Doughty, who had singled. The Bulldogs added a run in the seventh on a double by Hatcher and a single by Skinner. Logan Tanner gave MSU a cushion in the top of the eighth when he hit a double and drove in Rowdey Jordan and Tanner, both of whom had singled. Shortstop Lane Forsythe sealed the deal when he drove in Kamren James. MSU batters stroked 11 hits with the bottom third of the batting order, Hatcher, Skinner, and Forsythe accounting for seven of those hits. This was MSU's 20th game of the season. In the first 10 games the Dawgs committed 16 errors, but in the second 10 games they committed only six, a good omen.

On March 20 three MSU pitchers Will Bednar, Preston Johnson, and Landon Sims shutout the Tigers, allowing only five hits. Starting and winning pitcher, Bednar, threw five innings and gave up three hits; Johnson threw two innings and gave up nothing; Sims threw two innings and gave up two hits while earning a save. Meanwhile, four Tiger pitchers allowed the Bulldogs only four hits but three runs. Losing pitcher, London Marceaux, threw seven innings for the Tigers and gave up two hits, three walks, and one run.

The MSU website explained the scoring:

> In a game ruled by pitching, the MSU offense was able to put pressure on the LSU defense and execute some small ball to scratch across enough offense. State had four hits but used a sacrifice fly from Lane Forsythe to open the scoring in the fifth. An RBI single from Rowdey Jordan followed a leadoff walk and a wild pitch. In the ninth a one-out walk was followed by a double from Logan Tanner and an RBI ground out from Josh Hatcher. Luke Hancock was on base twice via walk, while Tanner walked, scored a run and singled. Forsythe, Hatcher, and Jordan contributed RBIs.

LSU denied the Dawgs an SEC road sweep the next day by outscoring them 8-3. State sent five pitchers to the mound, and they gave up a total of six walks and seven hits including two home runs. The Dawg's third pitcher, Jackson Fristoe, was charged with the loss. He threw four innings and gave up a run on three hits and two walks. LSU's winning pitcher, A.J. Lobos, threw six innings, giving up four hits, a walk, and two runs. Tanner Allen went one-for-two at the plate and drove in two of the visitors' three runs. Although a sweep at LSU was not in the cards for the Dawgs, they took home a series win and were off to a good start in SEC play.

On March 24, Mississippi State had a 17-4 record and were ranked #2 in the coaches' poll when they faced a North Alabama team that stood 1-17. It was simply no contest, MSU won 18-1. The Bulldog sent 10 pitchers to the rubber, and they gave up six hits, four walks, and one run while striking out 15 hitters. State hitters had a field day, garnering 14 hits and 14 RBIs. Four Bulldogs had multi-hit games. The North Alabama Lions committed five errors while MSU was flawless in the field.

Number-one ranked Arkansas, sporting a 16-3 record, came to the Dude on March 26 to begin a three-game SEC series with the 17-4, second-ranked Diamond Dawgs. What promised to be an important series for both teams turned into shock treatment for MSU and its fans.

The Razorbacks won the Friday game 8-2, jumping on MSU starting and losing pitcher Christian MacLeod for three solo home runs in the first inning. Designated hitter Matt Goodheart, right fielder Cayden Wallace, and center fielder Christian Franklin did the damage. Franklin hit another homer in the fourth, and MacLeod departed, having gone 3 2/3 innings and giving up five runs while striking out four batters. Six MSU pitchers struck out 13 Razorbacks. The Diamond Dawgs managed only four hits and two runs off Arkansas pitching. Winning pitcher, Patrick Wicklander, threw five innings and gave up two hits and a run. Lane Forsythe registered two of the Dawgs' four hits and one of their two RBIs.

In the Saturday game the Dawgs scored three more runs than they had Friday, but the Razorbacks did the same thing and won 11-5. MSU sent three pitchers to the mound with starter Will Bednar giving up six hits, a walk, and five runs while striking out 10 Hogs. Losing pitcher, Brandon Smith, pitched only one inning, but he gave up five runs on four hits and two walks. Of the 13 hits given up by State pitchers, six were of the extra-base variety, two doubles and four home runs. Bulldog pitchers did strikeout 16 of the porkers. MSU managed 10 hits, three of which were slugged by Tanner Allen, who hit a home run and a double while driving in two runs. The Hogs sent four pitchers to the slab with Caden Monke, who pitched only 2/3 of an inning, coming out the winner. Arkansas pitchers struck out 12 Bullies. After two games, MSU had already lost the series to the Razorbacks and faced the distinct possibility of being swept on their home field by the SEC West visitors.

Sunday didn't bring redemption for the Bulldogs. Arkansas won 6-4 to cap off a humiliating three-game sweep of the second-ranked Bulldogs. MSU's starter and loser, Jackson Fristoe, went 3 2/3 innings, giving up five hits and five earned runs while walking two batters and fanning seven. Houston Harding pitched 1 2/3 innings and gave up a run. In came star reliever Landon Sims, who threw 3 2/3 innings, a very long outing for him, of interesting baseball. Sims faced 15 batters, walked four, struck out five, and gave up no runs. MSU outhit the visitors 11-7 but managed two fewer runs. Four Dawgs—Scotty Dubrule, Tanner Allen, Josh Hatcher, and Brad Cumbest—got two hits each. Hancock and Logan Tanner hit homers. The Hogs' winning pitcher, Ryan Costeiu, threw 1 2/3 innings and gave up two hits and two runs. Jaxon Wiggins, who pitched two innings, earned a save. MSU had managed to score only 11 runs in the series. The Dawgs' one error cost them the game. On a play that should have resulted in the third out of the fourth inning, third baseman Kamren James's throwing error allowed four runs to score.

MSU slid to # 7 in the coaches' poll. But after sweeping the second-ranked team in the country on their home field, Arkansas dropped from #1 to # 2. Vanderbilt, which had the same record as Arkansas, 19-3, moved into first place. MSU now stood 17-7 overall and 2-4 in the SEC with 24 conference games left. The "Clarion Ledger" sports section's March 29 headline read, "**Back to the drawing board for MSU after series sweep.**"

MSU next played SEC rival Kentucky in a three-game series, beginning April 1 at the Dude. The Bulldogs needed to get well soon, and they did just that, sweeping the Wildcats 8-1, 3-2, and 4-3. In the Friday night game, starter and winner, Christian MacLeod, threw six innings, giving up two hits and no runs while striking out 11 batters. Rowdey Jordan, who hadn't been heard from much, hit his third home run of the season, drove in two runs, and scored three times in three official plate appearances. Kamren James went two-for-four at the plate, doubled, stole a base, and drove in four runs. Wildcat batters mustered only five hits.

In the Saturday game, the Bulldogs faced a 2-0 deficit going into the bottom of the sixth inning but rallied to tie the score. Brayland Skinner walked, and Rowdey Jordan singled, moving Skinner to second base. Tanner

Allen singled, scoring Skinner and sending Jordan to third. Luke Hancock drove Jordan home with a sacrifice fly to left field. Jordan scored what proved to be the winning run in the eighth as he singled, moved to second when Tanner Allen was hit by a pitch, advanced to third on a wild pitch, and scored when Luke Hancock hit his second sacrifice fly.

State produced only six hits, all singles, with Jordan accounting for three. Mr. Jordan was coming on strong as he increased his reached-base streak to 11 games. The Wildcats collected their two runs in the fourth inning. The second batter of the inning, John Rhodes, doubled to right field, and T.J. Collett promptly plated both Rhodes and himself with a home run to center field. Kentucky managed only five hits, with Rhodes and Collett each getting two. As the final 3-2 score indicates, both teams enjoyed excellent pitching. Winner Will Bednar started for the Dawgs and went six innings, striking out 10 hitters and giving up two runs on three hits and two bases on balls. Closer Landon Sims pitched two innings, faced seven batters, gave up no hits, and struck out two. Sims also started the game-ending double play as he fielded an attempted sacrifice bunt. Kentucky starter Cole Stupp went seven innings and gave up all of State's six hits and three runs.

The Sunday game was another one-run squeaker as the Dawgs edged the Wildcats 4-3. Six Bulldog pitchers went to the hill and combined to strike out 12 batters, give up six hits, five walks, and three earned runs. Winning pitcher, Jackson Fristoe, started and pitched five innings. He gave up three hits and two earned runs while walking four batters and striking out eight. Parker Stinnett picked up a save by pitching the final inning and giving up no hits or runs. Kentucky scored its three runs one at a time in the second, fifth, and eighth innings. Bulldog batters produced a total of seven hits, only one more than the Wildcats managed, but the Dawgs also scored one more run than the Cats. Two of the Dawgs' hits were home runs by Logan Tanner and Luke Hancock. Tanner also hit a double, and Jordan hit a triple. State scored all four of its runs in the first four innings and never trailed in the game. Kentucky's starting and losing pitcher, Zach Lee, went 3 1/3 innings and gave up six hits and all four of MSU's runs.

The weekend sweep of Kentucky not only boosted MSU's SEC record to 5-4, it also gave the Diamond Dawgs their 11th winning SEC series out of the last 14 they had played. Bouncing back from the sweep by Arkansas was a good omen. MSU's record against SEC opponents would not drop below .500 again in the 2021 season. MSU rose from #7 to #5 in the coaches' poll.

On April 6 the Southern University Jaguars came from Baton Rouge to Starkville to provide the mid-week competition for the Bulldogs. The Jags were overmatched and out of their league. Nine pitchers threw one inning each for the Dawgs, giving up a total of seven hits and one run. Meanwhile, State batters hit four doubles, three homers, and nine singles. Those 16 hits combined with five walks and three errors gave MSU an easy 15-1 victory.

After playing nine straight games at the Dude, MSU ventured to Alabama for a weekend series with the Auburn Tigers at "The Loveliest Village on the Plains." What once was a village is now a city with a population exceeding 76,000.

State was 22-7 overall and 6-4 in the SEC, while Auburn was 12-14 overall and 1-9 in the SEC. The weekend would increase MSU's stock and sink Auburn further in the SEC cellar as the Bulldogs swept the Tigers.

MSU won the April 9 Friday game 6-5. The win marked the third time in their last four games and the fourth time of the season that the Dawgs defeated their opponents by a single run. MSU played long ball with Tiger pitchers as the Dawgs' eight hits included three doubles and two home runs. Tanner Allen homered and drove in three of the Dawgs' runs. In a game with four lead changes, MSU took the lead for good in the eighth inning with the aid of a misplayed popup and a wild pitch. Christian MacLeod, who started for State, gave up two runs on five hits including two home runs, while striking out six batters over six innings. The Dawgs sent four other pitchers to the mound. Brandon Smith, who pitched 2/3 of an inning, giving up a hit and striking out two batters, earned the win, while Landon Sims registered a save by throwing two innings, striking out four Tigers, and giving up nothing. Auburn hitters produced seven hits and four RBIs with shortstop and leadoff batter, Ryan Bliss, accounting for two. Three Tiger pitchers — Cody Greenhill, Richard Fitts, and Carson Skipper — gave up eight hits. Skipper took the loss while throwing two innings and giving up a hit and a run and striking out three batters.

MSU benefited from an outstanding pitching performance from winning pitcher, Will Bednar, in the second game. The sophomore righthander threw seven innings, gave up four hits and one run, while walking none and striking out seven. The run given up was a homer off the bat of designated hitter Cam Hill in the second inning. Reliever Stone Simmons gave up the other Auburn run in the eighth while pitching 1/3 of an inning. Bulldog pitchers struck out 10 hitters and didn't walk a batter. MSU batters pounded out 11 hits including three home runs and a double. Rowdey Jordan, Kamren James, Luke Hancock, and Josh Hatcher all got two hits, and James drove in three runs. Tanner Allen's one hit drove in three runs. Auburn's runs came off a solo home run by catcher Cam Hill in the second and by a single by Ryan Bliss in the eighth that drove in Bryson Ware. In 3 2/3 innings, Tiger starting and losing pitcher, Hack Owen, struck out two hitters, while giving up nine hits including two homers, one walk, and six earned runs. Over the last 5 1/3 innings, Auburn relievers gave up only one run, but the game was already out of hand as the Bulldogs won 7-2.

After the game Head Coach Chris Lemonis commented to the "Clarion Ledger":

> I told the ball club after the game that I thought it was [Will Bednar's] best outing in our uniform. He is a power pitcher, so he usually dominates early [in the game] but, after seven innings, I don't think he came off of his [velocity] numbers. He threw great sliders, mixed in the fastball, and started to use his changeup, which is a nice piece of development against left-handed hitters.

The Sunday game that the Bulldogs won 19-10 was quite different from the previous two. The first inning was brutal for Auburn as the Dawgs scored nine runs off the Tigers' starter and loser, Joseph Gonzalez, in 2/3 of an inning. Carson Swilling finished the inning but not before giving up another run. The Tigers trailed 10-0 before coming to bat. Mississippi State's starter, Jackson Fristoe, gave up four runs in three innings and was relieved by winning pitcher, Houston Harding, who went three innings and gave up one run. The game featured 28 hits, 17 walks, and 29 runs as both teams' batters feasted on below-average pitching. Bulldog hitters managed 17 hits including four extra-base hits. Logan Tanner and Lane Forsythe hit doubles; Tanner Allen hit a triple, and Logan Tanner connected for a home run. Tanner Allen and Luke Hancock both had three RBIs, and Logan Tanner had five. Eight MSU players collected hits with Lane Forsythe, Luke Hancock, Kamren James, and Logan Tanner each posting three hits. Tanner Allen had two hits, and Rowdey Jordan was hit by a pitch four times, setting a school record. The Tigers' 11 hits included three big flies and two doubles. Errors were not needed to pad the scoring, but Auburn committed the game's only fielding miscue. The Tigers used eight pitchers, and the Bulldogs used six in this slugfest.

MSU center fielder and team leader, Rowdey Jordan, grew up in Auburn. Maybe in anticipation of his return to his hometown, Jordan, who had struggled at the plate early in the season, had padded his batting average 119 points going from .167 to .286 since the March 4 Southern Miss game. In the five games just prior to the Auburn series, Jordan had three multi-hit games. Jordan was 9-21 (.429) with seven RBIs and five runs scored in the previous five conference games he had played against Auburn. But he was 0-4 in MSU's first game of the 2019 College World Series against the Tigers. For this series, Coach Lemonis moved Jordan from third place in the batting order to the leadoff position. In this sweep of the Tigers in Auburn, native son Rowdey Jordan went 4-12 at the plate, drove in a run, and scored seven times. He was also hit by a pitch four times in the third game.

After the sweep of Auburn, the Dawgs stood 24-7 overall and 8-4 in the SEC and were ranked #4 in the coaches' poll. The Bulldogs' impressive second SEC sweep in a row had come on the road. MSU was about to go to Starkville for five straight home games, which would feature two out-of-conference foes and a weekend series with the Ole Miss Rebels.

The April 13 game against non-conference foe Arkansas State provided little suspense. The Dawgs led 6-3 at the beginning of the eighth inning, then their bats came alive in the bottom of the inning, and they scored 12 runs. The Red Wolves made an impressive comeback in the top of the ninth, scoring seven runs. Too little too late, MSU won 18-10. State's 15 hits included five homers and three doubles. Freshman Kellum Clark, normally an infielder, played left field, got one hit and drove in three runs, while fellow freshman shortstop Lane Forsythe registered three hits and drove in three runs. Rowdey Jordan got three hits, a single, a double, and a home run while scoring two runs and driving in two. Mr. Jordan had raised his once anemic batting average to .298. Dade Smith was the winning pitcher. Smith threw two innings, walked a batter, and struck out five. Arkansas State used seven pitchers. The last three relievers, none of whom pitched a complete inning, gave up 12 earned runs.

Ole Miss came to Starkville on April 16 for a weekend SEC series. The #6-ranked Rebels were 24-8 overall and, like MSU, 8-4 in the SEC. No doubt the Dawgs had little fear of the Rebels as MSU had handled them readily in recent years. During the 2017 season MSU went 4-0 against Ole Miss, which included a three-game SEC sweep in Oxford. MSU won two of those games by one run and the other two by two runs. In 2018 the Dawgs won three of four from the Rebels including two of three in SEC play at the Dude. In 2019 the Dawgs were 4-0 against the Rebels; that mark included another three-game SEC sweep in Oxford. The two teams did not play each other in the 2020 season because of COVID.

MSU and Ole Miss usually play four games each season, three SEC games and the Governor's Cup. The non-conference cup game is played at Trustmark Park in Pearl. Because of the COVID pandemic, there was no Governor's Cup game during the 2021 season.

The Diamond Dawgs won the Friday, April 16, game 5-2 as 10,291 fans filled the Dude. Ole Miss ace and future first-round draft choice, Gunnar Hoglund, pitched seven innings and gave up four hits and three runs while striking out nine. Derek Diamond pitched one inning and gave up three hits and two runs. The three hitters at the top of State's lineup accounted for six of the Dawgs' seven hits and all five of their runs. Rowdey Jordan went one-for-four, scored a run, and batted in a run. Tanner Allen went three for four and scored two runs. Kamren James went two-for-two and drove in four runs with a homer and a sacrifice fly. Ole Miss scored one of its runs in the third inning when first baseman Cael Baker singled; Jacob Gonzalez walked; Peyton Chatagnier singled Baker to third base, and he scored on an error by MSU shortstop Lane Forsythe. T.J. McCants accounted for the Rebels' other score with a solo home run in the fourth. Ole Miss managed only six hits off three MSU pitchers. Christian MacLeod started for the Bulldogs and pitched five innings, giving up four hits and two runs while striking out five. Winning pitcher, Preston Johnson, went two innings, gave up one hit, and struck out four batters. Closer Landon Sims pitched two innings and gave up a hit and struck out three batters.

The Saturday game, attended by 13,338 fans, proved to be an entirely different affair. Ole Miss sent super lefty Doug Nikhazy to the mound. In one of the best pitching performances these eyes have ever witnessed, Nikhazy completely shut down Bulldog hitters. He gave up one hit (a single by Brayland Skinner), two walks, and no runs. In contrast, Ole Miss batters pounded out 17 hits and scored nine runs while facing four Bulldog pitchers. The Rebels scored at least one run in six different innings. Five Rebels connected for more than one hit, with catcher Hayden Dunhurst leading the way by registering three. Ole Miss hitters stroked four doubles, a triple, and a home run. Every Rebel who batted reached base. MSU starting and losing pitcher, Will Bednar, threw three innings and gave up seven hits and six earned runs.

Both coaches commented on Nikhazy's gem:

Mike Bianco:

> I don't know how many opportunities you get to throw a shutout against your archrival at their ballpark against one of the largest crowds in baseball. He felt great. He looked like he was in total control. The last three innings, he really hit another gear. I wasn't going to take that away from him.

Coach Chris Lemonis commented to the "Clarion Ledger":

> He's one of the best arms in our league and the country. He got a lead, and he took that lead and just jammed it down our throats all day long. Three-pitch mix. It was just really good. We never got on to anything the whole day.

Mississippi State had to win the rubber game on Sunday to move its streak of four consecutive SEC series wins over Ole Miss to five. Recovering quickly from Saturday's humiliation at the hands of Nikhazy, Bulldog batters mustered 12 hits and seven runs to defeat the Rebels 7-5 and win their third SEC series in a row. Leadoff batter, Rowdey Jordan, shinned by going four-for-five at the plate, hitting a solo home run and scoring two runs. In the heat of the SEC schedule, Jordan had really come alive; he was now batting .308. Dependable Tanner Allen went one-for-three and drove in three runs. MSU starting pitcher, Jackson Fristoe, went 2 2/3 innings, gave up two hits and one run while striking out three hitters and issuing four bases on balls. Winning reliever, Houston Harding, threw 3 1/3 innings and gave up two hits and three earned runs while striking out five batters. Ole Miss started Drew McDaniel, who went 5 1/3 innings and gave up three hits and two earned runs while striking out four Bulldogs. Josh Mallitz went to the mound in the sixth inning for the Rebels. Mallitz faced three batters and gave up three earned runs on three hits without registering an out. Austin Miller replaced Mallitz, pitched 1/3 of an inning, gave up two hits and two runs and was tagged with the loss. Ole Miss batters connected for only six hits. Hayden Leatherwood hit two homers and a single and drove in three Rebel runs. The Sunday game drew 10,522 fans. The series, which was played on Super Bulldog Weekend, drew a total of 34,201 fans to the Dude.

After the Ole Miss series, the Bulldogs had to be feeling good about themselves. They boasted a record of 28-5 overall and 10-5 in the SEC and were ranked #4 in the country. Halfway through the SEC schedule they had won four of five series and had swept two of those. The sweep by Arkansas, which had been ranked #1 most of the season, and Nikhazy's gem were in the rearview mirror. The team had jelled in every aspect of the game, and the future looked bright.

On April 20 the University of Alabama at Birmingham came to Starkville for a non-conference game. The UAB Blazers didn't provide much competition as the Dawgs scored 19 runs on 17 hits. Designated hitter Logan Tanner went three for four at the plate and drove in five runs. Kamren James and Luke Hancock drove in three runs each. The Dawgs hit six doubles and three home runs off seven UAB pitchers. Ten pitchers marched to the mound for MSU, and none of them pitched more than an inning. Mikey Tepper started, pitched an inning, gave up a walk and no runs. The Dawgs scored four runs in the bottom of the inning, making Tepper the winning pitcher.

Next the Bulldogs traveled to Nashville to play a weekend SEC series beginning April 23 against Vanderbilt. The Vandy Boys were ranked #2 nationally with a 29-6 overall record and an 11-4 conference mark. The Commodores' roster included two of the very best pitchers in the country, Jack Leiter and Kumar Rocker. In the Friday game, Rocker, the son of former Auburn All-American football player Tracy Rocker, threw a complete game at the Bullies. He gave up three hits and two runs while walking none and striking out eight batters. Christian MacLeod started for MSU and was tagged with the loss after striking out seven batters and giving up four hits, four walks, and four runs while throwing 3 2/3 innings. Rowdey Jordan went two-for-four at the plate and scored one of the Bulldogs' runs.

On Saturday the Bulldogs turned the table on the home-standing Commodores by going up two runs in the first innings and never trailing in their 7-4 victory. Rowdey Jordan led off the game with a home run as his batting average stayed above .300. Catcher Logan Tanner, who went three-for-five at the plate, hit a homer and drove in three runs. Jack Leiter, son of former major league pitcher Al Leiter, did not perform as well as Rocker. Leiter pitched five innings, gave up six hits and four runs, and was charged with the loss. MSU starter and winner, Will Bednar, pitched five innings, gave up three hits, three walks, and a run while striking out eight. In 2 2/3 innings, closer Landon Sims faced 11 batters and gave up two hits and a run while walking a batter and striking out six. Vanderbilt batters tallied only five hits.

After the game Coach Lemonis commented to the "Clarion Ledger":

> We can take a punch as good as anyone right now. Last week it was Doug Nikhazy, and last night it was Kumar Rocker. In this league, you kind of get used to [seeing really good pitching], but we have some tough dudes. We really compete, too. If you look at some of the [pitchers] we have faced this year and the guys that we have beat, I give [our hitters] a lot of credit. People may knock our offense, but our guys compete, and they win. They put runs on the board when they need to. I am proud of them.

In Sunday's rubber game, the Vandy Boys got the best of the Diamond Dawgs by reversing Saturday's score and winning 7-4. The game started off well for the Dawgs as they knocked Vandy's freshman starting pitcher, Patrick Reilly, out of the game by scoring three runs in 1/3 of an inning. Houston Hancock's double scored Rowdey Jordan, who had walked and advanced to third on a throwing error and a failed pickoff attempt. Scotty Dubrule double scored Hancock and Kamren James, who had walked. The Dawgs scored their third and final run in the second inning when Mr. Reliable Tanner Allen (who had three of MSU's seven hits) delivered his sixth home run of the season. MSU led 4-2 in the fifth when Vandy scored three runs on shortstop Carter Young's home run to take the lead. The Commodores added two more runs in the sixth. Vandy's Chris McElvain relieved starter Patrick Reilly with two outs in the first inning, pitched 5 1/3 innings, and gave up five hits and a run while earning the win. Nick Maldonado threw the last 3 1/3 innings and earned a save. MSU's starter, Jackson Fristoe, suffered the defeat, pitching 4 1/3 inning, giving up four hits and five runs while walking two and striking out six. Four relievers also pitched for MSU and gave up a total of three hits and two runs.

Having won four SEC series while losing two, MSU now stood 11-7 in the SEC. Arkansas was ranked #1 when they swept MSU, and Vanderbilt had been ranked #2 when they took two of three from the Diamond Dawgs.

Texas A&M rolled into Starkville for an SEC series that started April 30. The Aggies were 24-19 overall and 4-14 in the conference. Fifth-ranked MSU looked to take advantage of an unranked team and enhance its SEC record. They did just that by sweeping the series, but it wasn't easy; two of the three games were won by a single run. Mississippi State was ranked #4 behind Arkansas, Vanderbilt, and TCU in the May 3 coaches' poll.

In the Friday game, the Bullies connected for 14 hits and scored eight runs against four Aggie pitchers. Tanner Allen boosted his batting average to .361 by going four for seven, which included a double and a home run. Allen also drove in two runs and scored three. His solo homer in the 12th inning was of the walk-off variety as he continued to establish himself as one of college baseball's brightest stars. Catcher Logan Tanner also homered and drove in three runs. Rowdey Jordan went two-for-six at the plate, scored a run, and bumped his average up to .301 from .299. A&M's starting pitcher, Dustin Saenz, threw 5 2/3 innings, giving up nine hits, two walks, and three runs. Losing pitcher, Alex Magers, pitched 1 1/3 innings and gave up one hit and one run, Tanner Allen's walk-off homer. Aggie batters banged out 12 hits including two doubles and two home runs. Coach Lemonis sent eight pitchers to the mound. Starter Christian MacLeod threw four innings and gave up seven hits and three runs while striking out three batters. Reliever Landon Sims pitched the last three innings, faced 10 batters, gave up no hits, walked one and struck out seven. Sims picked up his third win of the season.

Saturday saw the Dawgs win another squeaker, 3-2 in the first game of a doubleheader. Winning pitcher, Will Bednar, threw five-plus innings, gave up a solo home run to A&M first baseman Austin Bost, and improved his record to 4-1. Bednar struck out seven, walked three, and gave up five hits. Brandon Smith gave up A&M's other run while pitching two innings, giving up two hits and striking out a batter. Loser Bryce Miller started for A&M and gave up three runs on five hits and eight bases on balls and two wild pitches. The walks and wild pitches did the damage. State batters managed only six hits and one RBI. MSU hitters left 13 men on base while A&M hitters stranded seven.

Given an opportunity to sweep the series by winning the second game of the day, Dawg hitters were up to the task. MSU's 17 hits included a double and a home run as the home team won 10-5. Rowdey Jordan's two singles drove in three runs, as did Brad Cumbest's homer and two singles. State took the lead when the Dawgs scored two runs in the fourth inning on a Forsythe double and a single by Jordan. MSU added four more runs in the seventh. The Aggies scored two runs in the eighth, but MSU scored an insurance run in the bottom of the inning. A&M failed to score in the ninth -- final score, MSU 10, A&M 5. Jackson Fristoe started for MSU and gave up six hits and three earned runs in two innings. Winning pitcher, Houston Harding, came on in relief and gave up four hits, two walks, and no runs while striking out four batters over five innings. A&M sent four pitchers to the mound. Starter Nathan Dettmer threw 3 1/3 innings, gave up nine hits, and five runs and was tagged with the loss. Three relievers combined to give up eight hits and five runs.

For 21 consecutive games Dawg pitchers had produced double-digit strikeouts. That streak ended when only nine Aggie batters struck out in the last game of the series. Nevertheless, those strikeouts kept the Dawg pitchers leading the NCAA with 540 Ks for the season. The Dude welcomed 25,958 fans during the weekend series.

Coach Chris Lemonis commented to the "Clarion Ledger" on Houston Harding's performance in the final game:

> Well, to bridge the game like he did [was huge]. We were having a tough time, and we didn't have a lot in the bullpen, so for him to give us five shutout innings there after he came in with two on and no outs—I gave him the shirt after the game because I felt like it was the biggest moment of the game. He was able to help

us win and help us have a good bullpen late in the game.

On getting the sweep:
> I thought we played our best in the second game today, too. I thought the first two games, we were okay and we were still able to win games. I don't know if it was exams or graduation or whatever, I just felt like our energy was a little bit down. The third game, the most tired game, I thought we had the most effort, and I was happy to see them respond. I kind of jumped on them after the first game today. I felt like we missed a lot of opportunities, and I didn't want us to sit back and think about how we took the series. It's never about taking the series; it's about us winning the next game. I was really pleased with the way they played tonight.

The Bulldogs' sweep pushed their overall record to 32-10 and their SEC record to 14-7. The Dawgs had produced three weekend sweeps against SEC teams.

On May 5 the Diamond Dawgs were in South Carolina to take on the Citadel in a non-conference match up. Fourteen position players and seven pitchers saw action for the Bulldogs as the visitors won 10-2. Leading 4-1 in the top of the fifth inning, MSU put the game out of reach by scoring five runs. Dawg batters connected for 13 hits including three doubles and two homers. Brad Cumbest wielded a big stick, driving in four runs while hitting a single and a homer in four trips to the plate. Nine MSU batters got at least one hit with Lane Forsythe leading the way with three. Coach Lemonis sent seven pitchers to the rubber. They gave up a total of five hits including a triple and a home run. None of State's pitchers gave up more than one run. Winning pitcher, Cade Smith, started and gave up one hit and no runs while striking out three batters over three innings. Losing pitcher, Cameron Reeves, threw 2 2/3 innings for the Citadel, giving up four hits and four runs while walking three hitters and striking out three.

While in South Carolina the Dawgs went from Charleston to Columbia for a weekend series with South Carolina. The Gamecocks were 34 and 10 overall and 11-10 in the SEC. In the first game, winning pitcher, Christian MacLeod, threw seven shutout innings at the Gamecocks while giving up a hit, two bases on balls, and striking out six hitters. In the seventh inning the Dawgs sent nine batters to the plate and scored five runs. Kamren James's double drove in three of those runs. MSU mustered 12 hits including three doubles and claimed the game 9-0. Rowdey Jordan went two-for-three at the plate including a double,; he walked twice and scored four runs. Tanner Allen went three-for-four at the plate, scored two runs, and registered two RBIs. The Gamecocks used four pitchers with starter and loser, Brannon Jordan, giving up three runs and eight hits. He also walked four batters, struck out four, and threw four wild pitches.

After the game Coach Lemonis commented to the "Clarion Ledger":
On the series-opening win:

> I'm really satisfied. I thought we were good Wednesday night [against The Citadel]. We played a pretty complete game. Tonight, obviously better competition, but we're playing pretty clean right now. I thought we got a great start from Christian [MacLeod]. We had some really competitive at-bats. [Brannon Jordan] has pitched really well for them all year, and we were able to get a lot of hits off of him, and he hadn't given up many hits all year. We're playing pretty well right now.

On Pitcher Christian MacLeod:

> He was able to mix those two off-speed pitches all night, having his curve and his change was big for him. He was able to keep them guessing all night. I don't think there was a lot of hard contact. He had a good week of work. I think he was coming out and wanted to pitch well [after last weekend]. I've seen a little bit of a different Christian lately. "Hey, I'm going to go out there and pitch and give us a great chance to win." He did that tonight.

On Kamren James's night:

> It was huge because in this ballpark and the way they hit, they've got some home run hitters over there. You can walk a guy or make an error; [they] hit a homer and next thing you know, you're scrambling, and they've got all the momentum. When Kam got that hit, it separated the game enough to where you can take a breath.

In the Saturday game, MSU chased USC starter and loser, Will Sanders, early by scoring five runs off him in 2 1/3 innings. In his brief stint on the mound Sanders faced 14 MSU batters. He gave up a triple to Tanner Allen and a home run to Luke Hancock. Allen's triple scored Rowdey Jordan, who had singled. Hancock's homer drove in two runs. The Dawgs scored single runs in the second, third, and fourth innings and concluded their scoring in the fifth by putting a 3 on the board. Tanner Allen went four-for-five at the plate and drove in three runs. Rowdey Jordan went two-for-three, scored three runs, and collected an RBI. In total the Diamond Dawgs managed 14 hits including three home runs, a double and a triple off of six Gamecock pitchers. USC hitters faced three MSU hurlers and managed a total of eight hits including two home runs and scored six runs. Over six innings MSU starter and winner, Will Bednar, gave up three runs and struck out 13 batters. Landon Sims pitched the last two innings for the Dawgs and slammed the door on the Gamecocks by striking out three while facing only seven batters. The 9-6 victory won the series from USC, but there was a game left to play.

Coach Chris Lemonis commented to the "Clarion Ledger":

> On his team's early offensive success this weekend: [Our success is probably] Because Rowdey [Jordan] and Tanner [Allen] hit first. Those guys have gotten us off to a good start the last couple of weeks. They're locked in, and they give us a chance to score. They're playing well right now, and we are facing really good arms. On taking the series with one game left:

> It's huge. I just told them it's about tomorrow's game. What we've done the first two days should give us some confidence, but it's really about us getting the next game and having more wins than everybody else in our league. All we can control now is what we do tomorrow. Coming out and having a great game tomorrow puts us in a really good position.

In the Sunday game USC bounced back to defeat MSU 4-3 and avoid a sweep. With three players managing two hits each, the Gamecocks outhit the Dawgs 10 to nine. USC took a lead in the second inning by scoring two runs off MSU starter, Jackson Fristoe. David Mendham did the damage with a two-run homer to center field. Fristoe pitched three innings and gave up Mendham's homer and four bases on balls. State scored a run in the third and a run in the fifth to tie the score. The sixth inning saw MSU score another run that put the Dawgs ahead 3-2, a lead they carried to the bottom of the ninth. The Gamecocks rallied on a double by Jeff Heinrich that scored Noah Myers to tie the score and send the game into extra innings. In the 11th, the Gamecocks walked off with a 4-3 win when Mendham drove in Heinrich with a double. This was the first time the Dawgs had lost a game all season while going into the ninth with a lead. Maybe Landon Sims, who had pitched two innings and faced only seven batters on Saturday, should have entered the game for the Dawgs in the ninth. Neither team had many timely hits. The Dawgs left 13 men on base, and USC left 16. Brandon Smith pitched the last two innings for MSU, gave up three hits, and one run and was tagged with the loss. Kellum Clark went two-for-four at the plate for the Dawgs and scored a run when Kamren James hit a sacrifice fly to right field. Tanner Allen hit a solo home run to right field in the fifth inning, and Rowdey Jordan did the same thing in the sixth to close out MSU's scoring. The loss left the Diamond Dawgs with an overall record of 35-11 and a conference mark of 16-8.

MSU was back at the Dude on May 13 for a three-game set against the Missouri Tigers. The Thursday game resulted in a comeback victory for the Dawgs, who trailed 4-2 in the seventh inning but put three runs on the board in the bottom of the inning. Scotty Dubrule's infield single with two outs scored two runs and gave MSU the lead. Luke Hancock got on base three times with a base hit and a pair of walks and scored the eventual game-winning run from second base on Dubrule's infield single. Rowdey Jordan got on base twice with a hit and a walk and increased his reached-base streak to 32 games. Tanner Allen's first-inning double was the 54th of his career, and it tied him for sixth place on the career-doubles list. Preston Johnson, who followed Christian MacLeod and Brandon Smith to the mound and threw two shutout innings for the Dawgs, was the winning pitcher. Landon Sims threw the last two innings and earned a save. Sims faced only six batters and struck out four.

The second game was a different story. Singles are not as valuable as extra-base hits unless those singles drive in runs. In this game MSU hitters connected for nine hits, four of which went for extra bases, two doubles, a triple, and a home run. Tiger hitters produced 13 hits that included only one extra-base hit, a double. In the second inning, Josh Holt hit a double that advanced Josh Day, who had singled to third base. Both Day and Josh Holt scored when Mark Vierling singled. In the third the Dawgs took the lead by scoring four runs. An error, two walks, a wild pitch, a triple, and a single combined to push Rowdey Jordan, Kellum Clark, Tanner Allen, and Kamren James across the plate. Allen's triple that drove in two runs was the big hit. MSU increased its lead to five in the fourth when Rowdey Jordan's double to center field drove home Lane Forsythe, who had reached base on a fielder's choice. The Tigers scored a run in the fifth and three runs in the in the sixth to go ahead 6-5. The runs resulted from two singles, a hit by a pitch, a walk, and a wild pitch. MSU came back in the bottom of the sixth on a home run by Kellum Clark. Missouri put the game away in the ninth inning with three singles and a sacrifice bunt. Ace pitcher Will Bednar started for the Dawgs and went five innings, giving up seven hits, three runs, two walks, and striking out six. Stone Simmons pitched the final two innings and gave up four hits and one run and was charged with the loss.

After splitting one-run wins with the Tigers, The Dawgs needed to claim a victory on their home field to win their seventh SEC series. It didn't happen. The Tigers, who going into the Sunday rubber game had won only six SEC games, jumped on the Dawgs, who had won 17 SEC encounters early and often, and came away with a 16-8 win. The Bulldogs actually outhit the Tigers 16-15, but the Tigers' hits were more timely. Missouri batters drove in 14 runs while MSU hitters drove in seven. The Bulldogs left a lot of runners on base. The Tigers not only had timely hitting, they hit the longball, including four homers, one of which was a grand slam.

According to Head Coach Steve Bieser, this was a much-needed series win for the Tigers.

> Big series win for us. This is a character-building series is something that we've needed for a long time here. I'm proud of how they responded. We're coming in playing a really good team -- honestly, I felt like this was the best team on paper that we've played this season. We came out and played better than the other

team, and when you can do those things, you're going to have some success.

On May 18, MSU played the 24-24 Jacksonville State Gamecocks in the last regular season game at the Dude. The Dawgs came away with a 6-1 victory in a five-inning rain-shortened contest. MSU scored in each of the first three innings, and the Gamecocks scored their run in the fourth. The Bulldogs collected six hits including a two-run homer by Luke Hancock in the first inning and a double by Lane Forsythe. Hancock's two-for-three at the plate gave him his 14th multi-hit game of the season. Tanner Allen's single pushed his hitting streak to 13 games and his reached-base steak to 16. Rowdey Jordan went one-for-three at the plate, drove in a run, and raised his batting average to .310. Jordan's performance increased his reached-base streak to 35. MSU sent four pitchers to the mound including the winner, Parker Stinnett, who threw two innings, walked four batters, and struck out four but gave up no hits and no runs. Jacksonville State's starter and loser, Camden Lovrich, went one inning and gave up Hancock's two-run homer.

Sporting a 37-13 overall record, a 17-10 SEC mark and a #6 ranking in the coaches' poll, the Bulldogs went to Tuscaloosa to play Alabama. The Crimson Tide stood 29-19 overall and 12-14 in the SEC. This last SEC series of the season was extremely important to MSU. The Diamond Dogs needed to win the series to enhance their seeding in the upcoming SEC and NCAA Tournaments. Seeding for the NCAA Tournament was especially important because teams seeded 1-16 would host regional tournaments. Winners of those tournaments would play in Super Regional tournaments, and winners of the Super Regionals would advance to the College World Series.

The first game of the series, which resulted in a 4-2 victory for the Dawgs, was played on Thursday, May 20. The Dawgs scored all four of their runs in the seventh inning. Tanner Allen, who went two-for-five at the plate, hit his 12th double and drove in two runs. This splendid senior outfielder from Theodore, Alabama, was hitting a cool .390, and he had driven in 50 runs. Kellum Clark went two-for-four at the plate, hit a double, scored a run, and drove in a run. Lane Forsythe went one-for-four, scored a run, and drove in a run. Rowdey Jordan got a hit, which stretched his latest hitting streak to 10 games and his on-base streak to 36 games. Alabama's starting pitcher, Tyler Ras, held the Dawgs at bay for six innings, giving up no runs, but MSU got to him in the seventh. In 1/3 of an inning, Ras, who was charged with the loss, gave up a walk, a double, a single, and a another double while the Dawgs scored all four of their runs. Winning Pitcher, Christian MacLeod, threw seven innings for the Dawgs, giving up five hits and two runs while walking a batter and striking out 10. Landon Sims was his usual self over the final two innings. Sims faced eight batters and gave up a hit and a walk while striking out five.

Coach Lemonis commented to the "Clarion Ledger":

On Tanner Allen's approach at the plate:

> He is just really good. I don't even know if it is a hot streak; he just has the ability to barrel everything. You would be amazed how intelligent [he is] standing on deck and the process that he goes through [to get ready for an at-bat]. I am always hearing the comments he is making to [Jake Gautreau]. He is just a special hitter, and he plays with confidence. I do not think that there is anyone in the country with more confidence in the box.

On Christian MacLeod's night on the mound:

> I thought that his stuff was good. Just the liveliness of the fastball and he had a really good breaking ball tonight. He was really good from the get-go and mixed his pitches well. I feel like he got stronger as the game went on. I am not going to say that his fastball got better, but his pitches were [getting stronger] through the middle innings of the game.

In the Friday game, Mississippi State cruised to a 7-0 victory over the Tide on the good right arm of Will Bednar and seven RBIs produced by the first five men in the Dawgs' batting order. Bednar was magnificent, throwing eight innings, giving up three hits and two walks while striking out 11 batters. Rowdey Jordan went two-for-four, hit a double, and drove in a run. Tanner Allen went one-for-four, hit a double, and drove in two runs. Logan Tanner went one-for-five and drove in a run. Luke Hancock went one-for-four and drove in two runs. Kamren James went two-for-four, which included a solo home run. Alabama starter and loser, Dylan Smith, went 7 2/3 innings, gave up eight hits and six runs while walking none and striking out three batters. Of the three hits managed by the Tide, leadoff batter second baseman, Peyton Wilson, collected two; both were singles. The Dawgs completely dominated this game. Could they sweep the series?

In the series final, Alabama grabbed a two-run lead in the first inning and added another run in the second. The Tide held that three-run lead until the fifth when MSU put four runs on the scoreboard. The Dawgs added three runs in the sixth. Alabama did not score another run after the second inning, and MSU didn't score after the sixth. Alabama committed an error in the fifth and two in the sixth. Bama's errors were instrumental in the Dawgs' big innings. MSU won 7-3. Rowdey Jordan went one-for-four, hit a double, scored a run, and drove in a run. Jordan finished the regular season batting .310. He had simply been outstanding in SEC play. Mr. Consistency, Tanner Allen, went two-for-five and drove in a run. Allen capped off the regular season with a .387 batting average. Luke Hancock went two-for-four, hit a double, and drove in a run. All nine of State's starters got at least one hit. MSU's starting pitcher, Jackson Fristoe, threw two innings, gave up two hits, three walks, and three runs. Winning pitcher, Houston Harding, came on and went 5 2/3 innings. In an impressive performance, Harding didn't strike out a batter, but he gave up only two hits and two walks and no runs. Left-handed reliever, Landon Sims, came on in the ninth, gave up a hit and a walk before slamming the door. Alabama batters managed a total of five hits, all of them singles. The Tide sent five pitchers to the mound. Losing pitcher, Landon Green, threw only 1/3 of an inning, giving up two walks and a run.

Here is what Coach Lemonis told the "Clarion Ledger":

> I loved how we played all weekend. I thought that we had the same effort each game. We had a slow start today, but [Houston Harding] was really good. He was probably as efficient of a pitcher that we have had all year. We did not get the strikeouts that we are used to, but we had some quick and easy innings. He was sharp.
>
> We have been one of the top teams in the country all year. I do not know if we have fallen out of the top eight all year besides maybe #10 this week after stubbing our toe last weekend. It is what we have done in the league, playing in the toughest conference in the country. We put it on the line going out of our league

and played a lot better than a lot of people. Our first weekend out we played the Big 12 schools and had success. Then we had Southern Miss and Louisiana-Lafayette in the midweek. We had Kent State and Tulane at home in weekend series early. A lot of people do not spend as much time pushing themselves outside [their conference] like we did.

MSU lost only three of its 23 out-of-conference games all season.

The series sweep of Alabama was huge for Mississippi State. The Bulldogs swept four of 10 SEC series and won three others, two games to one. They had been swept by Arkansas (#1 in the country), and they had lost two other series 2-1. MSU finished the regular season with a record of 40-13, which included a 20-10 SEC mark. The Dawgs would be seeded #3 in the upcoming SEC Baseball Tournament. They would have a first-round bye and would have to lose twice to be eliminated. The May 24 coaches' poll ranked MSU at #6 in the country. The probability of MSU being one of eight national seeds in the NCAA Tournament was very high. A national seed would mean the Dawgs would host an NCAA Regional Tournament, and if they won the regional, they would host a Super Regional.

Post-Season Play

The Arkansas Razorbacks won both the SEC Western Division and the overall SEC Championships with a 22-8 conference record. Tennessee won the Eastern Division with a 20-10 SEC record, which tied Mississippi State for second overall in the conference. Arkansas was seeded first in the conference tournament, Tennessee second, Mississippi State third, and Vanderbilt, which had finished second in the eastern division with a 19-11 conference record, was seeded fourth. All four of those teams had a bye in the first round. Missouri in the Eastern Division, 8-22 in the SEC, and Texas A&M, 9-21 in the Western Division, did not qualify for the SEC tournament.

The SEC Baseball Tournament, played at Hoover Metropolitan Stadium in Alabama May 25-30, was not kind to the MSU Bulldogs. Some think that players, coaches, and fans downplay the importance of a team's performance in a postseason conference tournament when it is already certain that their team has already secured an invitation to the NCAA Tournament. The same folks realize that a team's performance in a conference tournament can mean a lot when the team needs a quality win or two to earn an invitation to the NCAA Tournament. Going into the SEC Tournament, MSU had no worries about getting an invitation to and hosting an NCAA Regional. There was little doubt that Mississippi State would be a national seed.

MSU was assigned to the bracket that included Kentucky, Florida, Tennessee, Alabama, and South Carolina. In the first round, Florida defeated Kentucky 4-1 and advanced to the second round to play Mississippi State. Eleventh-seeded Florida promptly sent MSU to the losers' bracket by thrashing on the Dawgs 13-1. This game got out of hand quickly for MSU. In two innings starting pitcher Brandon Smith faced 16 batters, threw 57 pitches, gave up eight hits, walked two, threw a wild pitch, struck out one, and gave up six runs. Two of the runs scored off Smith crossed the plate in the third inning as he departed in that inning after not registering an out. Cameren Tullar came in and finished the third while giving up four hits and three runs. MSU scored a run in the first inning, so at the end of the third, the Dawgs faced an eight-run deficiency that they were unlikely to overcome. The rest of the game was played and managed like the Dawgs had no chance to win. The carnage was stopped after the seventh inning by the mercy rule. A few numbers are revealing: the Dawgs had four hits, only one of which was of the extra-base variety, Tanner Allen's double. The Gators had 18 hits including four for extra bases. MSU used five pitchers, none of whom were named Will Bednar, Christian MacLeod, or Landon Sims.

Tennessee was regulated to the losers' bracket by 10th-seed Alabama by a score of 3-2. Second-seed Tennessee and third-seed MSU both ended the regular season with 20-10 conference records, and both lost their first tournament game. The Tennessee/Mississippi State losers' bracket game appeared to be an even match, but the Volunteers promptly sent the Bulldogs home, winning by a score of 12-2. In contrast to the Florida game, Coach Lemonis sent his two best starters, MacLeod and Bednar, to the hill along with his star reliever, Sims. It made little difference. In four innings MacLeod gave up five runs on five hits, walked a batter, hit a batter, and struck out four. Bednar threw two innings, gave up five hits and three runs, walked a batter, and struck out four. Stone Simmons pitched an inning and retired all three hitters he faced. Landon Sims started the bottom of the eighth and, believe it or not, got only one out while giving up five hits, a walk, striking out a batter, and allowing four runs. The game was halted after 7 1/3 innings by the run rule. Again, a few numbers explain a lot: MSU registered eight hits, Tennessee 15. The Dawgs managed only one extra-base hit, Rowdey Jordan's double. The Volunteers connected for four extra-base hits, including two homers. Surprisingly, super reliever Landon Sims was the losing pitcher. Perhaps MSU was more interested and focused on the upcoming NCAA Tournament than the SEC Tournament.

For their second SEC Baseball Tournament appearance in a row (there was no tournament in COVID 2020), The Bulldogs had laid an egg. They had been outscored 38-5 in their last four SEC Tournament games. LSU had run-ruled the Dawgs 12-2 in in a seven-inning game in the 2019 tournament. So, in their last three SEC Tournament games, MSU had been run-ruled. The Dawgs returned to Starkville to await news from the NCAA.

Tennessee went on to defeat Alabama in the third round and Florida in the semifinals to win the bracket. In the other bracket, Arkansas defeated Georgia and Vanderbilt in the first two rounds and dispatched #5-seed Ole Miss 3-2 in the semifinals. Tennessee and Arkansas faced each other in the championship game where the Razorbacks prevailed 7-2. Arkansas did not lose a game in the tournament. The Hogs added to their regular season championship the SEC Baseball Tournament Championship. Arkansas (46-10 overall and 23-9 in the SEC) maintained its grip on #1 in the May 31 coaches' poll. Mississippi State (40-15 overall and 20-12 in the SEC) dropped to #8.

When bids to the 64-team NCAA Division1 Baseball Tournament were announced, nine SEC teams made the field: Alabama, Arkansas, Florida, LSU, Mississippi State, Ole Miss and South Carolina. All but three SEC teams, Alabama, LSU, and South Carolina, were named national seeds and were to host regional tournaments. Five of the nine SEC teams, Arkansas, MSU, Ole Miss, Tennessee, and Vanderbilt, won their regionals and advanced to the Super Regionals. The Starkville Regional, which featured MSU, Samford, Virginia Commonwealth University (VCU), and Campbell, was played at Dudy Noble Field.

On Friday, June 4, the Mississippi State Bulldogs defeated the Samford Bulldogs 8-4. There was little doubt about who was going to start this important game. Will Bednar produced another win. Over seven innings, MSU's ace gave up six hits, including two homers and three runs, while walking a batter and striking out eight. Preston Johnson relieved Bednar and gave up a home run and struck out a batter in one inning of work. Stone Simmons pitched the ninth and walked a batter and struck out a batter. Samford's seven hits included three home runs and a double. MSU hitters smacked three doubles and a total of 11 hits. Rowdey Jordan went three-for-five and scored three runs. Tanner Allen went two-for-four, scored a run, and drove in a run. Allen's performance produced his 26th multi-hit game and extended his hitting streak to 19 games and his reached-base streak reached 22 games. Luke Hancock went three for three and drove in three runs.

On Saturday MSU faced VCU in the winners' bracket. VCU had beaten Campbell 19-4 in Friday's opening round. This time the Bulldogs administered a double-digit defeat on the Rams 16-4. Dawg batters pounded five VCU hurlers for 14 hits including three doubles and three home runs. Rowdey Jordan, who hit one of the doubles, went three-for-five, scored three runs and drove in two. Tanner Allen went three-for-five, scored two runs and drove in three. Kamren James went three-for-six, scored three runs and drove in two. James, Brad Cumbest and Kellum Clark hit home runs. MSU scored in six innings and put crooked numbers on the board in the first inning and the sixth. At the top of the sixth, the Rams trailed 6-1, but they soon closed the gap by scoring three runs. State opened the bottom of the inning leading 6-4 but exploded for nine runs to put the game out of reach. VCU aided the outburst by walking two batters, hitting a batter, committing an error and throwing a wild pitch. Losing pitcher, Michael Dailey, started for the Rams and gave up five hits, two walks and three runs. Andrew Ward pitched two innings and gave up all nine runs that MSU scored in the sixth inning. VCU batters registered eight hits including a double and two home runs. Winning pitcher, Christian Macleod, started for the Dawgs, pitched 5 2/3 innings, gave up five hits, four walks, and four runs while striking out a career-high 12 batters.

In the losers' bracket game played Sunday, Campbell defeated VCU 19-10. MSU faced Campbell Monday, June 7, with an opportunity to win the tournament. Should MSU win this game the Diamond Dawgs would be champions of the tournament and move on to the Super Regional Tournament, which would be played in Starkville. If MSU were to lose, they would play Campbell again to determine which team would be the champion and advance to the Super Regional that would be played elsewhere. It took only one game on Monday for MSU to dispatch Campbell and advance to the Super Regional.

MSU started Jackson Fristoe on the mound, but in a very uncharacteristic outing he lasted only 1/3 of an inning. Two walks, a flyout, a home run, and a hit batter caused three runners to cross home plate and chased Fristoe. In came winning pitcher, Houston Harding, who went five innings, giving up five hits, two walks, and two runs while striking out 10 batters. Landon Sims pitched the last three innings, giving up two hits while striking out four batters. Cade Boxrucker started for the Camels and gave up three hits including a home run and five runs while walking three batters. In 2/3 of an inning, reliever Ryan Chasse faced only three batters and gave up a walk. In came Thomas Harrington, who delivered an outstanding performance, going five innings, facing 20 batters, striking out three and granting a walk while giving up a home run. Boxrucker was tagged with the loss. Rowdey Jordan, who hit .533 for the tournament, went two-for-five and scored a run. Tanner Allen, who hit .583 for the tournament, went two-for-three at the plate, walked twice and scored a run. The Bulldogs scored all their runs in the first five innings. The Camels scored three runs in the first inning and two in the sixth to pull within one run of the Dawgs. But they could not score against Sims, who shut them down over the last three innings. Final score, MSU 6, Campbell 5.

The Dawgs had swept the Starkville NCAA Baseball Regional and would face Notre Dame in the Starkville Super Regional. This was MSU's fifth straight trip to a Super Regional. Notre Dame had hosted Central Michigan, the University of Connecticut and Michigan in the South Bend NCAA Baseball Regional. The Irish had scored 50 runs in its three-game sweep of the regional. They defeated Central Michigan 10-0, UConn 26-3 and Central Michigan again 14-2. At the end of the regular season on May 31, Notre Dame was ranked # 6 in the coaches' poll with a 30-11 record, and Mississippi had been ranked #8 with a with a 40-15 record. Now the Irish boasted a 33-11 record, and the Dawgs came in at 43-15. The stage was set for what turned out to be a real donnybrook of a tournament at Dudy Noble.

The first game played on Saturday, June 12, drew a Super Regional record crowd of 14,385 to the Taj Mahal of College Baseball. Excitement flooded the Dude for nine innings as the teams competed in a contest of wills. The Irish scored one run in each of the first four innings. The Dawgs countered with a run in the first inning and two in the third. Aided by a walk and two batters being hit by pitches, Notre Dame put three runs on the board in the top of the fifth to increase its lead to 7-3. MSU promptly played catch-up by scoring three runs with the help of an intentional walk and two errors in the bottom of the inning and trailed by only one run going into the sixth. Notre Dame failed to score in the pivotal sixth, ending a string of five straight innings of scoring at least one run. Mississippi State scored two runs in the bottom of the inning to take a one-run lead. Both teams scored one run in the seventh to end the scoring. The Dawgs outlasted the Irish 9-8. Rowdey Jordan went three-for-five at the plate, scored three runs and drove in two. Tanner Aallen went one-for-three, scored three runs and drove in a run. Kamren James went two-for-four with two RBIs and a run scored. MSU batters posted ten hits in the game, five of which were long balls. Jordan, Allen and Tanner Logan hit home runs while Jordan and Brad Cumbest hit doubles. MSU's starting pitcher, Will Bednar, threw 71 pitches over three innings of work. He gave up seven hits, two bases on balls, and four runs while striking out four hitters. Chase Patrick relieved Bednar and over 1 1/3 innings gave up three runs on three hits and a walk. Winning pitcher, Preston Johnson, relieved Patrick and threw 2 2/3 innings, giving up two hits and one run while striking out a batter. Landon Sims pitched the last two innings and gave up nothing while striking out three batters. Irish hitters managed 12 hits including three doubles and two home runs. Shortstop Zack Prajzner, who batted eighth for the Irish, carried the big stick in this game. He went three-for-four including a three-run homer and collected four RBIs. He also made two of the Irish's four errors. Surprisingly, Notre Dame used only two pitchers. John Bertrand started and over four innings gave up six hits and four runs. Tanner Kohlhepp, who was tagged with the loss, pitched four innings and gave up four hits and four runs.

Notre Dame stormed back and won the Monday game 9-1 to square the series at a game apiece. The Irish's starting and winning pitcher, Aidan Tyrell, put on a show, throwing 7 1/3 innings, striking out six batters, giving up five hits, three walks and one run. Reliever A Rao pitched 1 2/3 innings and walked a batter and struck out a batter. The Irish played better in the field, committing only one error, which didn't figure in the scoring. MSU's starting and losing pitcher, Christian MacLeod, threw five innings and gave up seven runs on five hits and two walks while striking out seven. Brandon Smith and Cade Smith closed out the game for the Bullies, with Brandon Smith giving up the Irish's last two runs.

MSU's only run came in the top of the first inning when Rowdey Jordan tripled, and Tanner Allen drove him home with a sacrifice fly. The Dawgs managed only five hits all game. Jordan's triple was their only extra-base hit. Allen's RBI was his 60th of the season. In contrast, the bottom part of the Notre Dame batting order was very productive. Six through nine-hole hitters collected seven of the eight RBIs the Irish generated. The ninth-place hitter, catcher D.J. LaManna, produced three of those RBIs. The Irish scored two runs in the first inning, four in the fourth, two in the sixth, and one in the seventh. Of the eight hits the Irish managed, one was a triple, and two were home runs. Bulldog fans, a large majority of the 13,971 in attendance, walked away from the Dude disappointed, but their coach was upbeat.

Coach Lemonis told the "Clarion Ledger":

> I think they are fine. I think we just got outplayed. I loved the way our guys went about their business tonight. Obviously, we don't want to make errors [2], but we had some really good at-bats. They just made plays. Cade Smith went out there late and pitched well. Like I said, it's baseball. You scratch it and get ready to go the next day, and our kids will be ready. They've played in this environment all year, and we've been in this 'Sunday game for the series' a lot this year, and our kids have always responded. I'm looking forward to seeing them play tomorrow.

The third game would decide which team would advance to the College World Series. It would be the most important game played to date at the new Dudy Noble.

Both teams scored a run in the first inning; right fielder Ryan Cole homered for the Irish, and Rowdey Jordan reached first base on an error and scored on a single by Kamren James. The second inning proved to be very encouraging for MSU and its legion of fans. Notre Dame put a zero on the board in the top of the inning, and the Dawgs followed with a six-spot. Two Irish pitchers gave up five walks, three singles, a sacrifice fly, and a home run in the frame. But a six-run lead after two innings was not safe when these two teams were playing. Both teams scored a run in the third inning, but in the fourth, the Irish put another zero on the scoreboard while MSU put up a 2. The Dawgs now led by eight. Notre Dame scored three runs in the top of the fifth to reduce State's advantage to five. MSU reacted by scoring a run in the bottom of the inning and moved the Irish deficient to six. The scoring ended in the seventh when the Irish scored two runs, and the Dawgs failed to score. Final score MSU 11, Notre Dame 7. The victory brought MSU's record to 45-16 for the season.

Bulldog batters pounded out 12 hits including four doubles and two home runs. Five Dawgs had two hits in the game. In four plate appearances, catcher Landon Tanner hit a double and a home run, scored two runs, and drove in three. Tanner Allen went two-for-four at the plate, hit a home run, and drove in his 61st and 62nd runs of the season. Allen was batting .392, Brad Cumbest .333, and Rowdey Jordan .326 after the Super Regional.

MSU's loyal fans showed up in droves again on a Monday night to witness their Bulldogs earn their third consecutive trip to the College World Series. The 11,754 people who walked through the gates at the Dude brought the three-game total attendance to 40,140, a record for an NCAA three-game series. MSU became the latest of ten schools that had earned a berth in the CWS three consecutive seasons since the Super Regional format was implemented.

Coach Lemonis told the "Clarion Ledger" about the kind of culture he was trying to build:

> Well, it was here when we got here. Obviously, when you decide to go to Mississippi State, you're going to a program where that's the aspiration. That's why we have the ballpark we do, the fan base we do. Our goal was to keep it moving and keep it moving forward. The nice part is all these young players in the program right now have experienced it, and they want it. That just continues to grow and sets the expectation higher. That's why I'm thankful that Tanner [Allen] and Rowdey [Jordan] decided to

come back. I'm so happy for them, and last year at this time, we didn't know what they were going to do. Coming back and being able to go to Omaha for a third time with the park packed just makes up for a lot that we lost last year.

The 2021 Men's College World Series

College football and basketball have a few schools which, for lack of a better term, are considered the elite or royalty of the sport. Think Alabama, Oklahoma, Ohio State, and Southern California in football, and Duke, Kentucky, North Carolina, and UCLA in basketball. NCAA Division 1 College Baseball also has an elite group of schools, and Mississippi State is one of them. The writers' working definition of an elite baseball school is one that has been to the CWS at least a dozen times and has won at least one championship. There are 11 such schools: Texas, Southern California, Arizona State, Miami, Arizona, Stanford, LSU, California State Fullerton, Oklahoma State, Florida, and Mississippi State. Four of these elite schools—MSU, Texas, Arizona, and Stanford—made it to the 2021 CWS. MSU is one of only five schools and the only SEC school to play in the CWS in five straight decades.

Three SEC schools won their Super Regionals and advanced to the CWS, Mississippi State 45-16, Tennessee 50-16, and Vanderbilt 45-15. Arkansas finished the regular season 46-10 and ranked #1 in the coaches' poll. The Razorbacks won the SEC regular season and tournament championships and the Fayetteville Regional that included Northeastern, Nebraska, and the New Jersey Institute of Technology. But they would not be competing in the CWS. North Carolina State, out of the ACC, which won the Ruston Regional, eliminated the Hogs in the Fayetteville Super Regional. The outcome of that Super Regional, which drew more than 33,000 fans, was simply shocking. The Razorbacks won the first game 21-2, but the Wolfpack captured the second game 6-5 and the decisive third game 3-2. The ACC was represented by both North Carolina State and Virginia in the CWS, and the Pac 12 was represented by Stanford and Arizona. Texas represented the Big 12.

As has been discussed, COVID cut short the 2020 season, and no CWS was played in 2020. COVID was still a problem in 2021, and it had a huge impact on the CWS. North Carolina State (NC State) was placed in bracket

1 with Stanford, Arizona, and Vanderbilt. NC State defeated Stanford 10-4 in first-round play and Vanderbilt 1-0 in the second round. Vanderbilt won its losers' bracket game against Stanford 8-5 and advanced to the semifinals to play NC State, where the Commodores won 3-1. Normally, because both Vanderbilt and NC State had lost only one game in this double-elimination tournament, they would play again to determine the winner of the bracket and earn the right to play the winner of bracket 2 for the championship. COVID protocols imposed by the NCAA forced a change. The Associated Press explained:

> Vanderbilt will advance to the College World Series finals after North Carolina State was forced to drop out because of Covid-19 protocols, the NCAA announced early Saturday. North Carolina State had only 13 players available during its 3-1 loss to the Commodores on Friday. The teams were scheduled to meet again Saturday afternoon in a winner-take-all bracket 1 final. The NCAA Division I Baseball Committee declared that game a no-contest. "This decision was made based on the recommendation of the Championship Medical Team and the Douglas County Health Department," the NCAA said in a statement. As a result, Vanderbilt will advance to the CWS Finals.

Mississippi State was placed in bracket 2 along with Tennessee, Virginia, and Texas.

On Sunday, June 20, the Dawgs played Texas in the first round, and pitching dominated the contest. The Diamond Dawgs managed only five hits. In four at-bats, Rowdey Jordan got two singles but didn't score or drive in a run. Kamren James went one-for-three at the plate and scored a run. Luke Hancock went one-for-four and scored a run. Brad Cumbest went one-for-three, accounting for the Dawgs' only extra-base hit, a triple, and drove in a run. State scored two runs in the fourth inning. A run scored when James walked; Hancock singled, sending James to third, and Scotty Dubrule hit a sacrifice fly, sending James home. The second run crossed the plate when Cumbest hit a triple, scoring Hancock. Texas pitcher Ty Madden performed well on the big stage. He went seven innings and gave up only four hits and two runs while striking out 10 Bulldogs. Hansen relieved

Madden and threw the eighth and ninth innings, giving up a hit and striking out two batters. Meanwhile, MSU pitchers Will Bednar and Landon Sims stifled Texas batters. Bednar went six innings and gave up one hit and one walk while striking out 15 batters and allowing no runs. Bednar's 15 strikeouts set a new MSU strike-out record for a nine-inning CWS game. It also tied Bednar for sixth place for a nine-inning game in CWS history. Sims pitched three innings and gave up three hits and a run while striking out six hitters. Texas's only run came on a home run by Mike Antico in the ninth inning. Bednar's 15 strikeouts and Sims' six set a new CWS record for a single nine-inning game, 21. Final Score MSU 2, Texas 1. Bednar was the winning pitcher and Madden the loser. In the well--played game, Texas made the only error. Mississippi State advanced to play Virginia in the second round.

MSU (46-16) played the Virginia Cavaliers (36-25) on Tuesday, June 22, in a nailbiter. When the Dawgs came to bat in the top of the eighth inning, they were trailing the Cavs 4-0. MSU starter Christian MacLeod lasted only 1 1/3 innings and gave up five hits, two walks, and four runs. Seven pitchers followed MacLeod to the slab for MSU: Preston Johnson, Chase Patrick, Parker Stinnett, Cameron Tullar, Cade Smith, Stone Simmons, and Landon Sims. Of those seven only Simmons gave up a run. The eight MSU pitchers combined to strike out six batters while giving up 12 hits, five runs, and four walks. Virginia's starting pitcher, Griff McGarry, allowed only two base runners while giving up no hits to the Dawgs through seven innings. Scotty Dubrule led off the eighth inning with a walk; Brad Cumbest flew out, and Kellum Clark smashed a two-run homer. Batting for Lane Forsythe, Josh Hatcher singled; Rowdey Jordan doubled, and Tanner Allen smacked a three-run homer. McGarry, who had given up two runs in the inning, was relieved by Zach Messinger, who gave up two hits and two runs without retiring a batter. Stephen Schoch came in and gave up two runs on two hits while pitching only 1/3 of an inning. Nate Savino got the last out of the eighth and one out in the ninth and gave up a hit and no runs. Kyle Whitten closed out the ninth, giving up only a walk. Final score 6-5, MSU. Cade Smith was the winning pitcher, and Schoch was the loser. Landon Sims registered a save for pitching 1 1/3 inning and giving up nothing. The Dawgs headed to the semifinals where they would face Texas, who had defeated both Tennessee and Virginia in the losers' bracket.

At the beginning of the season the Diamond Dawgs defeated Texas 8-3 in the State Farm College Showdown, and in the CWS they had sent the Longhorns to the losers' bracket by defeating them again 2-1. If MSU were to defeat Texas again in the Friday game, they would advance to the CWS finals. If Texas won, the teams would have to play again in the double-elimination format to determine which one would advance to play the winner of bracket 1. Going into the ninth inning the score was even, 5-5. Texas had scored one run in the first, second, and fifth innings and two in the seventh. MSU had scored two runs in the fist inning and three in the eighth. Texas scored three runs in the ninth inning, and MSU didn't score. The 8-5 Texas win extracted a measure of revenge for their previous two losses to the Dawgs and set up another game between the two teams to determine which one would advance to the CWS finals.

Mississippi State squared off again with Texas on Saturday, July 26. In the preseason coaches' poll, Texas had been ranked #10, and at the end of their regular season, the Longhorns had ranked #4 with a 42-15 record. This game would end the season in disappointment for one team and qualify the other team to face Vanderbilt, winner of bracket 1, in the championship series for all the marbles. The first time the two teams faced each other in the CWS, MSU pitchers Will Bednar and Landon Sims combined to stymie Texas by combining to allow four hits and one run while striking out 21 batters in the Dawgs' 2-1 victory. Will Bednar started again for MSU in this rubber game in the best-two-of-three matchup. Bednar threw 6 1/3 innings and allowed four hits, three runs, and two walks while striking out seven batters. Texas scored two runs in the top of the second inning on a walk to Ivan Melendez and a homer by Cam Williams. The Horns scored their last run in the fifth on doubles by Douglas Hodo and Mike Antico. Landon Sims relieved Bednar with one out in the seventh inning. Winning pitcher Sims closed out the game by throwing 2 2/3 innings, striking out four batters and giving up no hits or runs.

Texas pitcher Tristan Stevens started for the Longhorns and went five innings, giving up nine hits and three runs while walking a batter and striking out two. The losing pitcher, Cole Quintanilla, threw 3 1/3 innings, giving up three hits and one run while walking a batter and striking out five. MSU scored single runs in the third, fifth, and sixth innings, so the score was 3-3 at the beginning of the ninth. Texas could not score against Sims in the top of the inning. In the bottom of the inning, Brad Cumbest struck out; Kellum Clark was hit by a pitch, and Brayland Skinner came in as a pinch runner for Clark and promptly stole second base. Tanner Leggett's single to center drove in Skinner with the winning run. Final score MSU 4 Texas 3. MSU would face Vanderbilt in the finals of the CWS. Vanderbilt was the defending CWS and NCAA champions, having won the 2019 CWS and COVID having wiped out the scheduled 2020 event.

Vanderbilt was ranked #3 in the preseason coaches' poll. The Commodores lived up to their early billing by posting a 39-13 regular season record that included a 19-10 SEC slate. They had won two of three from MSU in SEC play. In the double-elimination SEC tournament Vandy defeated Ole Miss 5-4, lost to Arkansas 6-4, and was eliminated by Ole Miss 4-1. Going into the NCAA Tournament Vanderbilt was ranked #3 in the coaches' poll with a 40-15 record. The 'Dores hosted and swept the Nashville Regional by defeating Presbyterian 10-0 and Georgia Tech 4-3 and 14-1. In the Nashville Super Regional Vandy swept East Carolina 2-0 and 4-1. Vanderbilt sported a 45-15 record at the start of the CWS. Placed in bracket 1, they beat Arizona 7-6, lost to NC State 1-0, beat Stanford 6-5 and NC State 14-3 to advance to the CWS finals against MSU.

Vanderbilt extended its postseason winning streak to six games by defeating MSU 8-2 on June 28 in the first game of the CWS finals. Vanderbilt's starting pitcher, Jack Leiter, who would be the second pick in the upcoming Major League draft, gave up three hits and two runs while walking three batters and striking out six over six innings. Kamren James homered in the top of the first inning, and in the fourth, Logan Tanner singled home Tanner Allen, who had doubled to close out MSU's scoring. Nick Maldonado relieved Leiter and earned a save by slamming the door on the Bulldogs by giving up two hits and nothing more over the last three innings. Meanwhile MSU starter and loser, Christian MacLeod, didn't make it out of the first inning. In 2/3 of an inning, he gave up a single and a double, walked two batters, hit two batters, and allowed six runs. Five pitchers followed MacLeod to the mound for the Dawgs. Chase Patrick came on with two on base and two outs in the first inning. He gave up a three-run homer to Jayson Gonzalez; two of those runs were charged to MacLeod. Cade Smith, Brandon Smith,

KC Hunt, and Jackson Fristoe combined to give up two hits and one run over the last eight innings. This was the Bulldogs' third loss in the four games they had played against Vanderbilt in 2021.

The next day the Bulldogs counter-punched the Commodores in a big way. MSU's bats came alive and produced 14 hits including doubles by Logan Tanner and Kellum Clark. The Commodores' poor pitching and fielding aided the Dawgs' cause. Five Vandy pitchers issued 10 bases on balls, and the 'Dores committed three errors. Fourteen hits, 10 walks and three errors produced 13 runs for the Dawgs. Vanderbilt starter and loser, Christian Little, lasted only two innings, giving up three hits, four walks, and five runs. Little didn't register an out in the third inning, as all four of the runs the Bullies scored in the frame were charged to him. Four other pitchers followed Little to the mound. Patrick Reilly, Nelson Berkwich, Hunter Owen, and Donye Evans combined allowed eight hits and 11 runs. Four Bulldogs had more than one hit. Scotty Dubrule and ninth-place hitter Lane Forsythe led the way. Dubrule went two-for-six at the plate and drove in four runs while Forsythe went three-for-five and drove in two runs. Vanderbilt batters managed only four hits and two runs off MSU pitchers Houston Harding and Preston Johnson. Lefthander Harding started and gave up two hits, two walks, and one run over four innings. The winning pitcher, righthander Johnson, pitched the final five innings, giving up two hits, two walks, and one run while striking out seven batters. The Dawgs' win set up a championship game to be played the next day, June 30.

MSU faced a huge challenge in the championship game mainly because Kumar Rocker, who was 14-3 on the season would be Vanderbilt's starting pitcher. In 2019 Rocker threw a no-hitter that included 19 strikeouts in a win over Duke in an NCAA Super Regional. He was a freshman at the time. Vanderbilt claimed the 2019 CWS title. Rocker won both of his starts and was named the Men's College World Series Most Outstanding Player. He finished his freshman season with a 12-5 record. Rocker would go on to be drafted number 10 by the New York Mets in the first round of the 2021 Major League draft. The Mets never signed him because of a medical condition. Rocker would be selected by the Texas Rangers as the number-three overall pick in the 2022 draft, and he would sign with the Rangers. Mississippi State would send their ace starter, Will Bednar, sporting an 8-1 record, to the mound. The San Francisco Giants would draft Bednar as the 14 pick in the 2021 Major League draft.

Kumar Rocker lasted 4 1/3 innings against the Dawgs, giving up six hits, two walks and five runs. In the first inning, Rowdey Jordan singled, advanced to second on a fielder's choice, advanced to third on a throwing error by Rocker and scored on a sacrifice fly by Luke Hancock. In the second, two walks and a double by Jordan produced another run. In the fifth, Rocker gave up singles to Jordan, Tanner Allen, Hancock and Logan Tanner, and two more runs scored. Rocker was relieved by Chris McElvain, who gave up MSU's final four runs in the seventh. Tanner's solo homer and Kellum Clark's three-run homer accounted for the four runs. Two other pitchers, Luke Murphy and Thomas Schultz, went to the hill for Vanderbilt, and they gave up a total of two hits and no runs. Meanwhile, Will Bednar and Landon Sims were masterful on the big stage. They combined to shut out an outstanding Vandy team while allowing only one hit. Bednar pitched six innings, walked three batters and struck out four. Sims pitched the last three innings, gave up a hit and a walk and struck out four batters. Shortstop Carter Young managed to get Vanderbilt's only hit, a single to left field in the eighth inning. Final score, MSU 9, Vanderbilt 0.

On June 30, 2021, the Mississippi State University Bulldogs were the NCAA Baseball National Champions, having won the Men's College World series. The 50-18 Bulldogs were also #1 in all the polls, and the 49-18 Vanderbilt Commodores were #2. This NCAA championship was the first team national championship Mississippi State University had ever won. Starkvegas went wild, and MSU fans across the world celebrated the achievement. The celebration went on for days, and the satisfying feeling of winning the 2021 Men's College World Series will linger for years in the hearts of Bulldog fans.

Post-season awards rolled in. The National College Baseball Writers of America (NCBWA) and Baseball America named Tanner Allen and Landon Sims first-team All-Americans. The NCBWA also named Bednar third team All-American. The American Baseball Coaches Association named Coach Chris Lemonis NCAA D1 Coach of the Year and Tanner Allen, Landon Sims and Logan Tanner first-team All-South Region.

Ole Miss

CHAPTER 3
Ole Miss Baseball's Long Journey to the National Championship

According to the Ole Miss Baseball Media Guide, the University of Mississippi first fielded baseball teams during the 1890s. The 1893 team went 0-1-1; the 1895 team 0-2-1, and the 1897 team went 1-1. Very little is known about those three teams, not even the coaches' names. The 1-4 record for the 19th century was not encouraging. Ole Miss got into baseball seriously in the 20th century, and it has fielded baseball teams every year since 1900 except for the war years of 1913, 1944-45. From 1900-1921, Coaches T.H. Johnson, P.J. Murphy, (first name unknown) Ashford, Dr. W.S. Leathers, T.J. Keefe, J.C. Elmer, J.M. Acker, J.W. McCall, Edgar Moss, Casey Stengel, Fred A. Robins, Baxter Sparks, Chester Nobel, and five unknown coaches combined to compile a record of 103-102. The number of games played per season varied from four to 15 during those years. The Baseball Hall of Famer Casey Stengel got his nickname, The Old Professor, at Ole Miss. His 14-10 record with the 1914 Rebels was the best through 1922.

Pete Shields became Ole Miss's head baseball coach in 1923, and he held that position through the 1931 season. Shields posted a 114-59 record. His .657 winning rate is still the best for any Ole Miss baseball coach who coached more than one season.

Tad Smith was the Rebels' head baseball coach from 1932-1942 and from 1946-1950. Goat Hale coached the 1943 team to a 2-10 record. Tad Smith coached Rebel baseball when Ole Miss joined the SEC in 1933. He fielded his first SEC team in 1934. After being shut down for the war years, 1944-45, Ole Miss named Tad Smith athletic director and head baseball coach. Smith relinquished his baseball duties after the 1950 season to concentrate on his duties as athletic director. Smith's overall baseball record was 107-143 - 4. During the 16 years he coached the Rebels, only six teams posted winning records.

Coaches in the College World Series Era

Tad Smith coached Ole Miss Baseball in the first three years of the CWS era, 1948-1950.

Tom Swayze (1951-1971)

In 1951 the great Tom Swayze, one of Johnny Vaught's assistant football coaches, was appointed head baseball coach. Swayze would coach the Rebels from 1951 through 1971. His teams would win 361 games, lose 201, tie 2 and capture four SEC Championships. Swayze would take the Rebels to their first CWS in 1956.

Swayze's 1956 team won the NCAA District III Playoffs in Gastonia, North Carolina. The Rebels played five games in the double-elimination tournament and won four. Ole Miss defeated Tennessee Tech 4-3, and 3-2, lost to Duke 4-2 and defeated Duke 6-2 and 7-1. The tournament victory earned the Rebels their first CWS appearance. In the CWS the Rebels defeated New Hampshire 13-12 and Bradley 4-0 and lost to Minnesota 13-5 and to Arizona 7-3.

Coach Swayze's 1964 squad made another trip to the NCAA District III Playoffs in Gastonia. The Rebels defeated West Virginia 11-0, North Carolina 4-3 and 13-1 to advance to the CWS a second time. The Rebels went two and out in the CWS. They lost to Southern California 3-2 and to Arizona State 5-0.

The last Swayze-coached Ole Miss team to advance to the CWS was the 1969 version. They won the NCAA District III Playoffs in Gastonia again. The Rebels defeated Virgina Tech 7-6, North Carolina 6-5 and 5-2 to earn the Rebels a third trip to the CWS under the tutelage of Coach Swayze.

Thomas King Swayze was born March 15, 1909, in Yazoo City, Mississippi, and died at the age of 93 in Oxford, Mississippi, on February 1, 2003. He graduated from Raymondville, Texas, High School and attended Edinburg Junior College in south Texas. Young Tom Swayze returned to Mississippi and enrolled at Ole Miss in 1929. While at Ole Miss, Swayze played end on the football team and was a left-handed pitcher on the baseball team. He earned three letters in football and four in baseball. After graduating from Ole Miss in 1933, Swayze played professional and semi-professional baseball for several years in Tennessee, Mississippi, Georgia, North Carolina and Canada.

When his baseball playing days ended, Swayze began his coaching career as a football coach at Benoit, Mississippi. He left coaching briefly and entered the insurance business and later worked for a tire re-capping plant in Yazoo City. Moving to Moss Point, Mississippi, Swayze coached both basketball and football and became a high school principal. He soon returned to Ole Miss, where he would leave his mark on athletics in Mississippi and the SEC like no other person has.

Ole Miss Head Football Coach Johnny Vaught hired Swayze as an assistant in 1947. His newly created job was contact man and field representative. That meant Swayze was the South's first football recruiter. Tom Swayze was an assistant coach under Johnny Vaught, but he did not live in the great football coach's shadow.

Swayze cast a long shadow himself as a highly successful head coach. He made his own mark as the University of Mississippi's head baseball coach. Under Swayze the Rebels posted a .640 winning record in all of their games and a .620 record in SEC encounters. Eighteen of Swayze's teams had winning records. Swayze's teams won four SEC championships (1959, 1960, 1964, and 1969). He was named SEC Coach of the Year for each of those championship years. The 1967 Rebels lost to Auburn in the SEC championship series. Swayze's teams posted a 14-2 record in four NCAA District III Tournaments, and they advanced to the College World Series in 1956, 1964 and 1969. Swayze was named NCAA District III Coach of the Year three times.

Coach Swayze developed 38 All-SEC players, eight All-District players, and four All-Americans: Jake Gibbs, Don Kessinger, Bernie Schreiber and Jimmy Yawn. Five of Swayze's players—Jake Gibbs, Don Kessinger, Jack Reed, Joe Gibbon, and Steve Dillard—went on to play major league baseball,. Gibbon pitched for Coach Swayze at Ole Miss and played basketball for Coach Bonnie Graham. In 1956 Gibbon led the Rebels to the College World Series. In 1957 Gibbon was the second-highest scorer in college basketball, averaging 30 points a game. He went on to appear in 400 major league baseball games over a 13-year career.

When Swayze was head coach, the baseball Rebels played in the shadow of Vaught–Hemmingway Stadium on All-American Drive. In 1976 the baseball diamond was named Swayze Field. When the new Oxford-University Stadium opened in 1989, its playing surface was named Swayze Field. These days Ole Miss baseball fans are said to go "Swayze Crazy" during the baseball season.

Nine years after the first CWS, Coach Swayze's 1956 Ole Miss Rebels earned the right to play in the tournament. They were the first Mississippi team to do so. In a big upset the Rebels won the NCAA District III championship without the services of six key players who were ruled ineligible. The six players were ineligible because they had played four seasons of varsity baseball, and at the time the NCAA limited players to three varsity seasons. In the district tourney the Rebs beat Tennessee Tech twice, lost to Duke once and then beat the Blue Devils twice to advance to the CWS. The eight teams to play in the 1956 classic were the University of Arizona, Bradley University, the University of Minnesota, the University of Mississippi, the University of New Hampshire, New York University (NYU), Washington State College and the University of Wyoming. Each of the eight teams was seeking their first CWS title. The Rebels, who were labeled the Cinderella team, played in bracket 2 with New Hampshire, Bradley and Washington State. In the first round the Rebels beat New Hampshire 13-12, and in the second round they beat Bradley 4-0 on a one-hitter by Buddy Wittichen. In the third round they lost to Minnesota 13-5. Ole Miss was eliminated by Arizona 7-3 in the semi-finals. Minnesota won the title by defeating Arizona twice, 10-4 and 12-1. What would the Rebels' record have been if the six players ruled ineligible had been able to play? Unfortunately, we will never know.

Swayze's 1959 and the 1960 SEC champions were invited to participate in the NCAA District III Baseball Tournament. Ole Miss turned down both opportunities. Those outstanding teams were denied the opportunity to play in the NCAA Tournament because of Mississippi's misguided attitude about racial integration at the time. So, both teams lost the chance to possibly advance to the College World Series.

In 1960 Ole Miss won its second consecutive SEC championship with a 22-3 overall record and a 12-2 SEC mark. The Rebels finished fifth nationally in the Associated Press poll. Along the way, Coach Swayze's powerful team posted a 17-game winning streak and won all of their home games. The 1960 Rebels outscored their opponents 163-33, and during the 17-game win streak, the pitching was fantastic. The Rebel hurlers threw four shutouts and gave up two or fewer runs in 13 of the contests. Against SEC teams the Rebels scored 136 runs and gave up 20.

After being crowned SEC Western Division champions, the Rebels met SEC Eastern Division champion, Florida, in a two-game series that decided the overall SEC championship. One game was played in Gainesville and the other in Oxford. The Rebels prevailed in both games. After falling behind 7-0 in Gainesville, the Rebs stormed back to win 15-7. The Oxford contest resulted in a 6-1 Rebel victory.

While the Rebel team was denied the opportunity to play in the NCAA Tournament, accolades poured in for individual players. Star third baseman Jake Gibbs hit .424 and drove in 32 runs. He was named All-SEC and All-American. Pitcher Larry Williams, who earned All-SEC honors for the second time, posted a 7-2 record, struck out 80 batters and compiled a 1.80 earned-run average. Pitchers Denny Blomquist and Don Porter both posted 7-0 records. In addition to Gibbs and Williams, outfielders Billy Ray Jones (BA .281, 5 HRs), Jamie Howell (BA .304), and catcher Robert Khayat (BA .326) were named first-team All-SEC. Even with his .424 batting average, Jake Gibbs did not lead the team in hitting; that honor went to Chuck Tuohey, who edged him by batting .425. It's a shame that this great team did not get a chance to earn its way to the CWS.

Things had changed by 1964 when the Rebels won the SEC Baseball Championship and the District III title to earn a second CWS appearance. In 1963 the Mississippi State Bulldog Basketball team won the SEC championship. The team and its bold coach Babe McCarthy defied Mississippi's unwritten law against state schools playing against racially integrated teams and participated in the 1963 NCAA Basketball Tournament. Mississippi schools were now free to compete against integrated teams. Ole Miss completed the regular season with a 19-4 overall record including an 11-1 SEC mark. After losing the first game of the best two-of-three SEC playoff series 10-9 to Auburn, the Rebels defeated the Tigers 7-0, 5-0 to take the overall SEC championship. Moving on to the NCAA District III Tournament, the Rebs swept the field. They defeated West Virginia 11-0 and North Carolina 4-3 and 13-1 to earn their ticket to the CWS.

Coach Swayze had this to say about his 1964 team before they left for

Omaha:
> I think this year's team is the best balanced that I have ever had. By that I mean speed, pitching, power, defense, and just all-around balance. Also, I do believe that this team is the most dedicated one that I have ever had at Ole Miss.

The eight teams that participated in the CWS were Arizona State University, the University of Minnesota, the University of Maine, the University of Missouri, Seton Hall University, the University of Southern California, Texas A&M University, and Ole Miss.

The Rebels were ranked third in the nation behind Missouri and Arizona State and ahead of fourth-ranked Southern California when they went to the College World Series. In the CWS the Rebels lost to Southern California 3-2 and to Arizona State 5-0.

What happened in the loss to Southern California was outrageous. Simply put, the NCAA decided to go against the rule that was in effect at the beginning of the game. The "Clarion Ledger's" Wayne Thompson explained:

> Ole Miss and USC were playing their first games of the series with the Trojans, defending champions, holding a 3-1 lead in the top of the fifth inning when the rains came. But rather than rule it a postponed game – and the rules as printed gave them no other choice – that group [the NCAA] said it was a "suspended game" and ordered play to resume at the exact point on Tuesday night.
>
> The entire tournament was put back for 24 hours, and the two clubs had ample time to get in a full nine innings Tuesday without causing any further delay in the proceedings. So, in essence, they had no real excuse – or for that matter, any reason.

The game against Southern California began Monday night on June 8, but it wasn't completed until the next day. Southern California scored three runs in the second inning Monday off Rebel pitcher Richie Prine. Don Kessinger scored a run in the fourth inning after walking and being moved along by singles hit by Fred Roberts and Dennis Huffman. Rain stopped the game with USC batting with one out in the fifth inning and the score standing

USC 3, Ole Miss 1. When play resumed the next day, the Rebels' Bill McGlathery shut out the Trojans the rest of the game. But the Rebels were able to muster only one more run over the remaining five innings. Results: a 3-2 USC win and the Rebels in the losers' bracket.

Rain caused another delay, and Ole Miss and Arizona State did not play until Friday, June 12. In the 5-0 loss to the Sun Devils the Rebels garnered only two hits, both of which were singles off the Sun Devils' ace, Skip Hancock. This was only the second time the Rebels did not score all year; they had lost to Southern Mississippi 2-0 in the third game of the season. Ole Miss starting pitcher, Larry Higginbotham, gave up three runs and struck out seven batters over 5 1/3 innings.

The University of Minnesota won the 1964 CWS by defeating the University of Missouri 5-1 in the championship game. The Rebels finished the 1964 season ranked seventh nationally with an overall 24-7 record.

Coach Swayze's 1969 SEC Champion Rebels swept Florida 8-2 and 4-1 in the SEC playoffs and finished the SEC season 11-5 in the conference. Ole Miss advanced to the NCAA District III baseball tournament where they produced another sweep by beating Virginia Tech 7-6, North Carolina 6-5 and 5-2 to earn the Rebels' third CWS bid. After sweeping the district tournament, Coach Swayze said the 1969 team was the most improved Ole Miss team he had ever coached. Going into the CWS the Rebs had an overall record of 26-13.

The eight teams that won their way to the 1969 CWS were the University of Texas, Arizona State University, the University of Tulsa, the University of California at Los Angeles (UCLA), the University of Massachusetts, Southern Illinois University, New York University (NYU), and the University of Mississippi (Ole Miss). Playing in bracket 1, the Rebels lost to NYU 8-3, beat Southern Illinois 8-1 and lost to Texas 14-1.

The Rebels jumped ahead 2-0 in the fourth inning of the NYU game on a single by Archie Manning, a double by Whitey Adams, and a single by Eddie McLarty. Rebel starting and losing pitcher, Freddie Setser, gave up three walks and a single in the fifth inning, allowing NYU to go ahead 3-2. Both teams scored one run in the eighth inning, and the ninth started with NYU leading 4-3. NYU scored four runs in the top of the inning, and the Rebels failed to score in the bottom of the inning. Ole Miss managed only three hits while NYU touched Rebel pitchers for nine. Final score, NYU 8, Ole Miss 3. The Rebels easily dispatched Southern Illinois 8-1 in their next game, which was a win-or-go-home affair. But then they faced Texas. I will let Archie Manning, who played shortstop for the 1969 Rebels, explain. The following is from a 2014 Mississippi Sports Hall of Fame internet posting:

> Just recently, Archie Manning received a text from son Peyton Manning, who had just made a speech in Omaha. "Peyton said he had run into an old-timer in Omaha who remembered me hitting a triple in the College World Series," Archie Manning said. "I know one thing -- it wasn't off of Burt Hooton. None of us hit Hooton."
>
> Hooton, who went on to pitch successfully 15 years in the Major Leagues, and the Texas Longhorns eliminated Ole Miss 14-1, ending Manning's Omaha experience.
>
> "Nobody could touch Hooton's knuckle curve," Manning said. Ole Miss opened the 1969 CWS with an 8-3 loss to New York University. Then, the Rebels came back and eliminated Southern Illinois, the nation's No. 1 ranked team, 8-1 in the losers' bracket. Then came Hooton and Texas.
>
> "We had a really good team," Manning said. "Coach Swayze knew baseball. We had some football players and some basketball players. We all got along and just loved to play baseball."
>
> Manning said he enjoyed football, although it was often more like work. "College baseball," he said, "was just plain fun."

Coach Vaught said that Coach Swayze "had the ability to see the potential in a player better than any other coach I have known." It appears that as he was evaluating an athlete's football potential, he noted baseball potential also. His baseball teams were jam-packed with football players. Their numbers include Archie Manning, Robert Khayat, Jake Gibbs, Doug Elmore, Freddie Roberts, Dave Jennings, and Rodney Mattina.

Coach Tom Swayze's life and career are memorialized in three halls of fame. He was inducted into the Mississippi Sports Hall of Fame in 1978 and the American Association of College Baseball Coaches Hall of Fame in 1982. He was also named a charter member of the Ole Miss Sports Hall of Fame in 1986.

Jake Gibbs (1972-1990)

Jake Gibbs came to Ole Miss in the fall of 1957 from Grenada, Mississippi. Jake had been an outstanding high school quarterback and baseball player. In addition to becoming the Rebels' first All-American quarterback, Jake played and eventually coached Ole Miss Baseball.

Playing third base for the Rebels during the 1959, 60, and 61 seasons, Gibbs compiled a career .384 batting average and flashed great arm strength. Gibbs was named All-SEC in baseball all three years. Gibbs was named All-American in baseball in 1960 and 1961. Signed as a "Bonus Baby" by the New York Yankees in 1961, Jake spent 10 years with the Yankees organization as a catcher, thanks to that great arm. Over his major league career, Jake played in 538 games. His best year was 1970 when he hit .301. He finished his career with several broken bones and a .233 batting average.

With the retirement of Coach Tom Swayze, Gibbs returned to Ole Miss in 1971 as head baseball coach. In 1972 Jake's first team advanced to the College World Series. During Gibbs's 19-year coaching career, the Rebels won two SEC titles (1972 and 1977) and three SEC Western Division titles (1972, 1977, and 1982). When he retired from coaching in 1990, Gibbs had compiled a 486-389-9 record and was the winningest baseball coach in Ole Miss history.

In 2012 the SEC started honoring former baseball players who had excelled on the diamond by naming a small group of SEC Baseball Legends. Gibbs was a member of the group so honored in 2014. Jake Gibbs is the only athlete that has been honored as both an SEC Football Legend and an SEC Baseball Legend.

In 1972 Jake Gibbs took over a club that had gone 16-21 overall and 7-11 in the SEC during the 1971 season. Gibbs's first team accomplished an amazing turnaround, posting a 29-15 overall record including a 15-3 SEC slate. The Rebels won the SEC Western Division Championship and defeated Eastern Division Champion Vanderbilt 5-3 and 5-4 to win the overall SEC Championship. Proceeding to the NCAA District III Playoffs, Ole Miss defeated Jacksonville 9-3, lost to Virginia 9-3, defeated Florida State 8-3, defeated Virginia 9-0, and defeated #2-ranked South Alabama 8-4 and 12-1. Before their matchup in the regional tournament, South Alabama had won seven straight games against the Rebels over two seasons. After winning the SEC and district titles, the Rebels advanced to the CWS ranked #2 in the country by AP.

The 1972 College World Series participants were Arizona State University, the University of Connecticut, the University of Iowa, the University of Mississippi, the University of Oklahoma, Temple University, the University of Texas, and the University of Southern California.

Led by infielder and future major-leaguer Steve Dillard and right-fielder Paul Husband, the Rebels were stacked with outstanding players. Dillard was All- SEC Western Division, All-SEC, All District III, and third-team All-American. Barry Gaddis was All-SEC Western Division; Paul Husband was All-SEC Western Division, All- SEC, All District III, and All-American. Jim Pittman was All-SEC, and Dennis Starr and Norris Weese (the only CPA to be a starting quarterback in the Super Bowl) were All-SEC Western Division.

In the 1972 CWS, Ole Miss lost its first game to USC 8-6 and its second game to Texas 9-8.

Don Kessinger (1991-1996)

Donnie Kessinger went to Ole Miss in the fall of 1960 as a freshman. The Forest City, Arkansas, product had been a three-sport star in high school football, baseball, and basketball. He starred in both basketball and baseball at Ole Miss and is recognized as one of the greatest Rebel athletes ever. Kessinger also coached Ole Miss Baseball from 1991-1996.

During all three of his varsity years, which ended in 1964, Kessinger led Rebel Basketball in scoring, averaging 24, 22 and 21 points per game. His career average of 22 points per game over 70 games still ranks fourth on the Rebels' all-time scoring list. Kessinger scored in double figures in 33 consecutive games. He is only seventh on the field goals-attempted list with 1,411. Although he often lifted an amazing jump shot loose from long range, he shot 43 percent from the field. He also made 82 percent of his free shots. There was no three-point field goal in those days, and had there been, Kessinger's average would no doubt have been significantly higher because he often shot and connected from downtown. Kessinger set 18 Ole Miss basketball records. He was named All-SEC three times and All-American in 1964.

Although Kessingere would no doubt have excelled in the NBA, his heart and future lay in baseball. He came to Ole Miss to play baseball for Coach Tom Swayze. During his varsity years, 1962 through 1964, Kessinger played shortstop in spectacular fashion. In 82 games he hit .400, stole 44 bases, and drove in 55 runs. The Rebels posted an overall record of 58-24 including a 31-16 SEC slate. The 1964 Ole Miss team won the Western Division of the SEC, the overall SEC Championship, the NCAA District III Playoffs, and advanced to the College World Series, where they lost to Southern California and Arizona State. Kessinger was All-SEC each of his varsity seasons, and he was All-American in 1964. He was also All-NCAA District III in 1962 and 1964.

Known as Don rather than Donnie in his professional baseball career, Kessinger spent 16 years in the major leagues playing for the Chicago Cubs, the St. Louis Cardinals, and the Chicago White Sox. He ended his major league career in 1979, serving as player-manager for the White Sox. Playing shortstop, the most important defensive position, Don once held the National League record for the most consecutive errorless games, 54. Kessinger led the league in double plays four times and was a career .965 fielder. He made the National League All-Star Team six times and started four All-Star Games. He was twice the National League Gold Glove winner at shortstop.

Upon retiring from baseball, Don returned to Oxford, and his family has been in the real estate business there ever since. He was head baseball coach for Ole Miss from 1991-96, compiling a 185-183 record. His 1995 squad was the first Rebel team to record 40 victories in a season, and it advanced to the finals of the NCAA Regional Tournament, held at Florida State. Two of Don and Carolyn Kessinger's sons, Keith and Kevin, played baseball at Ole Miss, and Keith played basketball for the Rebels. Both sons signed to play professionally, and Keith "had a cup of coffee" in the majors, playing in 11 games for the Cincinnati Reds in 1993. Kevin suffered an injury that limited his professional career to two games in the minors. Keith often serves as a very enlightening color commentator on Ole Miss radio and television broadcasts. Kevin's son Grae Kessinger played for Ole Miss during the 2017-2019 seasons. As of July 2023, Grae was playing for the major league Houston Astros.

Pat Harrison (1997-2000)

Pat Harrison became Ole Miss's head baseball coach in 1996 and coached the Rebels during the 1997-2000 seasons. Harrison came to Oxford from Pepperdine University, where he compiled a record of 69-38-1 over two seasons. Harrison played and served as an assistant coach under the University of Southern California's legendary coach, Rod Dedeaux. Harrison had been an assistant coach at Washington State, Oklahoma, and ORU before being appointed head coach at Pepperdine. During his tenure at Ole Miss, Harrison compiled an overall record of 116-107, which includes a 48-69 SEC record. His best season at Ole Miss was 1999 when he led the Rebels to a 34-28 overall record including a 17-13 SEC mark. That performance earned the Rebels a trip to the NCAA Regional Tournament at College Station, where they lost to Long Beach State 4-3, beat Monmouth 12-3, and lost to Texas A&M 13-6.

Mike Bianco (2001 and counting)

Mike Bianco is a native of Seminole, Florida. He played baseball at Seminole High School, and he was selected by the Boston Red Sox in the 13th round of the Major League draft. He played college baseball at Indian River Community College and under Skip Bertman at LSU. He was the starting catcher for the LSU team that finished third in the 1989 CWS. He served seven years as an assistant baseball coach at Northwestern Louisiana State and McNeese State. While he was an assistant coach at LSU (1993-1997), the Tigers won three SEC Championships and two SEC Tournament titles. LSU also played in four CWS and won three national championships. In 1998, Bianco became head baseball coach at McNeese, where he coached for three years, compiling a 100-71 record. His 2000 team went 39-20, captured a share of the Southland Conference championship, and advanced to an NCAA Regional Tournament.

In early June 2000 Ole Miss named Mike Bianco head baseball coach after Pat Harrison resigned. Things were about to change drastically. Here is how olemisssports.com summarizes Bianco's time at the helm of Ole Miss Baseball:

> In 22 seasons leading the program, Bianco has delivered 18 post-season appearances, including eight Super Regional berths and a pair of trips to the College World Series. He has racked up 854 victories, holding an 854-485-1 (.638) record. Those wins are the most in Rebel baseball history and rank third all-time among coaches in the SEC. He also stands as the winningest and longest-active coach in the SEC among the sports of baseball, men's basketball and football. The Rebels have reached the 30-win plateau in each of Bianco's 21 full seasons, including ten 40-win campaigns, proving that the Rebels don't rebuild under Bianco—they reload.

In addition to the 2022 national championship, Bianco's Rebels have won four SEC Western Division titles, two SEC Tournament titles and one SEC regular-season championship. Ole Miss captured the SEC Tournament title in 2006 and again in 2018. The 2018 team became the second SEC team ever to win both a divisional and tournament title in the same season.

During Bianco's 22-year run, 126 Rebel players' names have been called in Major League drafts. Three or more Rebels have been picked in the draft for 18 consecutive complete seasons. During the period 2018-2022, 27 Rebs have been named in the draft.

Under Coach Bianco, 92 Rebel players have been named to various All-American or Freshman All-American teams. The 2022 national champion team included three All-Americans. CWS Most Outstanding Player Dylan DeLucia was named third-team All-American by Baseball America. Team captain Tim Elko earned third-team laurels from the NCBWA. Hunter Elliott was named to Freshman All-American teams by Collegiate Baseball, Perfect Game, and D1Baseball.

The Southeastern Conference has honored a number of Bianco's Rebels. Stephen Head was named SEC Player of the Year in 2004. Drew Pomeranz was the SEC Pitcher of the Year in 2010. Three Rebels have been selected

SEC Freshman of the Year: Seth Smith in 2002, Stephen Head in 2003, and Jordan Henry in 2007. Tim Elko was named SEC Scholar-Athlete of the Year in 2021.

Since 2004 the C-Spire Ferriss Trophy has been awarded to the Mississippi Collegiate Baseball Player of the Year. Six of Bianco's Rebels have won that award: Stephen Head (2004), Brian Pettway (2005), Scott Bittle (2008), Drew Pomeranz (2010), Auston Bousfield (2014), and Kemp Alderman 2023.

While Jake Gibbs was head coach, Ole Miss made a move toward excellence in baseball by opening Oxford-University Stadium at Swayze Field. The $3.75 million facility opened February 1989. A seating area beyond the right-field fence was added in 1993. Today, students fill up that area and celebrate Rebel home runs with beer showers. Under Bianco's leadership, O-U Stadium at Swayze field has been expanded and upgraded multiple times. It now has a seating capacity of 12,152, and during the 2022 season, Bianco's Rebels attracted an average attendance of nearly 10,000. The stadium is now part of a multi-million-dollar complex that includes outstanding locker and weight-training rooms, a players' lounge, a team meeting room, indoor hitting cages, and an indoor pitching tunnel. Ole Miss baseball facilities are among the best in the country.

Coach Bianco's winning teams have consistently drawn fans by the thousands to Oxford-University Stadium at Swayze Field. The team, the fans, and the venue combine to produce one of the best atmospheres in college baseball.

Since Mike Bianco became head coach in 2000, Ole Miss has ranked among the nation's top 25 attendance leaders every year. For 16 consecutive years Ole Miss has ranked in the top five. In 2021, the Rebels finished #1 in the nation in attendance. Ole Miss fans have given the Rebels a distinct home-field advantage. At the end of the 2022 season, Bianco's Rebels had won 73.2 percent of their home games while compiling a 542-198-1 record at Swayze Field. Under Bianco, the Rebels have hosted nine NCAA Regionals and three Super Regionals at OU-Stadium, making Ole Miss baseball a national brand.

Mike Bianco was inducted into the Indian River Community College Hall of Fame in 2003. In 2008 he was named to the All-Alex Box Omaha

Era Team by LSU. In 2010, he was inducted into the Seminole High School Hall of Fame. Mike Bianco was named the 2022 NCAA D1 Baseball Coach of the year.

CHAPTER 4
Ole Miss's 2022 National Baseball Championship Season

The Season in a Nutshell

Ole Miss was listed #5 in the country in the D1 preseason baseball rankings. This high rank was foreshadowed by a 2021 season in which Ole Miss compiled a 45-22 record and advanced to the NCAA Tucson Super Regional, where they lost two games to one to the University of Arizona. Nearly all of the key players on a powerful offense were returning for the 2022 season. The Rebels started the 2022 season 13-1 and rose to the top of the poll.

The Rebs won their first nine games while scoring 100 runs and giving up 28. Five of those nine games were won by the "run rule." That is, the Rebs were ahead by 10 or more runs before the ninth inning. The win streak was broken when they lost on March 5 to the University of Central Florida 1-0 in 12 innings. Ole Miss won the next four games, and they stood at 13-1 on March 13 before playing two games against Oral Roberts. The seven-inning, double-hitter games were necessitated by a rain-out on March 12. Ole Miss won the first game 6-2 and lost the second 8-4. In the last game before the beginning of Southeastern Conference (SEC) play, the Rebels lost to Southeastern Louisiana 5-1 in Hammond, La. Going into the 30-game SEC season, the Rebs were 13-3, having scored 147 runs to their opponents' 35.

But from March 13 through the first of May the Rebels lost 18 games and won only 11. Fourteen of those 18 losses were to SEC teams. On May 2, the Rebels stood 24-19 overall and 7-14 in the SEC; they were no longer even listed in the rankings. This mid-season swoon was punctuated by a lack of timely hitting, ineffective pitching, and spotty fielding. It seemed that the wheels had fallen off the Rebel Machine when Ole Miss bottomed out, tied with Missouri and Kentucky for last place in the SEC. They were in danger of not qualifying for either the SEC or the NCAA Tournament.

Then things turned around quickly and dramatically. The Rebels won seven of their last nine SEC games and defeated an outstanding University of

Southern Mississippi (USM) team in their only remaining non-conference game. Ole Miss finished the regular season 32-21 overall and 14-16 in the conference. The Rebels qualified for the SEC Tournament as they earned the ninth seed. The first day of the tournament #8 seed, Vanderbilt, defeated the Rebs 3-1 and sent them home. With a 32-22 overall record and a 14-17 record against SEC opponents, Ole Miss saw its future placed in the hands of the selection committee, which would determine which 64 teams would participate in the NCAA Tournament. It was highly doubtful that Ole Miss would make the NCAA Tournament.

Thirty-one teams that win their conferences' regular seasons or tournament championships automatically qualify for the field of 64. Then the committee chooses 33 at-large teams. Ole Miss was the last of the 33 at-large teams chosen. The selection committee made the Rebels the #3 seed in the Coral Gables Regional along with #1 Miami, #2 Arizona, and #4 Canisius. The Rebels swept the double-elimination regional, defeating Arizona 7-4, Miami 2-1, and Arizona 22-6. It was on to the Hattiesburg Super Regional, hosted by USM. Again, the Rebs went undefeated, shutting out the Golden Eagles 10-0 and 5-0. Ole Miss was off to Omaha for the 2022 Men's College World Series.

The eight winners of the NCAA Super Regionals are divided into double-elimination four-team brackets, and the winners of the brackets play best two out of three for the championship. Ole Miss was placed in a bracket that included Arkansas, Auburn, and Stanford. It took four games for the Rebs to win their bracket. They defeated Auburn 5-1, Arkansas 13-5, lost to Arkansas 3-2, and defeated Arkansas again 2-0. Oklahoma won the other bracket that included Texas, Texas A&M, and Notre Dame. The Rebels and the Sooners squared off in the championship series. Ole Miss won convincingly 10-3 and 4-2.

Coach Mike Bianco's Ole Miss Rebels were the 2022 NCAA CWS and national champions. After not being ranked at the end of the regular season, they were again ranked #1 in all the polls, and Coach Bianco was the National Coach of the Year. What follows is their amazing story.

Ole Miss Rebels Baseball 2022 – The Details

After losing the first baseball game of the 2020 season to Louisville 7-2 in Oxford on February 14, 2020, the Ole Miss Rebels ripped off 16 consecutive victories. All of those games were played before the SEC season was scheduled to begin. The March 11 game, which Ole Miss won 18-7 against the University of Louisiana Monroe, proved to be the last game of the season. The COVID pandemic brought the college baseball season to an abrupt halt. On March 12 the NCAA canceled all national championships for winter and spring sports. The SEC and Ole Miss canceled the remainder of all spring competition. The baseball Rebels were ranked #5 in the coaches' poll when the season ended. Seeing the promise their Rebels had displayed early in the season, Rebel Nation was devastated when the rest of the season was cancelled because of COVID. The Ole Miss roster was loaded with outstanding players such as pitchers Doug Nikhazy and Gunnar Hoglund and position players such as Tyler Keenan, Anthony Servideo, and Kevin Graham.

The Ole Miss 2021 roster brimmed with talent, as most of the key 2020 players returned to play a full season. Ole Miss was ranked #5 in the preseason coaches' poll. The Rebels finished the season 18-12 in conference play and went 3-2 in the SEC Tournament. Advancing to the NCAA Tournament, Ole Miss won the Oxford regional, which included Florida State, Southeast Missouri, and Southern Mississippi. The Rebels played Arizona in the Tucson Super Regional and lost to the Wildcats two games to one. Ole Miss finished the season with a 45-22 record and one win short of the CWS. The Rebels finished the season ranked #11 in the coaches' poll.

Going into his 22nd season as Ole Miss's head baseball coach, Mike Bianco and his staff of assistant coaches, Mike Clement, Carl Lafferty, and Chris Cleary, were under heavy pressure to coach this team to the College World Series. Over 21 years, Bianco had taken his Rebel teams to 17 NCAA Regional Tournaments and sevem Super Regionals while compiling an overall record of 812-462 (.621). The problem was that Bianco had won only one Super Regional (2014) to advance to the CWS. Many fans seemed to think that with the talent the Rebels had over the years, the great baseball facilities on the Oxford campus, and the tremendous fan support, there should have been several more CWS appearances. In fact, the great facilities, talent, and fan support were the direct results of Mike Bianco's many successes as Ole Miss's head baseball coach. The dissatisfaction with Coach Bianco would fester during the 2022 season but ultimately just about disappear based on the performance of his team.

Preconference Play

Ole Miss was ranked # 6 in the 2022 preseason in the coaches' poll. The Rebels kicked off the 2022 baseball season February 18-20 by hosting Charleston Southern in a three-game series at Oxford-University Stadium/Swayze Field. The Rebels swept the Buccaneers 9-3, 11-1 and 12-2. The last two games were run ruled at the end of the seventh and eighth innings, respectively, because Ole Miss was ahead by 10 runs.

In the February 18 contest, Rebel starting and winning pitcher, Derek Diamond, went five innings, giving up two hits, two walks, and two runs while striking out eight batters. Jack Washburn, Mitch Murrell and Mason Nichols followed Diamond to the mound and combined to give up three hits and one run while striking out six hitters. Ole Miss fielding was not so good; shortstop Jacob Gonzalez committed two errors, third baseman Reagan Burford one, and pitcher Jack Washburn one. Hayden Harris drove in two runs for the Bucs in the fourth inning with a double, and Ryan Waldschmidt homered in the seventh inning to end the Bucs' scoring. The Bucs collected a total of five hits in the game. Charleston Southern's starting and losing pitcher, Bryce Brock, pitched two innings and faced 12 batters. He gave up four runs on two hits, two walks, and a hit batter. Zac Robinson followed Brock to the mound, and he gave up four runs on three hits, a walk, a balk, and two hit batters. Four other pitchers went to the mound for the Bucs, and they combined to give up two hits, two walks, and one run over five innings. Hayden Dunhurst threw out a base runner who was trying to steal. The Rebels had seven hits, including a Tim Elko homer; six walks; three stolen bases, and five batters were hit by a pitch. Final score, Rebels 9, Bucs 3.

The Saturday game was ended by the run (mercy) rule when Charleston Southern trailed 11-1 after failing to score in the top of the seventh inning. The Rebels scored in each of the six innings they batted. The Bucs' starter and loser, Jerry Couch, threw 2 2/3 innings and gave up six hits and six runs. Reliever Ryan Gleason followed Couch and gave up two runs in two innings. Three other pitchers followed Gleason, and they combined to give up two runs. The Rebels' eight hits included doubles by Jacob Gonzalez, Peyton Chatagnier, and Ben Van Cleve and home runs by Elko and Hayden Leatherwood. The Rebels' starting and winning pitcher, John Gaddis, a lefty transfer from Texas A&M Corpus Christi, pitched four innings and gave up three hits, two walks, and one run while striking out three batters. Riley Maddox and Matt Parenteau, a transfer from Parker College, followed Gaddis to the mound. They shut the Bucs down completely.

Senior Drew McDaniel started and won the Sunday game for the Rebs. He went 3 2/3 innings and gave up two hits, one of which was a homer by Brooks Carter, and one run while striking out four batters and walking two. Three Rebel pitchers, Hunter Elliott, Dylan DeLucia, and Jack Dougherty, combined to give up one hit and one run the rest of the way. Ole Miss had a great day at the plate. Leading 3-1 at the start of the bottom of the fifth inning, the Rebels exploded for eight runs. The run rule came into play again when the Rebels scored a run in the bottom of the eighth inning. Sixteen batters connected for 12 hits that included doubles by Justin Bench and T.J. McCants and home runs by Keven Graham and Kemp Alderman. Final score, Ole Miss 12, Charleston Southern 2.

Opening day attendance was 11,146, the second-largest opening-day crowd in program history. Attendance for the weekend totaled 32,888, second in the nation and the third largest in program history for a three-game series.

In the February 23 mid-week game, the Rebels put on a show at Swayze Field against the Arkansas State Red Wolves. The Rebels scored 15 runs in five innings while the Wolves scored only five. The game was run-ruled at that point. Versatile senior Justin Bench played center field, went two-for-two at the plate, hit a double, and drove in four runs. Kevin Graham went three-for-four, hit a home run, and drove in seven runs. Hayden Leatherwood homered in his only at-bat. Ole Miss registered 12 hits, six walks, a hit batsman, and three stolen bases. In his first start as a Rebel, Jack Washburn threw three innings, giving up two runs, two hits, four bases on balls while striking out four batters. Dylan DeLucia relieved Washburn and went 1 2/3 innings and gave up three runs on four hits and two walks while striking out four batters. DeLucia's performance would soon prove to be an aberration. Winning pitcher Cole Baker threw only 1/3 inning and struck out the only batter he faced.

ASU batters generated their five runs on six hits and six walks. One of the hits was a home run struck by third baseman Ben Klutts, the only Wolf with an extra-base hit. ASU starter and loser, Walker Williams, went two innings and gave up five runs. Four Wolf pitchers followed Williams to the mound, and they gave up a total of 10 runs.

On February 25 the Rebels continued their winning ways when they faced Virginia Commonwealth University at Swayze Field. In this first game ever against VCU, the Rebels dispatched the Rams 10-4. Fielding errors played a big part in this game. All three Rebel errors resulted in unearned runs. Third baseman Reagan Burford, shortstop Jacob Gonzalez, and second baseman Peyton Chatagnier each committed an error. Chatagnier would not make another error all season. VCU committed five errors that led to three unearned runs. The Rebs' eight hits included four extra-base hits; doubles by Garrett Wood, Calvin Harris, and Reagan Burford; and a home run by Kevin Graham, his third in three games. Despite going 0 for 2 at the plate, Peyton Chatagnier drove in three runs with sacrifice flies. This was the third game in which starting catcher Hayden Dunhurst had been out with an injury. Sophomore Calvin Harris filled in admirably for Dunhurst. In this game, Harris, batting ninth, went two-for-three, scored a run, and drove in a run. Burford went one-for-two at the plate, scored a run, and drove in a run.

Four Rebel pitchers held the Rams to four runs on eight hits. Starter and winner, Derek Diamond, gave up five hits and two runs in five innings. Reliever Hunter Elliott threw two innings and gave up one hit and no runs, and reliever Mitch Murrell went an inning and gave up nothing. Mason Nichols pitched the ninth inning and gave up two hits and two runs. The Rams' starter and loser, Jack Masloff, pitched three innings and gave up three runs. Mason Delane followed Masloff to the slab and pitched four innings, giving up five runs. Joey Perkins and Chase Hungate followed and gave up a total of two runs.

The scheduled Saturday game was not played because of inclement weather. Sunday's weather was better, and the Rebels made the best of it by run-ruling the Rams 14-3 in seven innings. VCU scored all of its runs in the first inning on a walk, an error, a wild pitch, and a ground out. The Rams managed only two hits, a single, and a double. Rebel starter and winner,

Drew McDaniel, threw three innings, giving up three runs on one hit, three walks, and a wild pitch while striking out three batters. Reliever Jack Gaddis faced 10 hitters in three innings and gave up a hit and nothing else. Brandon Johnson pitched the last inning and gave up no hits and no runs. Meanwhile, Rebel hitters drove in 14 runs with 14 hits including a double, a triple, and three home runs. Kevin Graham hit the double; Peyton Chatagnier hit the triple, and Tim Elko, Jacob Gonzalez, and freshman football player Tywone Malone hit homers. The Rebs scored in every inning except the sixth. Led by Elko's three RBIs and Malone's two, seven Rebels drove in runs. The Rams sent five pitchers to the mound. Their first three pitchers each gave up four runs on a total of 12 hits and five walks.

The two wins over VCU pushed the Rebels' record to 6-0 and to #2 in the coaches' poll.

The Rebels faced the University of Louisiana Monroe Warhawks at Swayze Field on March 1. ULM brought a dismal 1-5 record into the contest. As would be expected, the Rebs dominated the game and walked away with a 10-2 victory. The Rebels stroked nine hits, four of which went for extra bases, off six Warhawk pitchers. Jacob Gonzalez went one-for-two at the plate, scored a run, and drove in a run while Ben Van Cleve went one-for-three, scored a run, and drove in a run, and Calvin Harris went two-for-two and scored two runs. Center fielder T.J. McCants wielded the big stick for the Rebs. He went three-for-four including a home run, scored two runs, and drove in three. Freshman lefty Hunter Elliott started for Ole Miss, pitched four innings, gave up two runs on three hits and a walk while striking out nine of the 15 batters he faced. Riley Maddox, Matt Parenteau, and Jack Dougherty shut out the Hawks over the last five innings. Over the last three innings Dougherty gave up three hits and struck out seven batters. Rebel pitchers threw extremely well with bases occupied, and they combined to strike out 17 batters. Out of 11 players who reached base for the Hawks, only two scored. Neither team committed an error.

Things got worse for the Warhawks in the second game, played March 2. The Rebels run-ruled ULM 11-1 in seven innings. The Hawks scored their first and only run in the top of the fourth inning when Jack Washburn balked a run home. Rebel first baseman and team captain, Tim Elko, came to bat with the bases loaded in the fourth and fifth innings. In the fourth,

Elko walked to force in a run. Elko's roommate and super hitter left fielder Kevin Graham followed him to the plate and promptly hit a grand slam. In the fifth inning Elko also hit a grand slam. Elko and Graham combined to drive in 10 of the Rebs' 11 runs. Calvin Harris, who was still catching in place of the injured Hayden Dunhurst, went two-for-three and drove in the other Ole Miss run. Jack Washburn started for Ole Miss, pitched five innings, gave up one hit, four walks, and one run while striking out seven batters. Mason Nichols, Jackson Kimbrell, and Wes Burton shut out the Warhawks in the sixth and seventh innings. Third baseman Grant Schulz registered the two hits the Warhawks mustered.

In early March, Ole Miss played its first road series of the season against the University of Central Florida Knights at John Euliano Park in Orlando, Florida. John Rhys Plumlee was listed on the Knights' roster as a junior outfielder. He had transferred from Ole Miss to UCF in January 2022. Plumlee, who starred as the Rebels' quarterback as a freshman but lost out to Matt Corral as a sophomore, played both football and baseball at Ole Miss. He had been a seldom used outfielder in baseball. The NCAA turned down Plumlee's request to be eligible to play baseball for UCF in the 2022 season. He had to sit out the season based on an NCAA rule. Plumlee watched from the stands as his former teammates competed against the team he would presumably play for in 2023. Plumlee went on to have a stellar season as the quarterback for the Knights' football team in 2022.

Ole Miss entered the March 4 game with an 8-0 record, and the Knights came in at 7-1. The three-game series would prove a good test for both teams. In the first four innings, UCF scored two runs, and Ole Miss failed to score. The fifth inning saw the Rebels grab the lead by scoring three runs in the top of the inning as T.J. McCants drove in Justin Bench and Kevin Graham with a home run. That lead was short-lived as the Knights scored three runs in the bottom of the inning on a homer by first baseman Nick Romano and a single by catcher Cole Russo that scored designated hitter Ben McCabe. In the top of the sixth inning, the Rebs tied the game at 6 when Peyton Chatagnier, Jacob Gonzalez, and Tim Elko all hit solo home runs. Ole Miss added two more runs in the seventh inning when Chatagnier hit his second home run with Reagan Burford on base. With the Rebels leading 8-6, the Knights scored the last run of the game in the eighth inning. Rebel starting pitcher,

Derek Diamond, threw 4 2/3 innings and gave up six hits and six runs while striking out seven batters. Freshman Riley Maddox registered his first win by throwing 1 1/3 innings and giving up no runs. Brandon Johnson claimed a save by pitching the last three innings and giving up four walks, no hits, and one run while striking out five. The Knights sent five pitchers to the mound. Starter David Litchfield went five innings, giving up six runs. Ben Vespi went two innings, gave up two runs, and was saddled with the loss. Ole Miss collected 10 hits, and UCF eight. Neither team committed an error.

On March 5, my wife, Dorothy, and I were in Ocala, Florida, visiting friends Bob and Wanda McRae, whom we had not seen in 40 years. I streamed the game on my iPad, and it was not a pleasant experience. In a 12-inning, 1-0 marathon, UCF handed Ole Miss its first loss of the season. There isn't much to say about the game because Rebel batters managed only three hits and struck out 16 times against two UCF pitchers, Connor Staine and Chase Centala, who were almost unhittable. Meanwhile, UCF batters managed seven hits off four Rebel pitchers. John Gaddis, Mason Nichols, Mitchell Murrell, and Hunter Elliott were also superb. Ellliott took his first loss when he faced seven batters in the 10th and 11th innings and gave up a run on a hit and two walks. Three double plays, including one in the 11th inning that doubled off a base runner on a fly out, kept the Rebs in the game. UCF committed the game's only error. The Rebels suffered another huge loss in this game. Left-fielder Kevin Graham went down with a broken wrist. After the game Coach Bianco said, "I don't know what we will do without Kevin Graham. He makes the lineup better with his play and the way he changes how pitchers approach other people." Graham would be out of the lineup for a month, and he would be sorely missed.

The Rebels roared back in the March 6 Sunday game and thrashed the Knights. Ole Miss bats came alive overnight, and the Rebs produced 15 hits while scoring nine earned runs. Included in the 15 hits were doubles by Gonzalez, Alderman, and Dunhurst and a triple by Calvin Harris. Harris suffered an oblique injury in the game, which would keep him out of the lineup for 19 days. Chatagnier went one-for-four at the plate. But with a sacrifice bunt and a sacrifice fly, he managed to drive in four runs. Five other Rebels drove in one run each. UCF bats remained cool. Drew McDaniel, Jackson Kimbrell, and Dylan DeLucia combined to give up one run on a

Dunhurst-passed ball, five hits, and three walks while striking out 11 batters. Kimbrell earned his first win, and DeLucia earned his first save. Playing left field in the place of Kevin Graham, the Rebs' regular designated hitter, Kemp Alderman, made an error while going three-for-four at the plate and scoring two runs. Reagan Burford played third base, made an error, went three-for-three at the plate, scored a run, and drove in a run. Errors and misplayed balls would prove to be problems for Burford, Alderman, and the Rebels. The Knights' starter and loser, Hunter Patteson, gave up seven hits and four runs in 3 2/3 innings. The six pitchers that UCF sent to the mound simply could not control the Rebels' hot bats. By winning the series, the Rebels left the Sunshine State with a 10-1 record. The March 8 coaches' poll ranked Ole Miss #3 in the country behind Arkansas and Vanderbilt.

SWAC school and in-state rival Alcorn State provided the March 9 midweek game. It was not much of a contest as the Rebels run-ruled the Braves in seven innings 16-1. Ole Miss's eight hits included doubles by Tim Elko, Reagan Burford, and Knox Loposer and a homer by Chatagnier, who went two-for-two, scored four runs, and drove in four. Five Alcorn pitchers issued a total of 14 bases on balls. The Braves managed only four hits, one of which was a first-inning home run by Jermel Ford. Rebel starting and winning pitcher, Jack Washburn, threw three innings and gave up three hits and a run while striking out four batters. Cole Baker, West Burton, Matt Parenteau, and Mitch Murrell followed Washburn to the mound for the Rebels and combined to give up a walk and strike out eight batters. The Rebels' record improved to 11-1, and the Braves fell to 0-8.

Next up for Ole Miss was a weekend three-game series with the Oral Roberts University Golden Eagles. ORU, which had long been well-respected in baseball, brought a 9-3 record to Swayze Field. Rebel starting and winning pitcher, John Gaddis, threw five innings, giving up seven hits and two runs while walking two batters and striking out seven. Mason Nichols and Josh Mallitz followed Gaddis to the mound for the Rebels. Nichols gave up two hits and nothing else over two innings while Mallitz gave up nothing while striking out three batters in two innings. All nine of ORU's hits were singles. Ole Miss batters were hit by pitches three times and collected 10 walks and 13 hits off five Golden Eagle pitchers. The results were 16 runs on the board for the Rebs. Peyton Chatagnier in three plate appearances hit a double, scored three runs, and drove in two. Tim Elko went three-for-three at the plate, hit a homer, and drove in seven runs. The Rebels put crooked numbers on the board in four innings with a 7 showing up for the fifth inning. Isaac Coffey was the starting and losing pitcher for ORU. He gave up eight hits, three walks, and seven runs over four innings. The teams had not agreed to a run-rule for this game, and the Rebs won 16-2 in nine innings.

The game scheduled for Saturday was rained out, and a double hitter was played Sunday, March 13. Both games were seven-inning affairs, and the teams split the double hitter with the Rebels winning the first game 6-2 and losing the second 8-4.

Derek Diamond improved his record to 4-0 in the first game by giving up a hit and no runs while striking out five batters over four innings. Dylan DeLucia pitched an inning and gave up three hits and two runs while striking out one hitter. Brandon Johnson finished the game, giving up two hits and no runs while striking out three over the final two innings. Rebel batters collected a total of seven hits, which included a double by Hayden Dunhurst, a triple by Chatagnier, and homers by Elko and McCants. Still playing left field in the place of the injured Kevin Graham, Kemp Alderman committed an error but went two-for-two at the plate and scored a run. Dunhurst and DeLucia also committed errors. ORU's starting and losing pitcher, Ledgend Smith, gave up all six Rebel runs on seven hits and two walks over 5 1/3 innings.

In the second game ORU saddled Ole Miss with its second loss of the season by winning 8-4. ORU collected 10 hits including two doubles and two home runs off six Rebel pitchers. Jack Dougherty started for the Rebels and pitched 2 2/3 innings, giving up five hits and four runs while walking a batter and hitting a batter. Hunter Elliott, who was tagged with the loss, came in and pitched two innings, giving up two hits, a walk, and a run while striking out three. Riley Maddox relieved Elliott and gave up three hits, a walk, and three runs during an inning of work. Jackson Kimbrell and Drew McDaniel combined to pitch the last inning and gave up no runs. Rebel hitters managed only six hits, but five of those went for extra bases. Jacob Gonzalez hit a two-run home run, and Hayden Dunhurst hit a solo shot. Justin Bench, T.J. McCants, and Reagan Burford doubled. Bench's double drove in a run. Meanwhile, seven Golden Eagles combined for 10 hits including doubles by Mac McCroskey and Dustin Demeter and homers by Jackson Loftin and Alec Jones. Second baseman McCroskey drove in two runs, and shortstop Loftin drove in three. The Golden Eagles' winning pitcher, A.J. Archambo, started, pitched five innings, and gave up five hits and all four of the Rebels' runs. Ole Miss's record dropped to 13-2, but the Rebels were ranked #1 in the country in the March 14 coaches' poll.

In their last game before entering conference play, Ole Miss traveled to Hammond, Louisiana, to take on Southeastern Louisiana University. The March 15 contest was a rare mid-week away from the friendly confines of Oxford-University Stadium and Swayze Field. The game appeared to be a mismatch, as the Rebels sported a 13-2 record while the Lions were 7-9. SLU made the records irrelevant by dispatching Ole Miss 5-1. The Rebels seemed to be sleepwalking through the game as they garnered only three hits and committed three errors. The Lions posted nine hits and were perfect in the field. In the top of the second inning Kemp Alderman doubled home T.J. McCants to give the Rebels a short-lived 1-0 lead. The Lions countered in the bottom half of the inning when Tyler Finke hit a solo homer to left field. SLU went on to score another run in the third inning on a wild pitch, two in the seventh and one in the eighth on a homer by Preston Faulkner. Nevertheless, losing pitcher, Jack Washburn, had a quality start for the Rebs. He threw five innings and gave up two runs on four hits and three walks while striking out five batters. Drew McDaniel, Matt Parenteau, and Riley Maddox each gave up a run while Mitch Murrell pitched the final inning and gave up nothing. Three SLU pitchers held the Rebels' bats in check. Starter and winner, Adam Guth, went five innings, giving up three hits, five walks, and one run while striking out three batters. Andrew Landry threw three innings and gave up nothing while striking out two hitters. Gage Trahan pitched the final inning and struck out two Rebels while giving up nothing. The Lions improved their record to 8-9, and the Rebels left town having completed their pre-conference schedule 13-3 and ranked #3 in the coaches' poll and #1 by D1 Baseball.

The Southeastern Conference Plus

The competition Ole Miss would face was about to stiffen dramatically. The Rebels would play 30 SEC games over the remainder of the season. The

SEC is unquestionably the best baseball conference in the country. Eighteen of those games would be played against teams in the SEC West, which featured five of the best teams in the conference. In addition, the Rebels would continue to play mid-week games against quality non-conference opponents.

Ole Miss traveled to Alabama to face Auburn in the first of 10 SEC three-game series. The Tigers brought a 13-4 record into the first game, which was played Thursday, March 17. When asked about playing the formidable Rebels, Auburn Coach Butch Thompson didn't seem to be impressed. He indicated that he had no idea why the Rebels would be ranked #1 in a poll.

The Rebels were impressive in the first game, beating the Tigers 13-6. The box score indicates that the game should have been closer. Both teams registered 14 hits. The Rebs had three doubles and three home runs. The Tigers had four doubles and two home runs. The Rebels had five walks and Auburn four. Ole Miss had eight RBIs to Auburn's six. The difference was fielding, Auburn committed five errors while Ole Miss was perfect in the field. Aided by Tiger errors, the Rebels scored six runs in the sixth inning. Both teams had six earned runs. Peyton Chatagnier, who went three-for-five at the plate, hit a double and scored a run. Tim Elko hit a double in three plate appearances, drove in a run, and scored a run. Reagan Burford hit a double and a homer and drove in two runs. Shortstop Jacob Gonzalez hit two solo homers; the first came on the second pitch of the game. Rebel starting pitcher, John Gaddis, went 3 2/3 innings, giving up seven hits and four runs. Dylan DeLucia relieved Gaddis, pitched 3 1/3 innings, gave up six hits and two runs and earned the win. Standing 6'1" and weighing 263 pounds, Auburn first baseman Sonny DiChiara is an intimidating batter. He showed why in this game by hitting a homer and driving in three of his team's six runs. Three other Tigers got multiple hits.

The Friday night game was altogether different. Auburn scored multiple runs off six Ole Miss pitchers and administered the Rebels' worst loss of the season, 19-5. The first three hitters in the Tigers' batting order, third baseman Blake Rambusch, center fielder Kason Howell, and first baseman Sonny DiChiara, combined to produce seven hits and 11 RBIs. Rambusch stroked two doubles while Howell and DiChiara homered. DiChiara also produced a sacrifice fly. Auburn scored six runs in the sixth inning and put crooked numbers on the board in four other innings. Rebel starter and loser,

Derek Diamond, threw 3 1/3 innings and gave up four hits, four walks, and five runs while striking out two batters. Diamond was followed by Mason Nichols, who threw 1 1/3 innings, gave up two hits, a walk, and three runs. Mitch Murrell pitched an inning and gave up one run. Then Rebel pitching completely collapsed. Wes Burton gave up two runs without registering an out. Jackson Kimbrell followed and did the same thing. Drew McDaniel pitched the last two innings and gave up eight hits, a walk, and six runs while throwing a wild pitch and striking out two batters. Rebel batters produced only six hits, including a double by Justin Bench and a no-doubter home run by Kemp Alderman. Auburn starting and winning pitcher, Hayden Mullins, threw five innings and gave up two hits, four walks, and a run while striking out three Rebels. Tim Elko went one-for-four at the plate and drove in two runs. The Tigers had squared the series and set up a rubber game for Saturday.

Proving themselves to be as resilient as the competition, the Rebels spanked the Tigers 15-2 in the Saturday game. Jack Dougherty started for the Rebs and won his first game, going five innings and giving up two runs on seven hits and three walks while striking out seven batters. The performance of these three pitchers boded well for the future. Rebel bats didn't slumber in this game. The 15 runs were produced by 19 hits including five doubles and three homers. The Rebels scored in six innings. Tim Elko went three-for-five at the plate, hit a home run, and drove in four runs. Peyton Chatagnier went three-for-six, scored two runs, and drove in three. Hayden Leatherwood and Kemp Alderman hit back-to-back homers in the sixth inning. Alderman went two-for-five at the plate and drove in two runs. Auburn batters managed nine hits but only two went for extra bases. The Rebels left Auburn with a 15-4 overall record and a 2-1 SEC mark. By the end of the season Coach Thompson would get to play the Rebels again, and maybe he would learn why the Rebs were #1; they were loaded with talent.

The University of Memphis sported a 12-5 record when it came to Oxford to play a mid-week game against Ole Miss. In the March 23 game, the Tigers provided plenty of competition for the Rebel team, now ranked #2 in the country in the coaches' poll. The Tigers jumped ahead 4-1 in the top of the second inning, but the Rebels countered, scoring seven runs in the bottom of the inning. Memphis went on to score four more runs, but the

Rebels scored three more runs to maintain the lead. Final score, Ole Miss 11, Memphis 8. Memphis produced nine hits, including two home runs and scored eight runs off seven Ole Miss pitchers. Rebel starting pitcher, Jack Washburn, went 3 1/3 innings, giving up four hits, a walk, and four runs while hitting three batters. Riley Maddox earned his second win by throwing 1 2/3 innings, giving up a hit, and striking out four batters. Five other Rebel pitchers combined to give up four hits and three runs over the last four innings. Ole Miss batters struck 14 hits with three of them being doubles by Jacob Gonzalez, Justin Bench, and Kemp Alderman. Gonzalez went four-for-five at the plate and drove in two runs. Bench went three-for-three and drove in three runs, and Reagan Burford went three-for-five and drove in two runs. David Warren started on the mound for the Tigers and failed to register an out in the second inning. He was tagged with the loss after giving up six runs, five hits, walking two batters, and throwing three wild pitches.

The Tennessee Volunteers came to Oxford for a three-game SEC series starting March 25. The Rebels (15-4) were ranked #2, and the Vols (19-1) were ranked #5 in the coaches' poll. But Ole Miss was ranked #1 by Baseball America, and Tennessee was ranked #1 by Perfect Game. So, the games could be billed as two #1s playing each other. Those high rankings no doubt contributed to the series drawing 33,348 fans to Swayze Field.

Three Vol pitchers put Rebel bats in a deep freeze where they stayed stone cold all Friday evening. Starter and winner, Chase Burns, threw seven innings, gave up two hits and one run while striking out 11 Rebels. Mark McLaughlin pitched an inning and gave up a hit and a walk while striking out two batters. Kirby Connell pitched the last inning, facing three batters and striking out one. Ole Miss hitters struck out 14 times while registering three hits and one run. Ole Miss's only run came on a home run struck by Tim Elko in the seventh inning.

Tennessee's bats were hot. In the top of the second inning, the Vols hit a triple and two home runs and scored six runs off Ole Miss starter and loser, John Gaddis, who lasted only 1 1/3 innings. Dylan DeLucia came in and pitched 6 2/3 innings, giving up five runs on four hits and two walks while striking out six batters. Matt Parenteau threw the last inning, giving up two hits and a run while striking out a batter. Four Volunteers hit home runs: Jared Dickey, Blake Burke, Trey Lipscomb, and Luc Lipcius. Both left fielder

Dickey and shortstop Cortland Lawson drove in three runs. That 12-1 beatdown at Swayze Field was not a pretty thing to watch.

The Saturday game wasn't much better for the Rebels as they fell again to Tennessee 10-3. The Vols connected for 17 hits including four doubles off four Rebel pitchers, starter and loser Jack Daugherty, Hunter Elliott, Mitchell Murrell, and Josh Mallitz. Daugherty gave up six runs on eight hits in 3 2/3 innings while Elliott gave up four runs on six hits and three walks over four innings. Murrell and Mallitz combined to give up no runs on three hits over the last 1 1/3 innings. In the bottom of the third inning, the Rebs' first two batters reached base on errors, but the next three batters flew out, popped out, and struck out. The Rebels came to bat in the bottom of the eighth inning trailing 10-0. Ole Miss tallied by two runs in the eighth when Tim Elko's home run, off a 100-mph fastball, scored Justin Bench. Kemp Alderman, who accounted for two of the Rebels' five hits, produced the final run when he hit a homer in the ninth inning. Meanwhi,le, Tennessee's bats were still smoking, and they were running wild on the bases. The Vols' 17 hits included five doubles, and they stole four bases while getting caught stealing twice. Vol pitchers Chase Dollander, Will Mabrey, Ben Joyce, and Watt Evans kept the Rebels in check the whole game. Starter and winner, Dollander, pitched 6 1/3 innings, giving up no runs on three hits and a walk while striking out ten Rebels. Evans threw the final inning and gave up a run on a hit while striking out two batters. Much to the detriment of their cause, 15 Rebel batters struck out in the contest.

Tennessee had already won the series before the Sunday game, but the Rebels still had a chance to salvage a game. It didn't happen. Tennessee won 4-3. Both starting pitchers, Derek Diamond and Drew Beam, shut their opponents out for three innings. Then Tennessee scored three runs in the fourthh inning and chased Diamond with two outs in the fifth. Diamond had given up three runs on six hits while striking out two batters. Riley Maddox went to the mound and threw two innings, giving up three hits and a run while striking out four batters. Brandon Johnson pitched the last 2 1/3 innings, giving up one hit, a walk, and striking out two batters. Drew Gilbert drove in two runs for the Vols, Lipscomb one, and Lipcius one as the Vols picked up a total of 10 hits. Catcher Hayden Dunhurst drove in all three of the Rebels' runs with a homer in the eighth inning. In the ninth, T.J.

McCants and Kemp Alderman struck out; Hayden Leatherwood reached base on an error, and Dunhurst struck out with the tying run on base. The Rebels totaled seven hits including a double by Hayden Leatherwood and Dunhurst's homer.

Leaving Oxford, Tennessee's overall record was 23-1 and 6-0 in the SEC. The sweep by Tennessee left the Rebels with a 16-7 record overall and a 2-4 SEC mark. The March 28 rankings saw Tennessee ranked #1 in two polls while Ole Miss fell to #10 in the coaches' poll and #9 in the Baseball America poll. After starting 9-0, Ole Miss had lost seven of their last 14 games. The only thing that might have been encouraging for Rebel fans about this series was that the Rebs committed only two errors while Tennessee committed six.

The Tennessee series would prove to be reminiscent of the one between Mississippi State and Arkansas played in late March 2021. In that series a 16-4 (2-1 in the SEC) MSU team, ranked #4 in the coaches' poll and #2 in the Baseball America poll, played 17-3 (2-1 in the SEC) Arkansas ranked #2 in the coaches' poll and #1 in the Baseball America poll in Starkville. Arkansas swept that series at Dudy Noble, dispatching the Bulldogs 8-2, 11-5, and 6-4. The Dawgs more than overcame that devastating series sweep. Could the Rebels do the same with the Tennessee sweep?

On March 29, the North Alabama Lions came to Oxford with a 6-16 record and provided the Rebels an opportunity to get back on the right track. They did just that as the Rebels run-ruled the Lions 20-3 in seven innings. The Lions' batters mustered just five hits and three runs. Four Ole Miss pitchers combined to give up five hits, five walks, and three runs while striking out 13 UNA batters. Winning pitcher, Jack Washburn, threw three innings, giving up three hits and one run while striking out four batters. The Rebels scored in all six innings they batted. Recovered from his injury, the very athletic and versatile Calvin Harris played left field. He batted ninth and went three-for-four at the plate with a double and a homer and drove in five runs. Mr. Versatility himself, Justin Bench, played third base, hit a homer, scored three runs, and drove in three runs. Eleven Rebels each drove in at least one run. The Lions' starting and losing pitcher, Austin Nichols, threw two innings, giving up two hits, a walk, and three runs. Four UNA pitchers followed Nichols to the mound, and all but one of them gave up at least three runs.

Ole Miss was 17-7 and 2-4 in conference play when they ventured into the Blue Grass State to play Kentucky, which was 17-9 and 2-4 in the SEC. On Friday, April 1, Coach Bianco sent Dylan DeLucia to the mound for the Rebs. DeLucia pitched brilliantly, throwing 6 1/3 innings and giving up three hits, a walk, and a run. John Gaddis relieved DeLucia and finished the seventh inning, giving up nothing. Brandon Johnson finished the game, throwing two innings, striking out five batters while not giving up a run. The Rebs won 2-1. Ole Miss needed a masterful performance on the mound because four Kentucky pitchers combined to surrender only five hits and two runs while striking out 14 batters. The Rebels scored a run in the first inning when Tim Elko hit a single that drove in Jacob Gonzalez, who had reached base on an error. T.J. McCants led off the ninth with a triple, but Kemp Alderman and Hayden Dunhurst struck out before Hayden Leatherwood drove in McCants with a single for the winning run. DeLucia was the winning pitcher in his first start of the season. This was a good omen for things to come. Kentucky's third baseman, Chase Estep, drove in the Cats' shortstop, Ryan Ritter, in the seventh inning, taking advantage of a DeLucia error, a passed ball, a stolen base, and Estep's ground out. Kentucky starter and loser, Mason Hazelwood, gave up one run in two innings while allowing two hits and a base on balls. McCants's triple was the only extra-base hit of the game. Both teams made only one error each, but both errors resulted in the other team scoring a run.

The Saturday game was a different story, Kentucky's bats were working, and Ole Miss's weren't. The Cats registered eight hits and scored nine runs while Ole Miss managed only four hits and scored only two runs. Kentucky hitters produced two doubles, a triple and two home runs. The Cats' Jacob Plastiak went to bat five times and hit two homers, driving in four runs. Rebel pitchers hit two batters and walked four. Kentucky base runners stole two bases and were picked off base once. The Rebels scored two runs in the first inning off Cat starter and winner, Darren Williams. Williams pitched 6 1/3 innings, giving up two runs, four hits, a walk, and a wild pitch while striking out seven Rebels. Hunter Elliott started for the Rebels and gave up two runs on four hits and two walks and hit a batter over 4 1/3 innings. Ole Miss loser, Riley Maddox, relieved Elliott and pitched 1 1/3 innings, hit a batter, walked a batter, gave up three hits and two runs. Derek Diamond relieved Maddox and over 1 1/3 innings gave up three hits and three runs while striking out a batter. Matt Parenteau pitched the last inning and gave up two runs on two hits. Kentucky's 9-4 win squared the series at one game apiece.

Ole Miss batters pounded out 13 hits and scored 10 runs while three Rebel pitchers allowed only eight hits and one run to take the Sunday game 10-1. The Rebel hits included doubles by Hayden Leatherwood, Reagan Burford, and Banks Tolley and home runs by Jacob Gonzalez, Tim Elko, and T.J. McCants. There was no score until the top of the fourth inning when the Rebels plated two runs on McCants's sacrifice fly that scored Elko, and Hayden Dunhurst's single that scored Kemp Alderman. Then the Rebels exploded in the fifth, scoring six runs. Mr. RBI Elko homered; Burford scored on a fielder's choice; Leatherwood doubled Alderman home, and Gonzalez hit a three-run homer. The Rebels went on to score single runs in the seventh and eighth.. Kentucky's only run came off chase Estep's homer in the fifth inning. Winning pitcher, Jack Washburn, started for the Rebs and threw five innings, giving up four hits and one run. He was followed by Jack Dougherty, who went three innings, giving up two hits and no runs. Jack Gaddis pitched the final inning and gave up two hits but no runs. The three Rebel pitchers struck out 11 Kentucky hitters. Kentucky sent seven pitchers to the mound. Starter and loser, Tyler Bosma, pitched 3 2/3 innings, giving up five hits and five bases on balls and two runs while striking out two batters. In 1/3 of an inning, Wyatt Hudepohl surrendered two hits, a walk, and three runs. All but one of the other four Kentucky pitchers gave up at least one run.

Ole Miss left the Blue Grass State with a 19-8 overall record and a 4-5 SEC mark. In the April 4 coaches' poll Ole Miss was ranked #8 and was #7 in the Baseball America poll.

On Tuesday, April 5, Ole Miss played Southern Miss at Trustmark Park in Pearl. USM was ranked #24 in the coaches' poll. I spent 20 years as a professor of accounting and an administrator at Southern Miss, and I attended this game with my son Craig, who is a Southern Miss alum. There was no score in the bottom of the second inning when Hayden Dunhurst drove in Reagan Burford and Kemp Alderman with a three-run homer. Aided by a throwing error by Rebel shortstop Jacob Gonzalez, USM countered by scoring three runs in the top of the third inning. The Golden Eagles scored single runs in fourth, fifth, and seventh innings. The Rebels scored four runs in the bottom of the seventh inning and took a one-run lead into the eighth when USM settled the matter, putting four runs on the board. USM collected 14 hits including three doubles, a triple, and a home run off seven Rebel pitchers. Six Golden Eagles registered at least one hit and an RBI. Derek Diamond started for the Rebels and gave up five hits and three runs over 2 2/3 innings. Over the next 4 1/3 innings Mason Nichols, Riley Maddox, Jackson Kimbrell, and Drew McDaniel combined to give up four runs on six hits. Losing pitcher, Brandon Johnson, pitched 2/3 of the eighth inning and gave up a three-run homer to USM third baseman Danny Lynch. Josh Mallitz pitched the last inning and gave up nothing. The Rebels managed six hits, including two doubles and a home run. USM used six pitchers. Tyler Stuart started, pitched two innings, and gave up a hit, two walks, and three runs off Dunhurst's home run. Garrett Ramsey, who pitched two innings and gave up two hits and no runs, was the winning pitcher. Landon Harper pitched 1/3 innings, gave up nothing, and earned a save. Final score, USM 10, Ole Miss 7.

Alabama showed up at Swayze Field on April 8 with a 17-12 overall record and a 4-5 SEC mark. Alabama scored a run in the top of the first, but Captain Tim Elko pushed the Rebels ahead with a two-run single in the bottom of the inning. The Rebels didn't score again until the ninth inning when left fielder Kevin Graham, who had been out a month with a broken wrist, crushed a two-run homer over the right-field wall. Meanwhile, the Crismon Tide had taken advantage of the Rebs' seven-inning drought by scoring two runs in each of the third, fourth, and fifth innings. Ole Miss managed only four hits all game while Alabama stroked 12. Final score, Alabama 7, Ole Miss 4. Hunter Elliott started on the mound for the Rebels, and in three innings he gave up three hits and three runs while walking one and hitting two batters. Dylan DeLucia came in and gave up two runs in the fourth inning, and in the fifth inning he gave up another two runs without retiring a batter. Shortstop Jim Jarvis and first baseman Drew Williamson provided the bulk of Alabama's offense. Leadoff batter, Jarvis, got three hits in five plate appearances and scored three runs. First baseman and fifth-hole hitter, Williamson, drove in three runs with a groundout and a double. Alabama's starting and winning pitcher, Garrett McMillan threw seven innings, giving up three hits, three walks, and two runs while striking out seven batters.

In the Saturday game the Rebels' bats came alive and pounded out 15 hits including three doubles and six home runs. Jacob Gonzalez hit three of the home runs and drove in six runs while Tim Elko, Reagan Burford, and Peyton Chatagnier each contributed a homer. Batting in the ninth hole, Chatagnier went three-for-five at the plate and scored three runs. The six homers were the most in a single game since the Rebs hit six against Arkansas-Pine Bluff in 2019. The contest was a back-and-forth affair that was tied 10-10 after nine innings. After scoring no runs in the first two innings, the Rebels scored two in the third and five in the fourth. After scoring three runs in the first five innings, Alabama scored three in the sixth and four in the seventh. The Rebels matched Alabama by scoring two runs in the eighth inning and one in the ninth. Alabama hitters collected a total of 12 hits off four Rebel pitchers. Alabama first baseman Drew Williamson feasted on Ole Miss pitching, going three-for-four at the plate and driving in five runs. Three pitchers went to the mound for Alabama, and Dylan Ray, who threw the last 2 1/3 innings, giving up a run on two hits and a walk while striking out two batters, was the winner. Rebel batters struck out 13 times and left seven runners on base. Alabama batters struck out eight times and left eight runners on base. Final score, Alabama 12, Ole Miss 10.

Alabama swept the series by posting a 7-3 victory over the Rebels in the Sunday game. In stark contrast to the Saturday game, the Rebels managed only four hits off three Alabama hurlers. But again, Mr. Elko showed up, going two-for-four at the plate with a home run and two RBIs. Kemp Alderman accounted for the Rebels' other run with a home run. Alabama's starting and winning pitcher, Grayson Hitt, threw 6 1/3 innings, giving up three hits, two walks, and three runs while striking out eight batters. The two relievers who followed Hitt gave up a total of one hit, one walk, and no runs while striking out three batters. Ole Miss starter and loser, Jack Washburn, threw three innings and gave up five hits, three walks, and three runs. Derek Diamond followed Washburn and pitched 4 1/3 innings, giving up two hits and two runs while striking out five hitters. Riley Maddox and Dylan DeLucia closed the game out as each gave up one run and one hit. Alabama batters managed nine hits including three doubles and three home runs.

When Alabama left town, their embarrassed host, the Ole Miss Rebels, stood 19-12 overall and 4-8 in the SEC. Having lost four consecutive games, Ole Miss fell completely out of the April 11 coaches' top 25 poll and the Baseball American poll. That was a very steep fall from the #8 and #7 slots in the previous polls. The Rebs would not be ranked again until the postseason.

The Murray State Racers came to Oxford Tuesday, April 12, with a 15-15 record. Rebel bats came alive again against non-SEC pitching, and Rebel pitchers controlled the Racers' bats for the whole game as Ole Miss won 8-2. Two big innings produced all eight of the Rebels' runs. In the first inning leadoff batter Jacob Gonzalez slapped out a single, and Justin Bench sent him home on a double to left-center field. Kevin Graham sent Bench home with a sac fly. Reagan Burford hit an infield single, and Tim Elko scored on a throwing error, 3-0 Rebels. The Racers scored their first run in the sixth inning when former Ole Miss Rebel Cade Sammons doubled to score pinch runner Wyatt Gardner. Murray State scored its other run in the 8th inning when Sammons scored on a wild pitch. The Rebs put the game out of the Racers' reach in the sixth inning when they scored five runs. Kemp Alderman singled and soon scored on a wild pitch. Gonzalez doubled, driving in Calvin Harris, who had singled, and pinch-runner Banks Tolley. Justin Bench doubled home Gonzalez, and Kevin Graham doubled home Bench. Ole Miss sent six pitchers to the mound. They combined to give up four hits and two runs. Starter and winner, Drew McDaniel, went five innings and gave up two hits, a walk, and a run while striking out eight batters. Murray State sent 10 pitchers to the mound, and they combined to give up eight runs on 14 hits, a walk, and a wild pitch.

Ole Miss traveled to Columbia, South Carolina, in a Thursday-Saturday series that began April 14. The Rebels were 20-12 overall and 4-8 in the SEC. But they blasted the Gamecocks 9-1 in the series opener. Ole Miss's starting and winning pitcher, Dylan DeLucia, threw 7 2/3 innings, giving up six hits, a walk, and a run while striking out four batters. Matt Parenteau closed for the Rebels, giving up two hits and nothing more over 1 1/3 innings. Both DeLucia and Parenteau were pitching to spots and getting groundouts and flyouts as they walked only four batters. DeLucia's performance, the longest by a Rebel starter all season, would prove to be a good omen of future success. Rebel batters produced 10 hits, including a double and two home runs. Ole Miss led 9-0 before the Gamecocks scored their only run in the bottom of the eighth inning. T.J. McCants hit a two-run homer in the second inning, and Reagan Burford hit a three-run dinger in the third. South Carolina sent three pitchers to the mound. Starting pitcher Aidan Hunter suffered the loss as he allowed seven runs over three innings. John Gilreath threw five innings, giving up two runs while striking out five Rebs.

Any balm that the Murray State and the first South Carolina games administered to the Rebels' bruised pride had little lasting effect. The Gamecocks won the Friday game 4-2 and the Saturday game 9-8. In the Friday game Tim Elko went four-for-four at the plate, hit solo homers in the first and sixth innings, and accounted for all of the Rebels' scoring and four of their six hits. Both Derek Diamond and Riley Maddox pitched well for Ole Miss. Diamond threw 5 1/3 innings and gave up five hits, including a three-run homer to Josiah Sightler, and four runs. Maddox went 2 2/3 innings and gave up nothing. The Rebels left five runners on base, and the Gamecocks left only one.

The Saturday game proved to be a nail-biter slugfest. Ole Miss batters stroked three doubles, a triple, and a home run. South Carolina batters countered with two doubles and three home runs. Rebel batters posted a total of 13 hits while USC batters totaled 11. Ole Miss went into the top of the ninth inning trailing 8-4. Reagan Burford led off with a walk; pinch-hitter Ben Van Cleve followed with a double; Justin Bench singled to drive in a run; Jacob Gonzalez singled to drive in a run; Kemp Alderman doubled to drive in both Bench and Gonzalez. The score was tied at eight runs apiece when the Gamecocks came to bat in the last of the ninth. Talmadge LeCroy led off with a walk and subsequently scored the winning unearned run on a sac fly by Jalen Vasquez. The Rebels left South Carolina with a 21-14 overall record and a 5-10 SEC mark.

Southeast Missouri State provided the mid-week competition on April 19. The SEMO Redhawks sported a 24-10 record when they squared off against the Rebels at Swayze Field on a sunny day that registered a high of 63 degrees. Another forgettable performance by the Rebels at the plate and in the field allowed the Redhawks to prevail 13-3 and to leave Oxford with a 25-10 record. The Rebels scored single runs in the fourth, eighth, and ninth innings. In the fourth Hayden Leatherwood singled and drove Kemp Alderman. who had doubled. In the eighth Tywone Malone hit a home run over the center-field wall, and in the ninth, John Kramer homered to right field. Meanwhile, SEMO put runs on the board in seven innings. Nine pitchers went to the mound for Ole Miss and combined to give up 12 hits, including two doubles and a home run, nine bases on balls, and a wild pitch. Rebel fielders committed three errors. Reagan Burford made two errors playing second base. Burford usually played third base, and the move to second was apparently made in an effort to rest Peyton Chatagnier, who had been struggling at the plate. The Redhawks threw four pitchers, who combined to give up 10 hits and three walks while the Redhawks played flawlessly in the field. SEMO's winning pitcher, Austin Williams, pitched three innings, giving up three hits and no runs while striking out four Rebels. Losing pitcher Drew McDaniel started for the Rebs and gave up three hits, two walks, and three runs while striking out two batters and hitting a batter over 1 2/3 innings. Max Cioffi threw 2/3 of an inning and gave up two hits, two walks, and three runs while throwing a wild pitch and striking out a batter. Coach Bianco had hoped that the 6'4", 225-pound Cioffi would be a reliable contributor in 2022. As a freshman in 2018, the relief pitcher had appeared in 14 games, pitched 23 innings, and produced a 1.96 ERA, the lowest on the staff for a pitcher who threw more than an inning. As a sophomore in 2019, Cioffi pitched in 16 games, producing a 2-2 record and a 4.45 ERA and played a key role in an SEC Tournament victory and a NCAA Regional win. In the 2020 season cut short by COVID, Cioffi made six appearances in relief, did not give up an earned run, and earned a save. He allowed just one run in eight innings pitched. He held batters to a .115 average while striking out 12 batters and walking none. In 2021 Cioffi made only one appearance, allowing a hit and a run while striking out three batters in 1 2/3 innings. He missed two months with a meniscus tear. Coming back late in the season, he allowed a run on three hits against North Alabama. Then he missed the rest of the season with a torn UCL. Cioffi was trying to return from Tommy John surgery. He ended the 2022 season with four appearances, going 2 2/3 innings, giving up three runs on three hits while walking three batters and striking out four.

Defending National Champion Mississippi State came to Oxford for a three-game series that started Thursday, April 21. Like the Rebels, the Bulldogs were in the midst of a disappointing season. The Dawgs stood 22-16 overall and 5-10 in the SEC. The Rebels were 21-15 overall and 5-10 in the SEC. Neither team appeared in the top 25 rankings, a very strange situation this far into a college baseball season. Mississippi State had been ranked #3 in the preseason coaches' poll but had dropped out of the ratings by March 7. Ole Miss had been ranked #6 in the preseason poll and had risen to #1 in the March 14 poll but had dropped out of the ranking by April 11. Ole Miss had dropped the last six games they had played against MSU in Oxford, and they had not won a three-game series against the Bulldogs since 2015.

In the Thursday game's rising star, Dylan DeLucia, improved his record to 3-0 by pitching a gem. In the Rebels' 4-2 victory, DeLucia hurled the Rebels' first complete game of the season, while striking out eight batters and giving up two runs on five hits and no walks. Both of the Dawgs' runs came on solo home runs. Brad Cumbest homered in the third inning, and Kellum Clark homered in the seventh. The Rebels played flawlessly in the field, and they produced four runs off four MSU pitchers. Kevin Graham slammed a three-run homer in the first inning. Hayden Dunhurst hit a solo home run in the fifth, accounting for the Rebels' last run. MSU starter and loser, Brandon Smith, threw six innings and gave up four runs on four hits and a walk.

The Friday game was a back-and-forth affair. MSU grabbed the lead 1-0 in the top of the first when first baseman Luke Hancock homered off Rebel starter Hunter Elliott. That lead was short-lived as the first three batters in the bottom of the inning, Justin Bench, Jacob Gonzalez, and Tim Elko, all hit home runs off MSU starter Preston Johnson. The Rebels increased their lead to 4-1 in the second inning when Peyton Chatagnier hit a solo homer. The Dawgs closed the gap to 4-3 in the sixth on a ground-rule double by center fielder Jess Davis off Rebel pitcher Riley Maddox that scored Brad Cumbest and a single by R.J. Yeager that scored Davis. MSU scored four more runs in the seventh on home runs by Hunter Hines and Kellum Clark to take a 7-4 lead. Continuing their onslaught against Rebel pitchers, the Dawgs scored their last three runs in the top of the eighth to move the score to 10-4. Ole Miss mounted a comeback in the bottom of the eighth, scoring three runs when Gonzalez drove in Hayden Leatherwood with a single, and Alderman doubled, driving in Gonzalez and Bench. Too little too late, final score MSU 10- Ole Miss 7. Elliott pitched four innings for the Rebs, giving up four hits and one run while striking out six batters. He was followed by

Riley Maddox, who pitched 1 2/3 innings, giving up five hits, a walk, and two runs. Losing pitcher, Jack Dougherty, threw 1/3 of an inning, giving up four hits and four runs. Mason Nichols pitched the last two innings and gave up no runs on two hits while striking out two. Preston Johnson started for the Dawgs and gave up nine hits, three walks, and four runs over five innings. Pico Kohn, who pitched 2 innings and gave up a hit and a walk but no runs, was credited with the win. K.C. Hunt threw the final two innings for the Dawgs, giving up three runs.

The rubber game played Saturday was important to both teams as their seasons seemed to be headed downhill. Ole Miss and MSU needed to salvage some pride and get on the right track. The Rebels had broken the Dawgs' streak of six consecutive wins on the Rebs' home field. But they still hadn't won a three-game series from the Dawgs since 2015.

As was to be expected, the Saturday game was a hard-fought contest between two bitter rivals. MSU won 7-6 in the 11th inning when Brad Cumbest got the only hit, a solo home run to left field, off Rebel ace reliever Brandon Johnson, who pitched 3 2/3 innings. The Rebels never led, but Jacob Gonzales tied the game in the bottom of the ninth with a homer off Pico Kohn with Justin Bench on base. Winning pitcher, K.C. Hunt, threw the last 2 2/3 innings for State and gave up no runs and no hits while striking out two Rebels. Derek Diamond started for Ole Miss and went four innings, giving up eight hits and four runs. Josh Mallitz pitched 1 1/3 innings and gave up two runs. Jackson Kimbrell and Jack Dougherty combined for two innings, giving up no runs. Kade Smith started for MSU and pitched 5 1/3 innings, giving up four runs on four hits while striking out six Rebels. An unusual occurrence transpired in the bottom of the sixth inning. MSU Coach Chris Lemonis sent left-handed pitcher Cam Tullar into the game to face left-handed hitter Hayden Leatherwood with the bases loaded. Coach Bianco countered by sending right-handed pinch hitter Ben Van Cleve to the plate. Tullar was immediately replaced by right-handed pitcher Jackson Fristoe. Bianco then sent switch hitter Calvin Harris to the plate to hit for Van Cleve. Tullar never threw a pitch, and Van Cleve never had an opportunity to swing at a pitch. Harris hit a sacrifice fly to drive in a run. Fristoe threw two innings and gave up a hit and a walk while striking out two Rebels. Pico Kohn threw two innings and surrendered two runs. Winning pitcher, K.C. Hunt, faced only eight batters over the last 2 2/3 innings, and he struck out two of them.

Both Ole Miss and Mississippi State were bottom feeders in the SEC after this series. Ole Miss at 6-12 was at the very bottom of the seven-team SEC West. MSU was one notch higher at 8-10. The only team with a worse SEC record was Missouri from the eastern division. Only 12 of the 14 SEC teams make it to the SEC Tournament. Both Ole Miss and Mississippi State were in danger of not making it to the SEC Tournament, much less the NCAA Tournament. There was one impressive statistic related to the Ole MISS/MSU three-game series played in Oxford: a total of 35,055 fans attended the three games. It is doubtful that any other state would support two struggling home-state teams like that in a three-game series, especially if both teams were losers in their conference.

Although the SEC series with Mississippi State was over, the Rebels would soon get another shot at the Dawgs. The Governor's Cup between the in-state rivals is played annually at Trustmark Park in Pearl. This game does not figure in the conference records of the schools, but it is a very important part of their rivalry. The 2022 game was played April 26, and the Rebels squared their record against MSU for the season with a victory.

Ole Miss jump-started the action in the first inning by scoring two runs when Jacob Gonzales hit a triple that scored Justin Bench, and Tim Elko's groundout scored Gonzales. The Dawgs drew even in the bottom of the inning. Logan Tanner and Luke Hancock scored on a single by Hunter Hines and a throwing error by Reagan Burford. There was no more scoring until the Rebels put three runs on the board in the fifth. Elko drove in Gonzales and Chatagnier with a single, and Kevin Graham hit a double, scoring Elko. Four of the Rebels' hits went for extra bases. Gonzales, Graham, and Hayden Leatherwood hit doubles, and Gonzales hit a triple. Neither team scored the rest of the game. Final score, 5-2 Rebels. Rebel winning pitcher, Drew McDaniel, pushed his record to 4-2 by throwing five innings. He gave up two runs on two hits, five walks, a wild pitch, and a hit batsman. Mason Nichols shut out the Dawgs for three innings, and Brandon Johnson earned a save by pitching an inning and giving up a hit and a walk while striking out two batters. MSU managed only four hits, all singles. Mikey Tepper started on the mound for the Dawgs and pitched four innings. He gave up two runs on two hits while walking three batters, hitting a batter, throwing a wild pitch and striking out four Rebels. Lane Forsythe, who was normally MSU's starting shortstop, relieved Tepper in the fifth inning. That didn't prove to be a very good move by Coach Lemonis, as Forsythe gave up three runs on four hits in 1/3 of an inning, and he was tagged with the loss. Cam Tullar and Drew Talley closed out the game for MSU, giving up no runs on one hit and striking out 10 Rebels over the last 4 2/3 innings.

Things got even more difficult for Ole Miss when they had to face Arkansas in Fayetteville. The Razorbacks were ranked #4 in the coaches' poll and had a record of 32-9 including a 12-6 SEC mark. Ole Miss stood 23-17 and 6-12 in the SEC.

The first game was played on Friday, April 29. Coach Bianco sent Dylan DeLucia, who had become the Rebels' pitching ace, to the mound and the right-hander did not disappoint. DeLucia pitched seven innings against the strong Hog lineup and gave up two runs on eight hits and two bases on balls while striking out nine batters. Double plays turned in the first three innings helped DeLucia's cause. The Hogs' two runs were actually scored in the eighth inning. DeLucia started the inning but did not register an out. He was relieved by ace reliever Brandon Johnson after Braydon Webb hit a two-run homer. Johnson threw two innings and faced only six batters, three of whom struck out. The Rebels scored one run in the fourth inning and three in the fifth. Kemp Alderman singled to right field to drive in Kevin Graham in the fourth inning. In the fifth, Tim Elko doubled to drive in Hayden Dunhurst, and Graham singled to drive in Elko and Justin Bench. Arkansas starting and losing pitcher, Connor Noland, dropped his record to 5-3 as he gave up 11 hits, two walks, and four runs while striking out three batters over eight innings. Evan Taylor closed for Arkansas by striking out two of the two batters he faced. Final score, Rebels 4, Hogs 2.

Hunter Elliott, who was emerging as a superstar freshman, started the Saturday game for the Rebels. Like Dylan DeLucia, he did not disappoint. The left-hander threw a career-high six innings, giving up three runs on four hits and a walk while striking out eight batters. Rebel reliever Jack Dougherty, who threw 2 1/3 innings, giving up three hits and three runs, was charged with the loss in a game that Arkansas won 6-3. The Hogs scored the first run when first baseman Brady Slavens slammed a solo homer in the first inning. In the top of the second, Rebel center-fielder T. J. McCants countered with a home run to right center field. In the third, Tim Elko hammered a 466-foot homer to center field to put the Rebels up 2-1. In the fifth, Hog center fielder Braydon Webb hit a two-run homer to put the Hogs up 3-2. The Rebels tied the score at three apiece in the eighth inning as Kemp Alderman scored when Peyton Chatagnier grounded into a double play. Arkansas won the game in the bottom of the ninth on a three-run homer struck by designated hitter Kendall Diggs.

When playing away from home, winning a rubber game in a three-game SEC series seems to be especially difficult. The difficulty is exacerbated when you have to face a truly outstanding team like Arkansas. The Sunday game proved to be a close-but-no-cigar game for the Rebs. RBI machine Tim Elko's single off Hog starter Jaxon Wiggins put the Rebels up 1-0 in the first inning when he drove in Justin Bench, who had walked and moved to second base on a wild pitch. Arkansas took the lead in the third when right fielder Chris Lanzilli hit a two-run homer off Rebel starter Derek Diamond. In the fourth, Kemp Alderman's single drove in Kevin Graham, and Elko and put the Rebels up 3-2. The Hogs countered in the bottom of the fifth on a two-run homer by catcher Michael Turner. The Rebels loaded the bases in the ninth inning but could not get a runner home. Arkansas took this important rubber game 4-3.

From March 13 through the first of May, the Rebels lost 18 games and won only 11. Fourteen of those losses were to SEC teams. On May 2, Ole Miss stood 24-19 overall and 7-14 in the SEC. The Rebels, who had great expectations at the beginning of the season, had hit rock bottom. This midseason swoon was punctuated by a lack of timely hitting, ineffective pitching, and spotty fielding. It seemed that the wheels had fallen off the Rebel Machine when Ole Miss bottomed out tied with Missouri and Kentucky for last place in the SEC. They were in danger of not qualifying for the SEC or NCAA Tournaments.

The Rebels' talent had not been reflected on the field, and Coach Bianco was being heavily criticized by fans and the media. Bianco and his staff's jobs were in jeopardy, and he had been making moves trying to find the right combinations on the field. Injuries had limited the play of three very important players -- Kevin Graham, Hayden Dunhurst, and T.J. McCants.

Things were about to change as Coach Bianco settled on a weekend pitching rotation and starting lineup.

On Friday, May 6, another bottom feeder, Missouri, came to Swayze field for a three-game series. The Tigers were 6-16 in the SEC, and the Rebels were 7-14. A get-well opportunity presented itself to the Rebels. The trouble was that Ole Miss had not played well in SEC action on its home turf. The Rebels played five three-game SEC series at home. Through three of those series, over nine games they had won only one. Tennessee and Alabama had swept weekend series at Swayze Field, and Mississippi State had won two of three there.

Dylan DeLucia, who had established himself as the Friday night starter, toed the rubber for the May 6 game with the Missouri Tigers. DeLucia gave up two runs in the first inning but didn't allow the Tigers to score over the next three frames. He ran into trouble in the fifth, allowing a run while not registering an out. In total DeLucia threw four innings and gave up three runs off eight hits and two walks while striking out four Tigers. Having scored three runs in the bottom of the first inning and one run in the third, the Rebels were ahead 4-3 when Mason Nichols relieved DeLucia. Nichols allowed two runs on two hits and a walk over 1 1/3 innings. Jack Dougherty, who was becoming more consistent on the mound, earned the win by throwing 1 2/3 innings and giving up a hit, a walk, and no runs. Brandon Johnson closed for the Rebs, giving up a hit and a base on balls and no runs over two innings and earning his sixth save. The Tigers registered 12 hits, but only one was for extra bases, third baseman Luke Mann's two-run homer. The Rebels managed only seven hits off three Tiger pitchers. That total included a double and homers by Kemp Alderman and Peyton Chatagnier. Alderman, who was beginning to look a lot like Tim Elko, went four-for-four and drove in three runs. Final score, Ole Miss 7, Missouri 5.

The Rebels brought hot bats to the Saturday game. They collected 13 hits including doubles by Justin Bench, Tim Elko, and Hayden Leatherwood and a home run by T.J. McCants. Kevin Graham and Kemp Alderman drove in runs with sacrifice flies. Missouri starting and losing pitcher, Spencer Miles, surrendered five runs off 10 hits and a hit batsman over six innings. The Rebels scored a run in the first inning, two in the fourth, and two in the fifth off Miles. In the seventh inning, Austin Cheeley came in and gave up three runs on one hit in 1/3 inning. The Tigers scored their only run in the first inning off Hunter Elliott, who had earned the right to be a weekend starter. After giving up the run, Elliott struck out two batters to get out of a jam. In total he pitched seven innings and gave up four hits, a walk, and a run while striking out nine batters. Jack Washburn came in and slammed the door on the Tigers, giving up a hit and striking out two batters over the last two innings. Final score, Rebels 8, Tigers 1.

In the Sunday game, starter Derek Diamond earned a win and evened his record at 4-4. Diamond threw five innings and gave up eight hits and two runs. Missouri bats generated 11 hits including two doubles and a home run, but the Tigers could plate only two runners. Both runs crossed the plate in the fifth inning when second baseman and nine-hole hitter Justin Colon smacked a two-run homer off Diamond. Four Missouri pitchers combined to give up 15 hits, three walks, and ten runs while throwing three wild pitches and hitting a batter. The Rebs' John Gaddis earned a save by pitching four innings, giving up three hits, a walk, and no runs while striking out three Tigers. Kevin Graham, who was back at full strength, led a 15-hit Rebel barrage at the plate, going five-for-five, hitting two homers, driving in two runs, and scoring two. Tim Elko went two-for-five at the plate and drove in a run with a home run. Final score, Rebels 10, Tigers 2. By sweeping the Tigers, Ole Miss had finally won an SEC series in Oxford. They had accomplished that feat in style by scoring 25 runs and giving up only eight over the three-game series. Ole Miss's record improved to 27-19 overall and 10-14 in the conference. A total of 24,817 fans attended the series between two teams at the bottom of the SEC standings. After this series, Captain Tim Elko said and posted on X (formerly Twitter), "Don't let the Rebs get hot." This pithy utterance became the Rebels' and Rebel fans' mantra for the rest of the season.

Next up was a Wednesday, May 11, rematch against the Southern Miss Golden Eagles in Hattiesburg. The Rebels, who had lost to the Golden Eagles 10-7 on April 5 at Trustmark Park in Pearl. USM, with a 36-12 record, came to this game ranked #11 in the nation in the coaches' poll.

The Golden Eagles scored first in the bottom of the second inning when first baseman Christopher Sargent sent a solo home run over the left-field wall. That proved to be the only score for Southern Miss as Rebel pitchers shut down the home team's bats the rest of the game. Starting and winning pitcher, Drew McDaniel, improved his record to 5-2 by throwing five innings and giving up a run on four hits and a walk while striking out eight batters. Three Rebel pitchers followed McDaniel and shut out the Golden Eagles the rest of the way. Brandon Johnson, who had become a powerful closer, did his thing by giving up a hit and a walk while striking out two batters and earning his seventh save. The four Rebel pitchers struck out 15 USM batters and gave up only five hits. Six Southern Miss pitchers gave up seven hits, two walks, two wild pitches, and four runs while striking out 10 Rebels. Matthew Adams, the Golden Eagles' starter and loser, went 3 2/3 innings and gave up four hits, a walk, and three runs. Justin Storm, who threw one inning, gave up the Rebels' last run. In the fourth inning, Kevin Graham hit a two-run homer, and Kemp Alderman hit a solo homer. In the fifth inning, Tim Elko drove in a run with a single. Final score, Ole Miss 4, Southern Miss 1. The game drew 6,346 fans, the largest crowd in the history of Pete Taylor Park. With this victory over the Golden Eagles, Ole Miss squared its regular season record against in-state rivals by going 2-2 against Mississippi State and 1-1 against Southern Miss.

Ole Miss traveled to Baton Rouge to take on the LSU Tigers, who were ranked #15 in the coaches' poll with a 33-15 overall record and a 14-10 SEC mark. This would be the Rebels' last road SEC series of the season. In the bottom of the first inning, center fielder Dylan Crews smashed a home run with right fielder Josh Pearson on base to put the Tigers up 2-0. The Rebels snatched the lead in the top of the second when Hayden Dunhurst drove in John Kramer, who had been hit by a pitch, and T.J. McCants, who had singled. Jacob Gonzalez singled to drive in Dunhurst and Peyton Chatagnier. Tim Elko capped off Rebel scoring in the fifth with a solo homer to left field. Shortstop Jordan Thompson homered to right field in the eighth to score the Tigers' last run. Final score, Ole Miss 5, LSU 3. Dylan DeLucia, now well established as Ole Miss's Friday starter, improved his record to 5-0 by pitching 7-plus innings and giving up three hits, two bases on balls, and three runs while striking out nine Tigers. The game was suspended on Friday night with the Rebels leading 4-2. It was completed Saturday before the start of game two. DeLucia demonstrated his value in an extraordinary way in this two-day affair. He threw 38 pitches Friday night, and when he surprisingly came back Saturday, he threw 79 more and claimed the victory. Few starting pitchers ever pitch on consecutive days. Dylan did it extremely well during this crucial series for the Rebs. Brandon Johnson, now firmly established as the Rebels' closer, threw the last two innings, facing six batters and striking out four. LSU's starting pitcher, Ma'Khail Hillard, saw his record fall to 5-1 as he lasted three innings and gave up four hits, two walks, and four runs while striking out four Rebels and throwing a wild pitch. The Rebels managed only six hits, but the Tigers managed only three. Both teams were flawless in the field.

It was all Ole Miss in the second game. Seven Rebels drove in a total of 11 runs. Of the Rebels' 12 hits, six were of the extra-base variety. Kemp Alderman and Peyton Chatagnier hit doubles; Justin Bench, Tim Elko, Kevin Graham, and Hayden Dunhurst hit home runs. Graham went three-for-five and drove in two runs. Meanwhile, freshman Hunter Elliott, who had established himself as the Saturday starter, put on a show. Elliott threw 6 2/3 innings, giving up one run, four hits, three bases, on balls, hitting two batters and throwing a wild pitch while striking out nine Tigers. This performance reminded the writer of the great Doug Nikhazy, who pitched during the previous three seasons for the Rebels. Nikhazy would allow batters to get on base, but it was very difficult to score on him. Josh Mallitz, who had been establishing himself as a valuable arm out of the bullpen, threw the last 2 1/3 innings, giving up a hit and a walk while striking out three Tigers. As the Rebels were excelling at the plate and on the mound, the Tiger batters, pitchers, and fielders were struggling. Six LSU pitchers gave up 12 hits, two walks, and hit two batters while striking out 11 Rebels. Three LSU fielding errors resulted in four unearned runs crossing the plate for the Rebels. LSU's starting and losing pitcher, Devin Fontenot, lasted only 1 1/3 innings and gave up three runs on three hits, a walk, and a hit batsman. Five pitchers followed Fontenot to the mound. Final score, Ole Miss 11 and LSU 1. The Rebels had now won the last two series played at LSU (2019 and 2022). The last time that happened was in 1964 and 1965.

The Sunday game gave the Rebels an opportunity to sweep a series from LSU, and they were up to the task. Ole Miss scored a run in the first inning and two in the second and never trailed. LSU tied the contest by scoring two runs in the third and one in the fourt, but the tie was short-lived as the Rebs put four runs on the board in the fifth. LSU scored a single run in the bottom of the fifth. Ole Miss scored a single run in the top of the eighth, and LSU scored another run in the bottom of the eighth. Final score, Rebels 8, Tigers 5. Ole Miss hitters were swinging big bats that blasted six extra-base hits, three doubles, and three home runs. Justin Bench, Peyton Chatagnier, and Hayden Dunhurst hit doubles, and Chatagnier, Hayden Leatherwood, and Kemp Alderman stroked homers. Five of the Rebels' eight runs came off home runs. Rebel starting pitcher, Derek Diamond, hurled 4 1/3 innings, giving up six hits and four runs while striking out five batters. Winning pitcher, John Gaddis, gave up a hit, a walk, and a run while striking out a batter. Closer Brandon Johnson earned his ninth save by throwing 1 1/3 innings, giving up a hit and two walks while striking out four Tigers. LSU's starting pitcher, Samuel Dutton, faced only one batter, Justin Bench, who singled and later scored. Jacob Hasty came in and gave up three hits and two runs over four innings. Losing pitcher, Eric Reyzelman, pitched an inning and gave up three hits, a walk, and four runs. Two other pitchers followed, and they gave up a total of three hits, a walk, and a run. Thus, Ole Miss completed its first-ever sweep of LSU in a three-game series in Baton Rouge, 11-1.

Ole Miss was no longer in danger of not making the SEC Tournament. At this point it was settled as to which two of the 14 SEC teams would not make the tournament. As of May 18, Missouri was 8-19 in the conference, and Mississippi State was 9-18. Both teams had three conference games left to play, and even if both swept those games, they could not match the Rebels, who stood 13-14 in the conference. Ole Miss stood 31-19 overall when Texas A&M came to Oxford for the final SEC series of the season. The Aggies brought an overall record of 33-16 to the game and an SEC mark of 17-10. A&M was ranked #11 in the coaches' poll and #4 by Baseball America.

Texas A&M led 7-0 when the Rebels came to bat in the bottom of the second inning. The Aggies had bolted ahead 3-0 in the top of the first inning and aided by two errors by Hayden Leatherwood, had added four more runs in the top of the second. The Rebs closed the gap to four runs in the bottom of the second by scoring three runs. By the end of the sixth, the Rebs had scored two more runs to close the gap to 7-5. That is as close as they got to catching A&M. The Aggies were held scoreless from the third through the seventh inning but scored a run in the eighth and two in the ninth. The Rebels didn't score after the sixth. Final score, A&M 10, Ole Miss 5. Losing pitcher, Dylan DeLucia, was not his usual dominate self. He started for the Rebs but lasted only 1 2/3 innings, giving up five hits, four walks, and seven runs while striking out a batter and throwing a wild pitch. DeLucia faced 15 batters and threw 57 pitches. Three Rebel pitchers, Jack Dougherty, John Gaddis, and Max Cioffi, followed DeLucia and gave up a total of three runs. Mason Nichols also threw 2 2/3 innings and gave up a run on two hits and a walk while striking out four Aggies. John Gaddis came on and pitched 1 1/3 innings and gave up three hits, two walks, a wild pitch, and two runs while striking out an Aggie. Max Cioffi threw the last 2/3 of an inning and gave up a walk and nothing else. A&M bats produced 14 hits including four doubles and two home runs. Winning pitcher Joseph Menefee relieved starter Nathan Dettmer in the fourth inning and gave up a hit, three walks, and a run over 1 1/3 innings. Only two of the Rebels' eight hits went for extra bases, Hayden Dunhurst hit a double, and Justin Bench hit a triple. Dunhurst went three-for-three at the plate, scored a run, and drove in three runs. Bench went two-for-three and drove in two runs.

Ole Miss got back to its winning ways in the Friday game by handing A&M a 14-6 defeat. The Aggies grabbed a 3-0 lead in the first inning. The Rebs countered by scoring a run in the bottom of the inning and, after A&M failed to score in the top of the second, the Rebs put two runs on the board in the bottom of the inning to tie the score. It was basically all Ole Miss after that as the Rebels scored two runs in the third, three in the fourth, three in the fifth, and three in the seventh. Meanwhile, the Aggies scored two runs in the fifth and one in the sixth. Rebel batters registered 17 hits including three doubles and two home runs off five Aggie pitchers. Although the box score indicates that Aggie pitchers did not issue an intentional walk, they definitely pitched around Tim Elko. The captain went zero-for-one at the plate but walked four times, scored two runs, and drove in a run with a sac fly. Justin Bench, Jacob Gonzalez, Kevin Graham, and Kemp Alderman did the heavy lifting for the Rebels. Bench got a single and a double and drove in two runs and scored two runs; Gonzalez got three hits including a homer and drove in two runs and scored two runs; Graham got three singles and drove in three runs and scored a run; Alderman got two hits, including a homer, scored a run and drove in four runs. Hunter Elliott threw the first four innings for Ole Miss, giving up four hits, five walks, and four runs while striking out three Aggies. Jack Washburn relieved and earned the win by going 1 2/3 innings and giving up two hits, two walks, and two runs while striking out a batter. Josh Mallitz closed and earned a save by pitching 3 1/3 innings and giving up two hits while striking out four Aggies. A&M sent five pitchers to the mound, all but one of whom gave up at least three runs. Chris Cortez, who came in to relieve starter Wyatt Tucker in the third inning, was tagged with the loss.

The May 21 contest against Texas A&M was the last game of the regular season. It was also the rubber game of the three-game SEC series. Ole Miss was 31-21 overall and 14-15 in the conference, and A&M was 34-17 overall and 18-11 in the conference. A win for the Rebels would bring them to .500 in the SEC and enhance their chances to be invited to the NCAA Baseball Tournament. It wasn't to be. Texas A&M took the series with a 12-5 victory over the Rebels. Going into the fourth inning, Ole Miss led 5 to 2, having scored a run in the second inning and four in the third while A&M had scored a run in the first and another in the third. Ole Miss didn't score after the third inning, but A&M exploded for seven runs in the top of the fourth and three in the ninth. A&M hitters were simply sizzling, stroking 13 hits, including a double, a triple, and six home runs to put 12 runs on the board. Derek Diamond started for the Rebels and didn't make it out of the fourth inning. Diamond gave up six hits, two walks, and four runs over 3 1/3 innings while striking out three batters. Losing pitcher, Drew McDaniel, came in and threw 1/3 of an inning and gave up three hits, two walks, and five runs while striking out a hitter. Freshman right-handed pitcher, Mason Nichols, who stands 6'5" and weighs 205 pounds, came on in relief. He had been coming along nicely, and he continued to be impressive by throwing 2 1/3 innings and giving up a hit, a walk, and no runs while striking out two Aggies. Brandon Johnson came in and gave up three hits, a walk, and three runs while striking out three batters over 2 2/3 innings. Max Cioffi came in for the last 1/3 of an inning and struck out the only batter he faced. Ole Miss batters managed seven hits, but five were of the extra-base variety. Justin Bench and T. J. McCants hit doubles, and Jacob Gonzalez, Hayden Dunhurst, and Peyton Chatagnier hit home runs. Home runs accounted for all of the Rebels' runs. Gonzalez and Dunhurst hit solo homers, and Chatagnier hit a three-run homer. A&M's starting pitcher, Ryan Prager, threw 2 1/3 innings and gave up four runs on four hits while walking two batters and hitting one. Winning pitcher, Joseph Menefee, threw four innings, giving up three hits, a walk, and a run while striking out six Rebels. Three other pitchers toed the slab for A&M and did not allow a hit or a run over the last 2 2/3 innings. At the end of the game and the regular season, the Rebels stood 32-21 overall and 14-16 in the SEC.

The Rebels were on their way to the SEC Tournament, but no one (except maybe the players and coaches) thought they were capable of playing .833 ball over 12 post-season games and winning the CWS.

Post-Season Play

Ole Miss was seed #9 in the 12-team SEC Baseball Tournament held in Hoover, Alabama. The teams seeded #5 through #12 opened tournament play on Tuesday, May 24, in a single-elimination format; double-elimination action started Wednesday. The Rebels played #8-seed Vanderbilt on Tuesday, and the Commodores eliminated the Rebels in a 3-1 game. The tournament reverted to double-elimination play Saturday, May 28. Tennessee, the #1 seed, went on to win the tournament by defeating the Florida Gators 8-5, and the Vols received an automatic invitation to the NCAA D1 Baseball Tournament.

The Ole Miss game against Vanderbilt seemed to validate the old saying, "Good pitching stops good hitting." (Yogi Berra maintained that good pitching stops good hitting and vice-versa.) Dylan DeLucia started for the Rebs and pitched 4 1/3 innings, giving up six hits, three walks, and two runs while striking out three batters, but he was tagged with his second loss of the season. Josh Mallitz came on and threw 3 2/3 innings, giving up a hit and a run while striking out five batters. Vandy scored single runs in the third, fifth and sixth innings. The two Rebel pitchers combined to produce an excellent pitching performance, as only two of Vandy's runs were earned. One of the Commodores' runs resulted from an error by star shortstop, Jacob Gonzalez. Vanderbilt's pitching was even better. Starter and winner, Carter Holton, threw six innings and gave up three hits, two walks, two wild pitches, and no runs while hitting a batter and striking out six Rebels. Nelson Berkwich threw an inning and gave up a run on a hit while walking a batter. Christian Little closed for the Commodores, giving up a hit and striking out four Rebs. Combined, the Rebels and the 'Dores sent 72 batters to the plate, and they produced 12 hits, only two of which went for extra bases; Vanderbilt had two doubles.

Ole Miss went back to Oxford with a 32-22 overall record and a 14-17 SEC mark (14-16 in the regular season) in hopes of a bid to the NCAA Baseball Tournament. Coach Bianco's 2002 and 2017 Rebel teams finished 14-16 in the SEC and did not make it to the NCAA D1 Baseball Tournament. Many, including the writer, did not think the prospects for the Rebels getting a bid looked good. Sixty-four teams receive bids to the NCAA D1 Baseball Tournament. Thirty-one bids automatically go to Division 1 conference champions, which are usually determined by conference tournaments. The other 33 bids are at-large selections made by the NCAA Baseball Committee. The Rebels had lost three of their last four games, finished below .500 against SEC teams, and had been swept twice at home. In fact, they had lost four of five SEC series at Swayze Field. But the Rebels had some things going for them. They had won 10 of their first 11 games. They played in the best conference in the country. They swept two of their last three SEC series including LSU in Baton Rouge. They had won eight of their last 11 games. The Rebels had gotten hot.

John Cohen, vice chair of the NCAA Baseball Committee, was Mississippi State's athletics director (who is now Auburn's athletic director) and former head baseball coach. Most Rebel fans thought that did not bode well for the Rebels. Chase Parham, in his outstanding book. "Resilient Rebels," revealed that just the opposite was true. He noted that Cohen was the Rebels' biggest supporter in the selection process and that he touted both Ole Miss and the SEC. As a graduate of both Ole Miss and MSU, I hope that information eases some of the animosity between the two schools' fans. Football coaches Lane Kiffin and the late Mike Leach had already helped make strides in that direction.

Ole Miss was the last at-large team selected to advance to the NCAA Baseball Tournament. Army Athletics Director Mike Buddie, who chaired the selection committee, said that Ole Miss was chosen over North Carolina State for the last slot. Buddie explained that the Rebels had performed a little better than the Wolfpack in their regular-season conference play. NC State had won four of 10 ACC series, and Ole Miss had won four of 10 SEC series. NC State's only series win against a team in the NCAA Tournament field came against Georgia Tech. Ole Miss had won its series against LSU and Auburn, both of whom were in the NCAA Tournament. NC State finished its season with a 36-21 overall record including a 14-15 Atlantic Coast Conference mark. Nine other ACC teams did make the tournament as did nine SEC teams. The selection of the Rebels over the Wolfpack was easy to question, but the decision was soon vindicated. The Rebels were about to get smoking hot.

Third-seeded Ole Miss squared off against second-seeded Arizona in the Coral Gables NCAA Regional Baseball Tournament on June 4, 2022. No doubt the Rebels had revenge on their minds since the Wildcats had eliminated Ole Miss two games to one in the 2021 Tucson Super Regional. Ole Miss had already meted out some punishment on Jay Johnson, who had been Arizona's coach in 2021. Johnson became head coach at LSU in 2022, and the Rebels swept the Tigers on their home field in May. Arizona carried a 37-23 record into the regional contest against the 32-22 Rebels.

A tropical storm delayed by 24 hours the start of the first game of the tournament. When the game finally got started, Arizona scored first. In the bottom of the second inning, the Wildcats' left-fielder, Chase Davis, and second baseman, Garen Caulfield, hit solo home runs off Rebel starter, Dylan DeLucia, to take a two-run lead. The Rebels pulled even in the top of the fourth when Jacob Gonzales hit a two-run homer. Arizona pulled ahead again in the sixth inning when third baseman Tony Bullard doubled to right field, scoring Chase Davis, who had walked, and right-fielder Tanner O'Tremba, who had singled. That lead didn't last long as Peyton Chatagnier pulled the Rebels even in the seventh by hitting a home run to left field, driving in Kemp Alderman. Ole Miss put the game away in the eighth as Chatagnier's double drove in Tim Elko and Kevin Graham. Kemp Alderman, who had moved to third base on Chatagnier's double, scored on an error by Davis. Peyton Chatagnier, the best fielding college second baseman these old eyes have ever seen, had experienced a severe batting slump earlier in the season and was now heating up at the plate. DeLucia pitched six innings and gave up four runs while striking out a career-high 12 batters. Winning pitcher, Josh Mallitz, threw three innings, giving up a hit and throwing a wild pitch while striking out five Wildcats. Brandon Johnson earned his 10th save by striking out three hitters and giving up a hit and a walk in one inning's work. Arizona's Garrett Irvin started on the mound and hurled 6 2/3 innings, giving up four runs on eight hits. Losing pitcher, Javyn Pimental, gave up two runs on two walks and a wild pitch while not registering an out. The Rebels were off to a promising start.

On Saturday, June 5, Ole Miss played the University of Miami at Alex Rodriguez Park Mark Light Field, the Hurricanes' home diamond. One of 16 schools hosting regional tournaments, Miami was a national seed at #6. If Miami were to win its regional, it would host a Super Regional against the winner of the Hattiesburg Regional Ttournament hosted by the University of Southern Mississippi, the #11 seed. If Miami did not win its regional and Southern Miss won its regional, Southern Miss would host the Super Regional.

Miami, seeded #1 in the regional, played and defeated #4 regional seed Canisius 11-6 to move on to the winners' bracket and play Ole Miss. The Sunday game was a classic pitching duel. Ole Miss managed five hits, Miami four, a season low. Ole Miss scored two runs, Miami one. Both teams struck out 14 times. Miami went ahead 1-0 in the sixth inning on a sacrifice fly by center-fielder Jacob Burke that scored third baseman Yohandy Morales, who had reached base on a walk, advanced to second on a wild pitch, and advanced to third on a hit. Ole Miss scored its two runs in the bottom of the seventh. Tim Elko doubled to left, driving in Jacob Gonzalez and Justin Bench, both of whom had singled. The Rebels used three pitchers—Hunter Elliott, Mason Nichols, and Brandon Johnson. Each performed in a manner that showed how dominant they had become over the course of the season. Freshman Elliott, in a bulldog performance reminiscent of Doug Nikhazy, started and threw five-plus innings, giving up three hits, five walks, and a wild pitch but only one run. Winning pitcher, freshman Mason Nichols, threw 2 1/3 innings, struck out three batters, and gave up nothing. Closer Brandon Johnson earned his 11th save by pitching the last 1 2/3 innings and slamming the door on the 'Canes by striking out three batters and giving up a hit. Miami used only two pitchers. Carson Palmquist started and went 5 1/3 innings, giving up two hits and four bases on balls while striking out 10 Rebels and throwing a wild pitch. Losing pitcher, Alex McFarlane, threw the last 2 2/3 innings, giving up two runs on three hits and two walks while striking out four Rebels. Ole Miss was one victory away from winning the regional.

Arizona and Canisius played the first game in the losers' bracket, and Arizona won 7-5, sending Canisius home. Arizona then won the right to play Ole Miss again by eliminating Miami 4-3 and playing its way out of the losers' bracket.

On Monday June 6, Ole Miss played Arizona in the championship round. It would take two wins over the Rebs for Arizona to win the regional, but Ole Miss could claim the title with a single victory. The Rebels must have still been angry about the 2021 Super Regional because they thrashed the Wildcats 22-6 and won the regional. The Rebels scored early and often, batting in eight frames and scoring in six. They scored eight runs in the sixth inning. Mr. RBI Tim Elko hit three home runs, drove in five runs, and scored six. Ole Miss collected seven bases on balls and 18 hits including five doubles and five home runs off seven Arizona pitchers. The rejuvenated Peyton Chatagnier even topped Elko in RBIs, sending six runs home while going four-for-six at the plate including a double and a home run. Six Rebel batters got two or more hits. Arizona starting pitcher, Chandler Murphy, lasted 1 1/3 innings and gave up three hits, two walks, and four runs. Losing pitcher, Eric Orloff, threw three innings and gave up three runs on two hits and a walk. The last of the seven pitchers Arizona sent to the mound gave up six hits and four runs over three innings. Derek Diamond started for Ole Miss but again failed to get past the fourth inning. Diamond went 3 2/3 innings and gave up six hits and five runs while throwing a wild pitch and striking out three batters. Winning pitcher. Jack Dougherty. who had been coming on strong, came in and evened his record at 3-3 by throwing 2 1/3 innings, giving up two hits and two walks and no runs while striking out four Wildcats. John Gaddis pitched the seventh and eighth innings, giving up two hits and a run while striking out four hitters. Jack Washburn pitched the ninth inning, faced three batters, struck out one, and gave up nothing.

Arizona batters managed 10 hits including three home runs, two by designated hitter Blake Paugh. Tim Elko was named the Coral Gables NCAA Regional's Most Outstanding Player.

Ole Miss was still hot and on the way back to Mississippi to face in-state rival Southern Miss in a Super Regional. This would be the Rebels' third consecutive and eighth overall appearance in a Super Regional under Coach Bianco. Unfortunately, the Rebs had won only one of their seven previous Super Regionals (2014) Only three other teams, Arkansas, East Carolina and Stanford, have ever made it to Super Regionals three consecutive years.

Southern Miss had won their regional tournament that included LSU, Kennesaw State, and Army. The Golden Eagles beat Army 2-0, lost to LSU 7-6, beat Kennesaw State 4-3, and then defeated LSU 8-4 and 8-7 to earn the right to host a Super Regional. Southern Miss carried a healthy 47-17 record into the NCAA Hattiesburg Super Regional while Ole Miss sported a more modest 35-22 mark. The teams split two games during the regular season.

The first game of the best two-of-three matchup was played on Saturday, June 11, at Pete Taylor Park on the Southern Miss campus. Dylan DeLucia, who was steadily improving his star status, started for the Rebs. Over 5 2/3 innings, DeLucia gave up four hits, two walks, and no runs while striking out nine Golden Eagles. DeLucia improved his record to 6-2 with the win. Jack Dougherty, who earned his second save, continued to impress by throwing the last 3 1/3 innings, giving up nothing while striking out a batter. USM's total of four hits included a double by Slade Wilks and a triple by Christopher Sargent. Meanwhile, Ole Miss hitters were generating 10 hits, 10 RBIs, and 10 runs off five USM pitchers. The Rebels also benefited from eight bases on balls. Ole Miss scored two runs in the third inning, one in the fourth, and seven in the sixth. Tim Elko went two-for-five at the plate and drove in three runs. Kevin Graham went one-for-five and drove in two runs. Calvin Harris went two-for-four, walked, and scored a run. Five Rebels drove in single runs. USM's starting and losing pitcher, Hurston Waldrep, threw five innings and gave up six hits, four walks, and five runs. Four other Golden Eagle pitchers combined to give up four hits, four walks, and five runs over the last four innings. The 10-0 win put Ole Miss one win away from a trip to the College World Series in Omaha.

Hunter Elliott was the Rebels' starting and winning pitcher in the second game. The freshman All-American phenom pitched 7 1/3 innings and gave up three hits and no runs while striking out 10 batters. He faced only 25 batters and retired 16 in a row. Elliott is human; he made an error. Sophomore Josh Mallitz pitched the last 1 2/3 innings and gave up a walk and struck out a batter. All three of the Golden Eagles' hits were singles. In contrast, Rebel bats produced five runs off 10 hits, including a double by Justin Bench and a home run by T.J. McCants. Ole Miss scored three runs in the fifth inning, one in the sixth, and one in the eighth.

When the Hattiesburg Super Regional ended on Sunday, June 12, Ole Miss had made a huge statement about just how far the team had come over the last few weeks. Coach Bianco and his staff now had firmly established front-line pitching. The team had consistent and timely hitting with the capacity to play long ball. Peyton Chatagnier was playing spectacularly at second base, and the overall fielding was excellent. The team had developed great confidence, and it was evident. Outstanding coaching and in-game decision-making along with the character of the players and player leadership had congealed to produce a potent team that was sure of itself. I have been following Ole Miss baseball since 1961. The Rebels' performance in this Super Regional was the most impressive this observer has seen in a short series. Before a total of 10,943 fans, a large majority of whom were Southern Miss loyalists, Ole Miss pitching twice shut out a hard-hitting, well-coached Southern Miss team at their home ballpark, and Rebel hitters produced 15 runs off a very good pitching staff.

The Rebels left Hattiesburg scorching hot having swept their Regional and Super Regional opponents by combined scores of 46-11. Despite their overall 37-22 record, it was a very confident group of Rebels who headed to Omaha and the Men's College World series. This would be the second appearance in the CWS under head coach Mike Bianco. In the 2014 CWS, the Rebels advanced to the semi-finals where they lost to Virginia 4-1.

The 2022 Men's College World Series

The eight teams that made it to the CWS were placed in two four-team brackets. Bracket 1 consisted of Texas A&M, Oklahoma, Texas, and Notre Dame. Bracket 2 included Stanford, Arkansas, Auburn, and Ole Miss. The fact that four of the eight teams, Texas A&M, Arkansas, Auburn, and Ole Miss, came out of the SEC West says a lot about the powerful conference. Two other soon-to-be SEC teams, Texas and Oklahoma, were also included in the eight-team field. This speaks volumes about the quality of college baseball played in the South and Southwest.

The Rebels played SEC rival Auburn in game 4 Saturday, June 18. Rebel ace Dylan DeLucia tamed the Tigers over 7 2/3 innings, giving up four hits and one run while striking out 10 batters. Auburn scored its run in the bottom of the seventh inning when second baseman Garrett Farquhar doubled, and first baseman Sonny DiChiara drove him home with a single. Josh Mallitz, who had developed into a very reliable relief pitcher, came in for the last 1 1/3 innings and caged the Tigers, giving up nothing while striking out three batters. I wrote this on November 30, 2022. later in the day I saw several items on the internet that said Mallitz had undergone Tommy John surgery and would probably be out of action for the entire 2023 season. It was a sad day for Ole Miss baseball. The Rebels scored two runs in the top of the first when Kemp Alderman singled, driving in Tim Elko and Kevin Graham, who had both singled. Kevin Graham slapped a solo homer to left field in the third inning to increase the Rebels' advantage to 3-0. Ole Miss added two more runs in the sixth when Peyton Chatagnier grounded into a double play that allowed Alderman, who had singled, to score, and T.J. McCants singled to drive in Calvin Harris, who had singled. Auburn's starting and losing pitcher, Joseph Gonzalez, threw five innings, giving up seven hits, a walk, and four runs while hitting two batters and striking out seven Rebels. Carson Skipper pitched the last four innings for the Tigers, giving up four hits and a run while throwing two wild pitches and striking out six batters. Kevin Graham got three of the Rebels' 11 hits including a double and a homer, drove in a run and scored two runs. Kemp Alderman, a budding star, went two-for-four and drove in two runs. Calvin Harris, a real gamer, went two-for-four at the plate and scored a run. The versatile sophomore, Harris, who had started games as catcher, right fielder, left fielder, and designated hitter during the season, would wind up leading the team in hitting with .336 batting average. Ole Miss advanced to play Arkansas in game eight on June 20.

When Ole Miss played Auburn in both teams' first SEC series of the season, the Rebels were ranked #1 in the coaches' poll. Auburn's head coach,

Butch Thompson, said that he had no idea why. After losing the SEC series 2-1 to Ole Miss and a critical game in the CWS, maybe Thompson learned that the Rebels should be in consideration for the #1 ranking. Auburn went on to defeat Stanford 6-2 in game 7, eliminating the Cardinals.

Hunter Elliott started on the mound for the Rebels in game 8 and earned his fifth win. The freshman pitched well through 6 1/3 innings, giving up six hits, two bases on balls, and three runs (only one of which was earned). Mason Nichols came in and threw 1 2/3 innings, striking out two Hogs and giving up nothing. Closer Brandon Johnson pitched the ninth inning and gave up two hits and two runs. Both runs were scored on first baseman Peyton Stovall's home run. Arkansas scored one run in the first inning, two in the second, and two in the ninth. Meanwhile, Rebel batters were feasting off seven Arkansas pitchers. The Rebels stroked 13 hits including three doubles and two homers. Ole Miss scored two runs in each of the first three innings, four in the fifth and three in the ninth. Tim Elko hit a two-run homer and drove in three runs. In four plate appearances, Calvin Harris, who was becoming more valuable daily, hit two doubles and a home run and drove in four runs. Kevin Graham went two-for-four and drove in two runs. Arkansas starting and losing pitcher, Zack Morris, lasted only 2/3 of an inning, giving up two hits, two walks, and two runs while throwing a wild pitch and hitting a batter. The loss was Morris's only one of the season against six wins. The other six Hog pitchers combined to give up 11 runs on 11 hits, eight walks, two wild pitches, and a hit batsman. Final score, Rebels 13, Arkansas 5. Arkansas went on to eliminate Auburn in game 10 by a score of 11-1 and earn the right to play the Rebels again on June 22.

In the 12th game, Ole Miss and Arkansas faced each other for the fifth time in 2022. The Rebels had won two games, and the Hogs had won two. The fifth game would reflect how evenly matched the teams were. Both teams scored in the second inning. Hog right fielder Chris Lanzilli hit a solo homer to left field in the top of the inning, and Rebel designated hitter Kemp Alderman countered in the bottom of the inning with a solo homer to left field. In the fifth, Hog designated hitter Brady Slavens hit a home run to center field, and Arkansas regained the lead. Catcher Michael Turner increased Arkansas's advantage to 3-1 with an RBI single that scored third baseman Caden Wallace, who had doubled. The Rebels loaded the bases with no outs in the bottom of the ninth but could push across only one run. Kemp Alderman led off with a single, and Arkansas brought in Brady Tygart to replace Evan Taylor on the mound. Two of Tygart's five pitches hit Rebel batters, Peyton Chatagnier and Hayden Dunhurst, to load the bases. Tygart, who had not registered an out, was replaced by Zack Morris. Hayden Leatherwood struck out, and T.J. McCants flew out. Then Justin Bench singled to drive in Alderman, but Jacob Gonzalez flew out to left field to end the game. Arkansas's starting and winning pitcher, Hagen Smith, threw five innings, giving up two hits, four walks, and a run while striking out eight Rebels. Zack Morris threw an inning and was credited with a save. The Rebels managed only five hits off Arkansas pitchers, and Kemp Alderman accounted for three of those. Losing pitcher, John Gaddis, started for the Rebels and over five innings gave up four hits, two walks, and two runs while striking out four batters. Jack Washburn threw two innings and gave up a run on two hits and a walk while striking out three batters. Jack Dougherty pitched the final two innings, giving up two hits and a walk while striking out three batters. Wallace, Lanzilli, and Slavens accounted for six of the Hogs' eight hits. Final score, Arkansas 3, Ole Miss 2. Arkansas had forced another game between the two rivals in the double-elimination tournament.

The June 23 contest between Arkansas and Ole Miss was the most important game either team played all season. The winner would play in the finals for the CWS and NCAA D 1 Championship, and the loser would go home greatly disappointed. It is difficult to determine which team in this game was more highly motivated. Neither had ever won a CWS and NCAA title. Both Ole Miss and Arkansas had been severely disappointed in 2021 because neither of their powerhouse teams made it to the CWS. Ole Miss had been eliminated by Arizona in the Tucson Super Regional, while Arkansas had been eliminated by North Carolina State, a team they beat 21-2 in the first game, in the Fayetteville Super Regional.

In the third game against Arkansas, Coach Mike Bianco sent Dylan DeLucia, with a 7-2 record, to the mound. Arkansas countered with Connor Noland, with a 7-6 record. Both DeLucia and Noland pitched brilliantly as the closeness of the two teams' talent was again demonstrated. Noland pitched eight innings, giving up seven hits and two runs while striking out seven Rebels. Evan Taylor relieved Noland in the ninth inning and gave up nothing while striking out a batter. DeLucia pitched the game of his life against an outstanding Arkansas ball club. It was something to behold. The Ole Miss ace pitched all nine innings, faced 32 batters, gave up four singles, did not walk or hit a batter, and did not throw a wild pitch. Kevin Graham hit a double in the fourth inning that drove in Justin Bench, who had singled and moved to second when Jacob Gonzalez grounded out. Tim Elko singled in the seventh and was driven home when Calvin Harris singled and was thrown out at second attempting to stretch a single into a double. Final score, Ole Miss 2, Arkansas 0. After this game, Ole Miss stood 40-26, and Arkansas was 43-21. They had split six games during the season. A total of 71,081 fans walked through the turnstiles at Charles Schwab Field to see the three games between the Rebels and Razorbacks.

Ole Miss moved on to face Oklahoma, who had defeated Texas A&M twice and Notre Dame once in bracket 1 to advance to the championship round. In the June 25 game, the Rebel bats caught fire. Ole Miss batters assaulted five Sooner pitchers for 16 hits including two doubles and four home runs while scoring 10 runs. Oklahoma batters managed only five hits, of which only one, a double, went for extra bases. Coach Bianco started the steadily improving Jack Dougherty on the mound. Ole Miss scored two runs in the first inning on singles by Elko and Graham, two wild pitches, and an error. The Rebels added to their lead with a run the second inning on a single by Harris, a wild pitch, and a single by Bench. The Rebs scored another run in the third when Elko connected for a solo home run. Dougherty retired the first 15 batters, and the Rebels led Oklahoma 4-0 before Sooner second baseman Jackson Nicklaus hit a single off Dougherty's first pitch in bottom of the sixth inning. The Sooners proceeded to chase Dougherty, scoring two runs on three hits, a walk, and an error. There were no outs, and the bases were loaded when Mason Nichols took the mound. Dougherty had thrown five-plus innings, which constituted a quality start that was just what the Rebels needed. Nichols threw two innings and faced seven batters, striking out five and giving up a walk but no runs. Josh Mallitz finished the game, pitching two innings, giving up a run on two hits and a walk while balking once and striking out four batters. The Rebels went on to score four more runs in the eighth inning.

Kemp Alderman led off the Rebel eighth inning with a base hit to right.

Peyton Chatagnier followed with a single to center. Then the Rebels made CWS history with three straight home runs. McCants hit one into the Ole Miss bullpen, and the Rebels led 6-2. The offense wasn't done. Harris, from just across the Missouri River in Iowa, sent a ball 430 feet in that direction, and the score was 7-2. Bench put the icing on the cake by launching a homer to left for the first back-to-back-to-back home runs at the College World Series since it moved to Charles Schwab Field, and the first in CWS history since LSU accomplished the feat against Mississippi State in 1998. The back-to-back-to-back jacks were hit by the eighth-, ninth- and first-place hitters in the Rebel lineup.

Oklahoma managed its last run in the eighth inning, and the Rebels added two more runs in the ninth. Tim Elko went four-for-five at the plate, hit a homer, and scored three runs. Justin Bench went two-for-five, hit a home run, and drove in two runs. T.J. McCants, who went one-for-two, hit a two-run homer. Calvin Harris went two-for-four including a solo home run. Peyton Chatagnier went three-for-five at the plate while hitting a double and driving in a run. Hard-hitting Kemp Alderman went two-for-five including a double and scored a run. Kevin Graham went one-for-five while driving in a run and scoring a run. The first two Oklahoma pitchers gave up eight of the 10 runs scored by the Rebels. Losing pitcher, Jake Bennett, threw 6 2/3 innings and gave up four runs on seven hits and three wild pitches while striking out 10 Rebels. Reliever Chazz Martinez gave up four runs on six hits and a walk over 1 1/3 innings. Three other Sooner pitchers gave up three hits and two runs over the last 2 1/3 innings while striking out two batters. Final score, Ole Miss 10, Oklahoma 3. The Rebels were a win away from being crowned the champions of NCAA Division 1 Baseball. The second game of the finals would be a do-or-die situation for the Sooners.

In an effort to square the championship series, Oklahoma head coach Skip Johnson, who has a reputation of being an excellent pitching instructor, sent Cade Horton to the mound. Horton is an outstanding athlete who originally committed to Ole Miss. He is from Norman, Oklahoma, and was flipped by the Sooners by an offer to play baseball and football. Horton didn't make it on the football field at Oklahoma, but he starred in baseball. When not pitching, Horton played shortstop for the Sooners. He was drafted #7 overall in the 2022 Major :eague draft. Horton showed how good he was in the 7 1/3 innings he pitched against the red-hot Rebels. He gave up four hits and two runs while striking out 13 Rebels and hitting a batter. The 13 strikeouts established a new CWS record.

Ole Miss's Hunter Elliott started and put zeroes on the board through six innings, but getting through the sixth was a struggle. Oklahoma had runners on first and third with one out. Then right fielder John Spikerman bunted toward the mound and apparently reached first safely while Jackson Nicklaus scored from third base. The Associated Press described that play and its aftermath:

> Jackson Nicklaus had been hit by Elliott leading off the inning and was on third after a sacrifice and wild pitch. He came home on Spikerman's bunt, but Bianco asked for a video review when Spikerman was called safe at first. Bianco said he rarely looks at replays on the scoreboard, but he did this time. He said he thought Spikerman was out of the running lane and came onto the field to request the video review. "Credit goes to the scoreboard guy," Bianco said.
>
> Spikerman knocked off Elko's glove as he ran through first, with the ball ending up in foul territory. The call was overturned, with Spikerman ruled to have been inside the baseline as he ran through the bag, requiring Nicklaus to return to third base. [Coach] Johnson questioned whether Bianco made his request within 30 seconds after the play ended, as required by the rules. He didn't dispute the final ruling. He just didn't like how it came about. "If we mess with the fabric of the game by getting computer umpires," he said, "I think I'll just go fishing."

Elliott retired the next batter and got out of the inning without the Sooners scoring.

Ole Miss put the first run of the game on the board in the bottom of the inning when Jacob Gonzalez homered to right center field. OU made that one-run lead disappear in the top of the seventh inning. Hunter Elliott started the seventh for the Rebs and retired the first two batters. Then Jackson Nicklaus doubled to score Jimmy Crooks, who had singled. Mason Nichols came in and pitched to two batters, walking one and hitting one. Wallace Clark, who had walked, advanced to third base. Sebastian Orduno was hit by a pitch; Kendall Pettis walked, advancing Orduno to second and Nicklaus to third while driving Clark home with the second run of the inning. Winning pitcher, John Gaddis, who had deferred his admittance to medical school to pitch one season for the Rebels, came in and threw 1 1/3 innings, giving up a walk and striking out two Sooners. Ole Miss closed all the scoring by putting three runs on the board in the bottom of the eighth inning. When Horton gave up a single to T.J. McCants, Oklahoma head coach Skip Johnson replaced him with Trevin Michael, and things went bad quickly for the Sooners. Bench singled; Gonzalez singled and drove in McCants while Bench moved to third. Bench scored, and Gonzalez advanced to second, and on a wild pitch, Gonzalez scored on another wild pitch. Brandon Johnson, who had not allowed a run in nine of his last 11 outings, struck out all three Oklahoma batters in the bottom of the ninth, earning a save and securing Ole Miss's first College World Series title and the NCAA D1 2022 National Baseball Championship. Final score, Ole Miss 4, Oklahoma 2. The college baseball world had let the Rebels get hot, and when they did, they sizzled their way to a national championship.

There were four Crocketts among the 25,972 fans who passed through the turnstiles for the championship game: me, my son Clint, and his two sons, Will and Wes, all of whom are big baseball fans. It truly was a day to remember for the Crockett guys!

Probably 20,000-plus of the 25,972 fans at the final game were Rebel fans. They soon covered the field and celebrated with the team for more than an hour. Celebrations broke out in the city of Oxford and on the Ole Miss campus. Rebel Nation had been waiting for a national baseball championship for a long time, and they flooded Oxford and the Ole Miss campus when the players and coaches arrived home. Rebel Baseball was the toast of Mississippi as Mississippi State Baseball had been just a year ago.

Postseason Awards
Mike Bianco – D1 Baseball 2022 Coach of the Year

Tim Elko – 2022 MLB Draft Pick (Round 10 - Chicago White Sox)
2022 NCBWA Third Team All-American
2022 College World Series All-Tournament Team
2022 Coral Gables Regional MVP
2022 Ferris Trophy Finalist
2022 ABCA All-South Region (First Base)
2022 Second Team All-SEC
2022 SEC Community Service Team

Jacob Gonzales – 2022 USA Baseball Collegiate National Team
2022 Coral Gables Regional All-Tournament Team
2022 First Team All-SEC

Hunter Elliott – 2022 Freshman All-American (Collegiate Baseball, Perfect Game, D1Baseball)
2022 USA Baseball Collegiate National Team
2022 Coral Gables Regional All-Tournament Team
2022 All-SEC Freshman Team
2022 SEC Freshman of the Week (Week 12, Week 13)

On July 26, 2023, I interviewed Ole Miss Head Baseball Coach Mike Bianco in his office at Oxford – University Stadium on the Ole Miss campus.

I asked if he felt any additional pressure beginning the 2022 season because Mississippi State had won the national championship in 2021. He basically said that he did not and that coaches must learn to not let pressure affect the way they do things. He said his wife, Cami, had a saying that helped – "Stay in your own dugout."

Coach Bianco noted that the 2022 team had all the components necessary to be successful: hitting, pitching, and fielding. As the season's record shows, it took a while to figure out the proper roles of the individual pitchers. Fielding was somewhat questionable early, but in SEC play it was very good. Hitting was good throughout the season, especially when Kevin Graham was in the lineup. Graham suffered a wrist injury that kept him out of the lineup for about a month, and the Rebs really missed him. Graham's situation illustrates how injuries to key players can affect a team.

Coach Bianco said that player leadership played a big part in the Rebels' 2022 success. Interestingly, he said that when he was a young coach, he did not understand the importance of player leadership, but he had learned its value. Tim Elko, Kevin Graham, and Justin Bench were excellent leaders, but other members of the team who did not get as much publicity, such Max Cioffi, provided leadership also. Leaders arise during the ups and downs of a season, not in fall practice. At the end of a season, it is clear to coaches who the leaders were and how valuable they were.

When asked what his personal high and low points were during the 2022 season, Bianco mentioned the regular-season series with Arkansas at Fayetteville as the low point and the series sweep of LSU at Baton Rouge as the high point. The Arkansas series was the seventh SEC series of the season, and the Rebels lost two out of three games. After having won the first game 4-2, the Rebs dropped the last two, 6-3 and 4-3. It was the third consecutive SEC series that the Rebs had lost two games to one. A sweep or two wins against the Hogs could have changed the trajectory of the season. The late-season sweep of LSU, 5-3, 11-1, and 8-5, was instrumental in getting a bid to the NCAA Tournament.

When asked about the uniqueness of the Rebels' last-in-last-standing performance in the NCAA D1 2022 Baseball Tournament, Bianco revealed an interesting perspective. He thought that the last-in-last-standing aspect had received some misplaced emphasis. People who know college baseball know that the NCAA Baseball Committee did not consider Ole Miss the 64th-best team in D1. This is aptly demonstrated in that they were the #3 seed in the four-team Coral Gables Regional. Thirty-one teams automatically qualify for the tournament because they have won their conference titles. The NCAA Baseball Committee chooses the other 33 at-large teams. The selection committee and others familiar with college baseball knew that Ole Miss was better than a number of teams that got automatic bids. Coach Bianco believes that it is not unreasonable to think that the last-in-last-standing phenomena will occur again.

Bianco believes that intuitional support is vital to the success of college baseball and that the Ole Miss administration provides excellent support for his team. He pointed out that the fans actually make it possible for the institution to provide the needed support. That is, baseball fans who buy tickets and attend games ultimately provide the financing for great facilities and other amenities needed for success. Coach Bianco made it a point to say that for a number of years OU Stadium had been sold out before the season started. He also thanked me for being a season ticket holder for years.

We discussed the effects of the transfer portal and the players being allowed to benefit from their name, image, and likeness (NIL). Bianco noted that there have been many changes in college baseball during his coaching career, and he expects changes in the future; he says coaches will just have to make adjustments. NIL affects recruiting, but there are many other considerations, and it might not affect some recruits at all. The transfer portal makes it possible to rebuild a roster more quickly. The transfer portal and timing of the Major Leagues draft and the 40-player roster limitation imposed by the NCAA combine to complicate roster management.

The recent NCAA rule change that in effect eliminates volunteer coaches and allows three paid assistant coaches is a good thing and overdue. If he could change one thing about college baseball, Bianco would change the NCAA's rule about the number of baseball scholarships allowed. He would increase the limit from 11.7 to 25 full scholarships.

.

Pearl River Community College

Chapter 5
Pearl River Community College, 2022 National Junior College Athletic Association (NJCAA) Division II National Baseball Champions

Pearl River County Agricultural High School (PRCAHS) began operations in September 1909 in a three-story building on a 20-acre plot of land adjacent to Poplarville, the county seat. Later that fall, the 1908 Mississippi law that allowed the creation of public agricultural high schools was ruled unconstitutional by the state supreme court because it did not provide "separate but equal" educational treatment for whites and African Americas. Twenty public agricultural high schools had been founded under the old law. After the court decision, all but three of them closed because of the loss of state funding. Pearl River County citizens rescued PRCAHS by making it a private school. The Mississippi Legislature soon fixed the problem by passing a law that created opportunities for both races. PRCAHS became a public school again.

At the beginning of academic year 1921-22, freshman college classes were added to PRCAHS's offerings. By the 1925-26 academic year, the institution was Pearl River College, having added sophomore-level classes. Pearl River College became the first two-year public college in the state and was later renamed Pearl River Junior College. Today the school is Pearl River Community College (PRCC), and it boasts four locations: the main campus in Poplarville, the Forrest County Center and Lowery Woodall Advanced Technology Center in Hattiesburg, and the Hancock Center is in Waveland. PRCC's primary service area includes Pearl River, Hancock, Forest, Jefferson Davis, Lamar, and Marion counties in South Mississippi.

In August 2005 Hurricane Katrina struck PRCC campuses in Poplarville and Waveland, doing more than $40 million in damages. The sports facilities on the main campus suffered major damage. PRCC has been repaired and rebuilt with private and public funds, and it sports one of the finest community college baseball facilities in the country. In 2023 Pearl

River Community College had a student population of more than 6,000 in academic programs and more than 5,000 in workforce-related programs.

The Junior College Baseball World Series (JUCO World Series) was first played in 1958 to determine a national champion. In 1993 The National Junior College Athletic Association (NJCAA) divided its membership into three divisions, and it has conducted an annual college world series for each of the divisions since that time. The baseball divisions are based entirely on the number of scholarships that individual schools can award to baseball players. D1 schools can offer up to 24 full scholarships, room, board, tuition, and fees. D2 schools can offer only tuition, books, and fees. D3 schools cannot offer any athletic scholarships. Schools in all three divisions can and do play each other in regular-season games, but the post-season regional tournaments and world series are divisional affairs. Mississippi community college teams play in NJCAA Division II. In 2006 Jones Junior College (now Jones College) was the first Mississippi school to win the NJCAA Division II College World Series.

Pearl River Community College has been winning baseball championships since it won its first Mississippi state championship in 1939. Although the Wildcats did not win the state title in 2002, they won the National Junior College Athletic Association Division II Region 23 Championship and advanced to the NJCAA D II World Series. The Wildcats won 27 consecutive games in 2004 and won the state championship. In 2018 PRCC won its third Mississippi Association of Community Colleges Conference (MACCC) Championship. Although PRCC didn't win the state championship in 2019, the Wildcats won the Region 23 title and made its second appearance in the NJCAA D II World Series. The Cats won their fourth state MACCC Baseball Championship in 2021 and their fifth in 2022. In 2022 PRCC's baseball team played 56 games, won 45, and lost 11 for a winning percentage of .804. Their 2022 conference record was 22-6, giving the Wildcats a .786 winning percentage. The 2022 team also won the Region 23 title and PRCC's first NJCAA D II World Series title, signifying the national championship.

In his sixth year as PRCC's head baseball coach, Michael Avalon and his assistants, Slater Lott and Brandon Pennington, took their team on a long journey that brought a national title to Poplarville, Mississippi. Coach

Avalon has a rich baseball history. He played baseball at Holmes Community College and was second-team All-American his sophomore year. He spent his junior year at Lincoln Memorial University in Tennessee and then transferred to the University of West Alabama, where he completed his playing career in 2004. Avalon was a graduate assistant at UWA in 2005 and 2006 when West Alabama won Gulf South Conference Championships in 2005 and was runner-up in 2006. The Tigers reached the NCAA Division II Regionals both seasons. Avalon served as an assistant coach at East Central Community College for five years before being named head coach at Mississippi Delta Community College. He spent five years at MDCC and took the Trojans to four MACCC playoffs.

In 2017, Avalon's first season at PRCC, his team posted a 28-19 record. In 2018 the Wildcats were off and running. They posted a 38-11 record and won PRCC's third state championship. The 2019 team was even better; they were ranked in the top 10 all season while posting a 41-14 record, winning the NJCAA Region 23 Championship and advancing to the NJCAA Division II College Baseball World Series in Enid, Oklahoma. The Wildcats went 0-2 in this World Series, but better things lay ahead. After 16 games, the 2020 season was cancelled by COVID. The Wildcats held a 12-4 record at the time. With COVID in the rear-view mirror, Coach Avalon's team went 36-9 in 2021, won the MACCC Championship, and Avalon was named MCAAA Coach of the Year. At the beginning of the 2022 season the Wildcats were ranked #1 in the country. Then came the magical season when all the pieces were in place, and the stars aligned.

Preconference Play

Mississippi community college teams usually play games on two days each week of the season. Doubleheaders are played both days. The first contest is a nine-inning game, and the second one lasts only seven innings. A mercy rule or run-rule comes into play under certain conditions. In a seven-inning game, the run-rule comes into play if a team leads by 10 runs after five innings. In a nine-inning game when a team is ahead by eight runs after seven innings, the run-rule ends the game.

PRCC's season started on the right foot on February 9 when the homestanding Wildcats swept Baton Rouge Community College, 11-1 and 5-0.

Both games were seven-inning affairs. In the first game, PRCC batters punished four BRCC pitchers, amassing 13 hits including home runs by John Griffin Bell, Tate Parker, and D.K. Donaldson. Meanwhile, starting and winning pitcher, Dakota Lee, and two relievers held BRCC to one run on three hits. In the second game, PRCC starter and winner, Leif Moore, who had recovered from Tommy John surgery, threw 3 2/3 innings and gave up a hit but no runs. He was followed by four relievers, who gave up a total of two hits and no runs. Wildcat hitters were still hot as they generated five runs on nine hits including home runs by D.K. Donaldson, and Alex Perry.

Two days later the Wildcats played the Sun Chiefs of Coastal Alabama – South and won 10-4 and 15-5. The first game went nine innings as the Wildcats continued their hot hitting, producing eight hits including home runs by Tate Parker, Ian Montz, and Preston Soper, who combined to drive in a total of eight runs. Winning pitcher, Sam Hill, threw four innings and gave up five hits and three runs while striking out four batters. Hill was followed by four relievers, who gave up a total of one hit and one run. PRCC run-ruled the second game in five innings. Six Wildcats registered RBIs: Tate Parker, D.K. Donaldson (2), Ian Montz (2), Triston Hickman, Logan Walters (3), and Preston Soper. Surprisingly, no PRCC batter hit a home run as they generated only two extra-base hits, a double, and a triple. Winning pitcher, Turner Swistak, threw two innings, giving up three hits and three runs. Four relievers followed and combined to give up two runs on two hits. The Wildcats, who didn't make an error, benefited from the Sun Chiefs' five errors.

On Sunday, February 20, in Decatur, Mississippi, PRCC played Southeastern Iowa Community College out of Burlington. In a barnburner, the Wildcats beat the Blackhawks 9-8. The nine-inning encounter saw several lead changes as one or both teams scored in every inning except the third and seventh. Entering the bottom of the ninth inning the score was tied 8-8 when freshman designated hitter Alex Perry's second home run of the day clenched the victory. Southeastern registered eight hits including two homers and a double off four PRCC pitchers including winning pitcher, Cole Tolbert, who threw the last two innings. PRCC hitters managed nine hits including three homers and a double off six Southeastern pitchers.

In the second game PRCC and Jones College out of Ellisville, Mississippi, put on a show. The Wildcats run-ruled the Bobcats 19-8 in eight innings. Five Jones pitchers gave up 13 hits including four homers and 11 walks. The Wildcats stole five bases and committed four errors while five Jones pitchers gave up 10 hits and six walks. Base runners for both teams ran wild as Jones runners had four stolen bases, and PRCC runners stole five. One inning proved the Bobcats' undoing. The PRCC website explains:

> The Wildcats did all of their damage in the fifth inning with two outs, scoring six runs after the first two batters were retired. [Ian] Montz and Ryan Burt each drew a walk before a [Taylor] Woodcock single brought Montz home. [Gabe] Broadus drew a six-pitch walk to load the bases, and in stepped [Alex] Perry. The freshman delivered once again, driving all three runners in with a triple. Two pitches later, [Tate] Parker hit his second two-run home run in as many innings to put Pearl River ahead 14-5.

On Tuesday, February 22, PRCC played Coastal Alabama – East in Brewton, Alabama. Both games were seven-inning affairs, and the Wildcats won the first 3-2 but lost the second 6-2. The first game was a pitching duel that was tied 2-2 going into the seventh inning. Coastal had tied the score in the bottom of the sixth with a solo homer. In the top of the seventh the Wildcats reclaimed the lead when Wes Harrison doubled to drive home Triston Hickman. The Coastal Warhawks put a runner on base in the bottom of the inning, but he didn't score. Turner Swistak started for PRCC and went 5 1/3 innings, allowing two runs on three hits while striking out six. Reliever Landen Payne, who threw 1 1/3 innings, was the winner.

The Wildcats' opening-season, seven-game win streak came to an end in the second game, which Coastal won 6-2. While both teams managed seven hits, the Warhawks' hits drove in six runs while the Wildcats drove in only two. PRCC's Sam Hill, who threw 4 2/3 innings and gave up four runs on four hits, took the loss and evened his record at 1-1.

On Sunday, February 27, PRCC played in Millington, Tennessee, against North Iowa Area Community College and Dyersburg State Community College in the Babe Howard JUCO Classic. The #4-ranked Wildcats won the first game against NIACC 5-4 and lost to Division I DSCC, 8-6.

In the first game, the NIACC Trojans took a lead, 1-0, in the bottom of the first inning. It was the last lead they would enjoy as the Wildcats scored four runs in the top of the second. Over nine innings the Trojans scored single runs in four innings, forcing extra innings. The Wildcats scored their final and winning run in the 11th when right fielder Ian Montz hit a home run over the center-field wall. Cole Tolbert, who pitched the last 3 2/3 innings for PRCC and gave up three hits but no runs, was the winning pitcher.

It took an extra inning to settle the second game against the DSCC Eagles, as the score at the end of nine innings was 6-6. This game featured more action as both teams managed nine hits. PRCC's Alex Perry hit a solo home run, and Logan Walters hit two home runs and drove in three runs. Unfortunately, this was not enough, as three DSCC players, Jalen Fithian, Andy Martin, and Grant Davis, each drove in two runs. The Eagles scored four runs to tie the game in the eighth inning on three walks and two singles. Neither team scored in the ninth, but in the top of the 10th, Dyersburg State took an 8-6 lead on a two-run triple. PRCC sent seven pitchers to the mound. Reliever Landen Payne threw 1 1/3 innings and suffered the loss.

After the doubleheader, Coach Avalon commented:

> We got to play two of the better teams that we will play this year. It was good to find a way to win game one. We played well for the first seven innings in game two and just didn't finish it against a quality opponent. We want to play well enough to beat teams like that, but we have to do a better job of doing the small things. We just have to get a little tougher in some situations.

When the calendar turned to March, the PRCC Wildcats boasted an 8-2 record. On March 2 they enhanced that record to 10-2 by traveling to Tuscaloosa, Alabama, and defeating the Shelton State Community College (SSCC) Bucs 6-1 and 3-2.

In the first game the Wildcats scored two runs in the second inning, which proved to be all of the scoring in the first six innings. PRCC's Turner Swistak and SSCC's Tate Robertson pitched masterfully over those innings. Winning pitcher, Swistak, gave up two hits and a walk while striking out six batters and allowing no runs. Losing pitcher, Robertson, struck out four batters and allowed two runs on five hits and a walk. The Wildcats scored two runs in the top of the second inning when Alex Perry hit a two-run home run. In the seventh, PRCC added four more runs when Logan Walters hit a grand slam off reliever Jack Hoppenjans, who threw only 1/3 of an inning, giving up four runs, two hits, and a walk. The Bucs scored their only run in the seventh. Cole Tolbert threw two innings for PRCC and gave up a hit, a walk, and a run.

The second game was a different story as the Wildcats scratched out a 3-2 victory while Sam Hill, Bobby Magee, and Landen Payne combined to give up only four hits and two runs. Payne was the winner, as he threw the last three innings, striking out five batters and giving up one hit and no runs. SSCC sent four pitchers to the mound, and they gave up only three runs on five hits and two walks. Three of the Wildcats' five hits went for extra bases while the Bucs did not manage an extra-base hit.

Coach Avalon said after the sweep:

> Any time that you can win two on the road is great, but it is especially great getting it done somewhere like Shelton State. It's a tough place to play, and they're a quality team. We're thankful to get back with two wins. We've played extra innings in three of the last four ball games, so seeing us stay in there, stay tough, battle, and come out with the win says a lot about our ball club.
>
> As we finished up this eight-game road trip, I challenged our team to really finish strong. We looked at this trip in the pre-season and knew that it was going to be a tough stretch for us. Now that it is out of the way, I think that we learned a lot. I was very proud of our guys today because I felt like we learned how to travel. That's something that new guys have to learn how to do as far preparing yourself for the game on the road. We were very organized today, and I was very proud of our guys for that.

Back at home in Poplarville on March 5, the Wildcats played the Eagles of Coastal Alabama – North (CACCN) with both games being seven-inning affairs.

The home-field advantage didn't show up in the first game, as PRCC lost. The Wildcats led 3-2 going into the top of the fifth inning when the visitors scored three runs to take the lead. In the bottom of the inning, the Wildcats tied the score at 5-5 by scoring two runs. The Eagles scored a single run in the sixth, while PRCC failed to score in the sixth or seventh frames. Final score, CACCN 6, PRCC 5. While both teams scored two runs on sacrifice flies, neither team hit a home run. The two teams produced a total of four extra-base hits as both had two doubles. PRCC managed nine hits and the visitors seven. Gabe Broadus led PRCC at the plate, going three-for-four with a double, and Blake Hooks was two-for-three. The Eagles threw Graham Holland four innings and winning reliever, Jace Dunsford, three. PRCC threw five pitchers with starter Will Passeau throwing four innings, and Harper Johnson going 1 2/3 innings and giving up the winning run.

The home-field advantage showed up in the second game. Dame Fortune (or Lady Luck) shined as the Wildcats reversed the first game score and walked away with a 6-5 victory while collecting only four hits off three Eagle pitchers. Tate Parker produced two of the Wildcats' hits. He went two-for-four at the plate, including two homers, scored two runs, and drove in three. Right-fielder Matt Mercer hit a homer and drove in two runs. Meanwhile, Wildcat pitchers gave up 12 hits including a double and two home runs. Coastal scored two runs in the second inning and three in the fifth and led the game 5-4 going into the bottom half of the last inning. Tate Parker's two-run homer in the seventh inning walked it off for the Wildcats. Coastal threw three pitchers with reliever Jace Dunsford pitching the last 2/3 of an inning and being charged with the loss. PRCC sent three pitchers to the slab. Leif Moore went 4 2/3 innings and gave up nine hits and five runs while striking out five batters. Byrion Robinson followed, throwing 2/3 of an inning and giving up one hit. Winning pitcher, Blake Hooks, closed out the game, going 1 2/3 innings, giving up two hits and a walk while allowing no runs.

Conference Play Plus

A doubleheader was scheduled with the Northwest Florida State College Raiders for Tuesday, March 8. The games were cancelled because of bad weather. So, the Wildcats' next two games were played March 12 against the Northwest Mississippi Community College Rangers at Poplarville in Dub Herring Park. These were the first Mississippi Association of Community Colleges Conference (MACCC) games of the season.

The visiting Rangers came out ahead in the first game by a score of 6-4.

PRCC had six hits, and the visitors had eight, but the Rangers managed two doubles, a triple, and a home run. NWMCC took the lead in the second inning and kept it until the seventh when the Wildcats scored four runs to tie the score at four runs apiece. The Cats didn't score again, but the Rangers added a run in the eighth inning and another in the ninth to seal the victory. Turner Swistak started on the mound for PRCC and threw five innings. Bobby Magee followed and threw two shutout innings. Losing pitcher, Cole Tolbert, came in and over 1 2/3 innings gave up two runs. Five Ranger hitters each drove in a run while first baseman Wesley Lester swung a big bat, going three-for-four and driving in three runs. NWMCC used four pitchers; reliever John Luke Martin, who threw one inning, gave up no runs and earned the win.

The second game was a seven-inning affair in which the #2-ranked Wildcats escaped with a 10-9 victory in a contest that saw the Rangers outhit the Cats 13 – 6. Designated hitter Ryan Lee hit two homers and drove in four runs for the visitors. Wildcat second baseman Taylor Woodcock went two-for-three at the plate, hit a home run, and drove in a run. The Rangers sent five pitchers to the mound, and only starter Braden Sanders, who pitched 2 1/3 innings and gave up four runs, lasted two innings. Losing pitcher, Jaylon Buckley, threw 1 1/3 innings and gave up four runs. The Wildcats also sent five pitchers to the slab, and only starter Sam Hill, who lasted 2 1/3 innings and gave up three runs, lasted more than two innings. Winning pitcher, Landen Payne, went two innings and gave up two hits and no runs.

On Wednesday, March 16, PRCC faced conference rival Jones College in Ellisville. The Wildcats swept the two games, winning 8-0 and 2-1 to push their overall record to 13-4 and their conference mark to 3-1.

PRCC run-ruled the Bobcats 8-0 in the first game that lasted eight innings. It wasn't much of a contest as the Wildcats outhit the Bobcats 14 -5, and five of the Wildcats' hits went for extra bases. Alex Perry, D.K. Donaldson, and Blake Hooks hit doubles, and Tate Parker and Logan Walters hit home runs. Parker's home run bounced over the fence off the glove of the Bobcats' left fielder. Meanwhile, winning pitcher, Dakota Lee, who pitched seven innings, and Bobby Magee, who pitched one inning, shutout the Bobcats, giving up five hits and only one extra-base hit, a double by Colson Harris. Jones's starting and losing pitcher, Dalton Tanner, went 4 2/3 innings, giving three runs. Tanner was followed to the mound by Cade Mattison and Peyton Bell, who combined to give up five runs off eight hits.

The second game was a seven-inning pitchers' duel. PRCC's starting and winning pitcher, Leif Moore, threw a complete game, giving up one run, three hits, and a walk while striking out five batters. JC's only run crossed the plate when left fielder DeeJay Booth hit a homer in the seventh inning. JC's starting and losing pitcher, Andrew Nix, went 4 1/3 innings, giving up four hits and two runs while walking two and striking out five. Drew Druckenmiller, who threw the last 2 2/3 innings for the Bobcats, didn't give up a run. Final score, PRCC 2, JC 1.

Coach Avalon captured the significance of this sweep of PRCC's South Mississippi and conference rival JC by saying:

> I know this is the first time in six years that we have come over here and got a sweep. This is not an easy place to do it. This is a quality program, and they're a good team. Our pitching was outstanding. We had some big hits, but we left some runners on in both games. We must get better there. We know that, and we're going to keep working on it. It was a great day, and I am very proud of them. This is two big wins for our program and school, and we're thankful for them.

The Wildcats, now ranked #3 in the country, traveled to Baton Rouge, Louisiana, to play LSU Eunice, ranked #1, and Baton Rouge Community College on Friday, March 18. In two nine-inning games against non-conference foes, the Wildcats defeated the LSUE Bengals and lost to BRCC Bears.

In the first game, the Wildcats scored two runs in three innings and one run in four innings while the Bengals scored four runs in the second inning and one in the eighth. PRCC registered 16 hits including four doubles. One of the doubles was struck by Tate Parker, who went four-for-five at the dish, scored two runs, and drove in four. Five other Wildcats drove in one run each. Sam Hill started on the mound for PRCC, threw two innings, and gave up three runs on three hits, one of which was a homer. Winning pitcher, Turner Swistak, relieved in the third inning and went five innings, giving up no runs. Cole Tolbert finished for the Cats, going two innings and giving up one run on a home run struck by Parker Coley. LSUE sent five pitchers to the mound. Starter and loser, Cade Hart, threw 1 2/3 innings and gave up four runs. The other Bengal pitchers combined to give up six runs. Final score, PRCC 10, LSUE 5.

In the second game, BRCC built an early 6-0 lead while their starting pitcher, Gavin Green, held Pearl River scoreless. But the Wildcats scored twice in the sixth inning and six times in the seventh to take an 8-6 lead into the bottom of the ninth. The Bears scored three runs in the ninth to secure a 9-8 victory with a walk-off single. PRCC sent nine pitchers to the slab, which was the most hurlers used in any game all season. Starter, Will Passeau, went two innings, giving up three runs, and loser, Landen Payne, threw 2/3 of an inning and gave up three runs. Reliever Mason Long pitched the seventh for the Bears and gave up one hit while striking out two batters, earning a win for his effort. While PRCC batters produced 12 hits, they did not hit well with runners on base. Twenty-two times Wildcat batters had an opportunity to drive in runs but failed to do so. BRCC pitchers gave up only one walk, while PRCC pitchers gave up 10.

The Wildcats were back home in Poplarville on March 23 for a date with conference foe, the East Central Community College Warriors. PRCC won the first game by what looked like a football score, 22-17. The game was wild, to say the least. The story is best told by using aggregates. Both teams used six pitchers. Of the 12 pitchers used, nine threw fewer than two innings. The 12 pitchers gave up a total of 10 walks and 40 hits including five doubles and three home runs. PRCC's winning pitcher, Ryan Burt, threw three innings, allowing a run on two hits. ECCC's losing pitcher, Grant Edwards, threw two innings, giving up five hits and five runs. ECCC scored eight runs in the top of the first inning and did not lose the lead until the bottom of the seventh when PRCC scored five runs. One or both teams scored in every inning except the sixth. Pearl River's shortstop and leadoff batter, Gabe Broadus, had seven at-bats. Both teams stole three bases. ECCC's pitchers hit six batters. PRCC turned two double plays while ECCC turned none. A total of 14 players had at least one RBI.

The Wildcats swept the two games by run-ruling the #5-ranked Warriors 14-4 in the second game. PRCC starter and winner, Leif Moore, threw two innings and gave up six hits, four walks, and four runs. Reliever Blake

Hooks threw the last four innings, giving up nothing and striking out four hitters. PRCC had two big innings, mustering six runs in the first inning and five in the fourth. Wildcat batters produced 14 hits with Gabe Broadus and right fielder Ian Montz each getting three. Broadus, Montz, and catcher Matt Mercer each hit homers. ECCC starting and losing pitcher, David Burton, faced only six batters and gave up four hits including two homers, two walks, and six runs without registering an out. Three ECCC relievers gave up a total of eight runs on 10 hits and two walks.

After the sweep Coach Avalon said:
> I'm smiling. I'm pretty proud. That was impressive. Credit to them, they swung the heck out of the bat. That's a tough day at the office and one to be very, very proud of. That's a quality team. They punched us early, but we punched back and finished the fight.

The #3 PRCC Wildcats were 19-5 overall and 7-1 in conference play when the Coahoma Community College (CCC) Tigers, who were 6-12 overall and 1-7 in the conference, came to Poplarville on March 26. As their records and the doubleheader showed, the two teams were far from being evenly matched. PRCC run-ruled the Tigers in both games.

The Wildcats jumped on the Tigers in the bottom of the first inning, scoring two runs. CCC halved the lead in the top of the fourth on a solo homer by Erick Lopez. PRCC extended the lead in the bottom of the fourth by scoring four runs. After that it was all Wildcats, and by the time two were out in the bottom of the sixth, they had run-ruled CCC 11-1. The Wildcats banged out 14 hits including two doubles and a home run. CCC starting and losing pitcher, Keshun Patterson, threw four innings and gave up seven runs. All but one of PRCC's position players had at least one hit, and two of them had three hits. Winning pitcher, Will Passeau, threw five innings, giving up four hits and two walks and a run while striking out seven batters.

After the game Coach Avalon said of Passeau:
> His stuff is really good. He was up to 93 miles per hour today. He had good stuff and a good breaking ball. They put a couple of good swings on him early, and he had to find himself. That's a big start for a freshman that hasn't done that yet. That was

his first start against a conference opponent. He settled in and pitched well.

The second game was even worse for the visiting Tigers. At the end of 4 ½ innings, PRCC led 15-4, resulting in a second run-rule victory. The Wildcats garnered 15 runs on 15 hits including three doubles and four home runs. Alex Perry had two homers and a double as he drove in seven runs. CCC starting and losing pitcher, Caleb Smith, who lasted only 2/3 of an inning, gave up seven runs. Reliever Tanner Grimes followed and gave up eight runs in 1 1/3 innings. Winning pitcher, Sam Hill, threw three innings, giving up two hits but no runs. Byrion Robinson threw an inning and gave up a hit but no runs. All four of CCC's runs were charged to Jordan Belsome, who pitched one inning. CCC's center fielder, Bryland Skinner, went 1-3 at the plate and drove in two runs. Skinner had played for Mississippi State on their 2021 National championship team, and in 2023 he played for the University of Memphis. Alex Perry, who scored three runs led the Cats, went three-for-four with seven RBIs. Broadus, Parker, Donaldson, and Woodcock each produced two hits.

After the game Alex Perry said:

> I haven't been swinging it well. Today I was seeing it. The coaches told me to lock in and see the ball, and I did that. They threw me a fastball early in the count, and I didn't miss it. In my next at-bat, I had a full count and got a good pitch to hit and was able to get that one out, too.

On March 29 PRCC's four-game winning streak came to a halt at the hands of conference rival Mississippi Gulf Coast Community College. The Bulldogs handed the Wildcats a 9-7 loss in the first game in Perkinston. Going into the game, PRCC was ranked #1 with a 20-6 overall record and an 8-2 conference mark. Gulf Coast was 10-15 overall and 5-5 in the conference. At first glance it looked like the Wildcats should have won the high-scoring contest. The Wildcats outhit the Bulldogs 10 to eight. The Bulldogs' hits were simply timelier than the Wildcats'. Middle reliever, Luke Reed, who pitched six innings for the Bulldogs, giving up four runs off six hits and two walks, was the winning pitcher. Reliever Landen Payne, who threw 2

1/3 innings, was the Wildcat's losing pitcher, giving up five runs on two hits and two walks.

The second game saw a reversal of fortunes as the Wildcats squared the series with a 9-2 victory. The Bulldogs managed only three singles and scored only two runs, while the Wildcats scored nine runs off 10 hits. In the seven-inning game, PRCC's starter and winning pitcher, Leif Moore, threw five innings, allowing three hits and two runs. Cole Tolbert followed Moore and gave up nothing over two innings. MGCCC sent four pitchers to the mound including starter and loser, Noah Nicholson, who gave up five hits and five runs over 2 2/3 innings. Catcher Matt Mercer hit two homers and drove in three runs for the Wildcats. D.K. Donaldson also hit a homer and drove in three runs for the Cats.

The calendar turned to April, and PRCC stood 20-6 overall.

On Saturday April 2 the #1 ranked Wildcats split two games against East Mississippi Community College (EMCC) in Poplarville. EMCC sported a 15-9 overall record, but they were 10-1 in the conference, putting them in first place. The visitors won the first game, 4-2. EMCC's hitting was very efficient as they did not leave a single runner on base, and one of their nine hits, a third-inning home run by first baseman Wesley Sides, produced three runs. EMCC's starting and winning pitcher, Kylan Stepter, went six innings, allowing no runs. Reliever Andrew Lewis registered a save by pitching three innings and giving up two runs. The Wildcats managed only five hits, one of which was a solo home run by Alex Perry. Sam Hill suffered his second loss by giving up seven hits and four runs in three innings. Reliever Dakota Lee threw six innings, giving up two hits and no runs.

PRCC bounced back in the second game, winning 4-3. The Cats scored two runs in the second inning and one in the fourth, while EMCC scored one in the third and two in the sixth. The PRCC website explains how the tie was broken, and the victory was won:

> It was truly a fitting end to the No. 1 Pearl River baseball team's doubleheader against East Mississippi. After missing 22 games due to injury, team captain John Griffin Bell stepped into the batter's box in the bottom of the ninth inning and put a ball into play that led to a walk-off victory and series split for the

Wildcats.

EMCC starting pitcher, Cole Davis, threw 6 1/3 innings and gave up three runs. Reliever Gabe Garner, who was charged with the loss, went 1 2/3 innings and gave up one hit, two walks and one run. Reliever and winner Blake Hooks, the fourth Wildcat pitcher, threw one inning giving up one hit while striking out two batters.

On April 6, PRCC traveled to Wesson, Mississippi, to play Copiah-Lincoln Community College (CLCC). The Co-Lin Wolves were simply no match for the Wildcats' hot bats and stingy pitching.

In the first game PRCC run-ruled the Wolves. Gabe Broadus and Matt Mercer both drove in four runs while Ivan Montz drove in three. Winning pitcher, Will Passeau, threw two innings and gave up five hits and three runs. Ryan Burt followed Passeau and threw two innings, giving up one hit and no runs. Harper Jordan closed out the game, going one inning and giving up two runs. Co-Lin batters collected only five hits, but one of them was a three-run homer struck by first baseman Kenner Bizot. Co-Lin's starting and losing pitcher, Andrew Smith, didn't make it out of the first inning. He threw 2/3 of an inning and gave up eight runs. Noah Freeman relieved and gave up four runs in a single inning. Two other relievers combined to give up three runs. Final score in five innings, PRCC 15, Co-Lin 5.

The second game wasn't much better for the Wolves as they managed only one hit and one run off three Wildcat pitchers. Starter and winner, Lief Moore, threw four innings, giving up a walk and striking out two batters. Moore was followed by Byrion Robinson, who gave up two walks while striking out two batters over two innings. Turner Swistak closed out the seven-inning game for the Wildcats, giving up the Wolves' only hit and only run. Meanwhile, PRCC managed eight hits off four Wolves pitchers, all singles. Those hits were effective, as they drove in seven runs. Gabe Broadus went three-for-five at the plate and drove in two runs, and John Griffin Bell went one-for-four and drove in three runs. After the second game Coach Avalon said:

> We pitched it really well in game two. This is a tough place to play; it's an offensive ballpark. They're a quality lineup. This is just a tough place to play. I'm proud of these wins. We did what

we needed to do. We jumped on them and scored early. We led throughout the day, which is hard to do. We're thankful for that. It was a good day for Wildcat baseball.

Coach Avalon had this to say about Gabe Broadus, who stole five bases in the second game:

Gabe is a sparkplug. We mess with him and J.G. [John Griffin Bell] and we think that putting J.G. behind him in the lineup kind of pushed him. He had a great day. That's what he's capable of. He can make a lot of things happen. He's an electric player, and I'm really proud of the day he had.

The Wildcats left Wesson with a 23-7 record that included an 11-3 conference mark, which put them in first place in the conference.

PRCC next played Holmes Community College at a neutral site, Sports Force Park in Vicksburg, on April 9. The first game was a nailbiter as PRCC put crooked numbers on the scoreboard in four innings but trailed the HCC Bulldogs 11-9 going into the top of the ninth. Holmes had scored in every inning but the seventh and had gone ahead of PRCC by scoring three runs in the eighth. The ninth inning saw PRCC score three runs in the top of the inning off reliever and loser, Jackson Dollar. Cole Tolbert shutout the Bulldogs in the bottom of the inning. Starting pitcher, Sam Hill, threw the first 4 1/3 innings, allowing four runs. Reliever Blake Hooks threw 2/3 of an inning, giving up one run, and Landen Payne tossed an inning, allowing two runs. Tolbert pitched the final three innings and gave up three runs on three hits and a walk while striking out three Bulldog hitters and earning the win. With Tate Parker going five-for-five at the plate, including three homers, the Wildcats punished three Bulldog pitchers with 14 hits that produced 12 runs. The Bulldogs countered with 10 hits that included three home runs and three doubles.

The second game was another matter. Four Wildcat pitchers shut out the Bulldogs on three hits. PRCC hitters connected for eight hits including three doubles and three home runs while scoring 11 runs. Gabe Broadus, Tate Parker, and Logan Walters stroked doubles, and Alex Perry, Matt Mercer, and Ian Montz hit homers. Perry drove in three runs, and Montz two. PRCC starting and winning pitcher, Dakota Lee, threw four innings, giving up three hits while striking out six batters. Two relievers followed Lee, each pitching a single inning and giving up no runs. The game was run-ruled after six innings with the score PRCC 11, HCC 0. Brody Wilkins was the Bulldogs' starting and losing pitcher. He went 3 1/3 innings, giving up five hits and nine runs.

On April 12, the Wildcats were back home in Poplarville, playing the Hinds Community College (HCC) Eagles. The first game went about as well as a coach could hope for. In one of the best pitching performances of the season, Turner Swistak threw a shutout at the Eagles while giving up five hits. PRCC's defense did not commit an error, and Swistak faced only 23 batters in a game that resulted in the Wildcats run-ruling the Eagles 10-0 in six innings. The Eagles' starting and losing pitcher, Justin Wilson, tossed 4 1/3 innings, giving up seven runs. Reliever John David Gunn threw an inning, giving up three runs. The Wildcats connected for 11 hits including two doubles and a home run. Ian Montz was two-for-three at the plate and hit a grand slam homer.

The second game belonged to the Eagles from the get-go. HCC scored two runs in the first inning, one in the second, and two in the third as they led the Wildcats from wire to wire. The Cats scored two runs in the second and two in the seventh in the seven-inning contest. Hinds' batters garnered nine hits while PRCC batters managed seven hits, which included a home run by designated hitter Preston Soper. The Eagles sent four pitchers to the slab. The starter and winner, Kendrick Bershell, pitched three innings and allowed two runs. Three relievers followed and gave up a combined total of two runs. PRCC threw five pitchers. Starting pitcher, Leif Moore, was charged with his first loss, bringing his record to 5-1. He threw only 1 1/3 innings, giving up three runs. The four relievers who followed gave up a total of two runs. Final score, HCC 5, PRCC 4.

In another home series, PRCC took on Itawamba Community College (ICC) on April 15. The Wildcats got back to their winning ways by trouncing the Indians 15-7 in eight innings. Leading the way for PRCC was Taylor Woodcock, who was four-for-six at the plate with a home run, two doubles, and seven RBIs. Gabe Broadus produced three hits and an RBI in six plate appearances. Four other Wildcats each got two hits and drove in a total of three runs. Four of ICC's runs were scored in the top of the first inning. PRCC put a 6 on the scoreboard in the third and never trailed after that. Indian batters managed eight hits off three Wildcat pitchers. ICC sent three pitchers to the mound. Starter and loser, Taylor Tarver, threw 3 1/3 innings, giving up six runs. Wilson Varner followed and gave up 10 hits and seven runs over three innings. Reed Hale finished, giving up two runs over 1 1/3 innings. Winning pitcher, Dakota Lee, brought his record to 3-0 by throwing five innings and giving up six runs. Will Passeau relieved in the sixth and threw a third of an inning, giving up a run.

The Wildcats won the second game 5-2, and good pitching was much more on display. Winning pitcher, Cole Tolbert, threw 5 2/3 inning in the seven-inning affair. In his second start of the season, Tolbert gave up four hits, two walks, and two runs while striking out four batters. Byrion Robinson followed Tolbert, faced one batter, and gave up a hit. Landen Payne finished on the hill, throwing 1 1/3 innings and giving up nothing. Eight PRCC batters produced eight hits including a double by Matt Mercer that drove in two runs and a home run by Ian Montz that drove in two runs. ICC's starting and losing pitcher, Collin Babin, threw a complete game, giving up eight hits, four walks, and five runs while striking out two Wildcats. Not only was the pitching good but so was the fielding. Neither team made an error, and both teams turned two double plays.

An April 20 doubleheader against the Meridian Community College (MCC) Eagles at Meridian resulted in a split. Both teams were in the NJ-CAA's top 10; PRCC was #2 and MCC #8. The Wildcats won the first game 5-3 and lost the second game 8-5. Pearl River's pitching shined in the first game. Turner Swistak started, and Cole Tolbert finished. They combined to allow 10 hits and three runs over nine innings while walking two and striking out seven Eagles. They gave up only one extra-base hit, a homer by Braden Luke, who went three-for-three at the plate and drove in two runs. Wildcat hitters produced seven hits, and one of those was a home run by John Griffin Bell, who went two for three and drove in two runs. Tate Parker got two hits and drove in two runs, one on a sac fly. MCC's starting and losing pitcher, Cole Boswell, threw 4 1/3 innings, giving up four hits and four runs while striking out five Wildcats. Three other pitchers followed Boswell and combined to give up a run on three hits and two walks.

> Coach Avalon remarked about the first game:
> Turner was good today. His velocity in the seventh inning was still as good as it was in the first inning. That's what we needed. He gave us a good start, and we need him to do that again next time out.

In the second game PRCC fell behind 3-1 in the second inning, and although they scored a run in the fifth and three in the seventh, they never caught up. MCC added a run in the third and four in the fifth to take the seven-inning contest 8-5. MCC's Chandler Cline went two-for-three at the plate, hit a homer, and drove in four runs. Each team managed only five hits. D.K. Donaldson went one-for-three and accounted for one of PRCC runs by hitting a homer. Tate Parker drove in two runs for the Wildcats with a home run. Meridian's Alec Sparks threw a complete game, giving up five hits and five runs and striking out seven Wildcats. PRCC sent seven hurlers to the slab including starter and loser, Leif Moore, who pitched two innings and allowed four runs. The split sent PRCC home with an overall record of 29-9 including an MACCC record of 17-5.

The PRCC Wildcats went on the road to Moorhead, Mississippi, to play the Mississippi Delta Community College (MDCC) Trojans on April 23. It turned out to be a very good trip for the #2-ranked Wildcats.

The first game started with a bang as PRCC's Ian Montz put three runs on the scoreboard with a home run. MDCC countered in the bottom of the first inning by putting two runs on the board. Unfortunately for the Trojans, they didn't score again in the seven-inning game, while the Wildcats scored 10 more runs to win 13-2. The Wildcats' starting and winning pitcher, Sam Hill, was terrific. After giving up two unearned runs in the first inning, he shut out the Trojans for 4 1/3 innings. Ryan Burt pitched the last 1 2/3 innings and didn't allow an MDCC hitter to reach base. The Trojans managed only three hits, all singles. Meanwhile, the Wildcats generated eight hits including home runs by Broadus, Montz, and Mercer. Losing pitcher, Patrick Martin, threw 6 1/3 innings, giving up nine runs on seven hits. In the seventh inning, MDCC sent three relievers to the mound, and in 2/3 of an inning they combined to give up four runs on one hit and six walks. Final score, PRCC 13, MDCC 2.

The second game was a pitching duel through the first seven innings. PRCC's starter, Dakota Lee, gave up one run over five innings, and winning pitcher, Landen Payne, gave up one run over the last three innings. MDCC's starter and loser, Haden Luke, gave up four runs on eight hits and four walks over 7 1/3 innings. The score was tied at one run each at the end of seven innings. The Wildcats scored six runs in the top of the eighth, and the Trojans scored a single run in the bottom of the inning. MDCC collected five hits, and PRCC managed 12. Five Wildcats produced two hits, and four Cats drove in a total of seven runs. Final score, PRCC 7, MDCC 2.

> Coach Avalon remarked:
> I'm very proud of them. We knew there was a chance that today could go like it did. This is a tough place to play. In game one, we did what we needed to do. We jumped on them and were able to finish. Looking at their schedule so far this year, sometimes they have gotten beat in the first game but won the second one. That arm tonight in game two was as advertised. He's a really good player. I'm proud of our at-bats and how we battled until the end.

After sweeping MDCC on the road, PRCC came home to Poplarville, hoping to sweep the Southwest Mississippi Community College (SWMCC) Bears and close in on an MACCC championship. The April 26 matchup offered just such an opportunity.

The first game illustrated the importance of timely hitting and the long ball. PRCC registered 11 hits including three doubles and two home runs. Southwest collected 14hits including two doubles and one homer. Wildcat Logan Walters drove in two runs on a first-inning home run. PRCC designated hitter Preston Soper drove in four runs, three of which came on a homer with two men on base. D.K. Donaldson hit a double, driving in two runs. Four of Southwest's runs came on a grand slam by left fielder Brady Wilson, who went three-for-four at the plate and drove in a total of five runs. Turner Swistak started for PRCC and gave up 13 hits and five runs over five innings. Winning pitcher, Will Passeau, threw the last four innings, giving up one hit and a walk while striking out six Bears. Josh Miller started for SWMCC and lasted 5 2/3 innings, giving up seven hits and four runs. Three relievers followed Miller including loser Austin Boarden, who pitched the last 2/3 of an inning and gave up three hits and four runs. Final score, PRCC 9, SWMCC 5.

The second game was a blowout as PRCC scored 10 runs in the bottom of the first inning and rolled to a 14-3 run-rule victory in five innings. The PRCC website explains:

> Pearl River came out of the gate on fire in game two, plating an incredible 10 first-inning runs. Bell was walked to open the contest. Broadus and Parker then loaded the bases with a pair of singles. The first run scored when Perry was hit by a pitch. Bases loaded walks from Montz and Donaldson then brought the next two runners across the plate, making the score 3-0. A ball off the bat of Mercer was misplayed by the third baseman, allowing another runner to score. In almost identical fashion to his home run in the first game, Walters crushed a hanging slider over the left-field wall for a three-run homer and 8-0 Pearl River lead. After Broadus reached base on a single, Parker went down in the strike zone to hit a two-run homer over the wall, pushing the lead out to 10-0. The blast was Parker's 15th homer of the season and pushed him into a tie with Simon Landry for career home runs with 33.

PRCC scored four more runs in the third inning while Southwest scored its three runs in the top of the fifth. Pearl River accumulated nine hits including three homers and a double. Gabe Broadus and Tate Parker had three hits and scored three runs apiece. Ian Montz went two-for-two with a double and a home run and drove in five runs. Logan Walters hit a three-run homer. PRCC starter, Leif Moore, threw three innings without allowing a run. Reliever Harper Jordan threw 2/3 of an inning, walking one, and reliever Mason Smith struck out the only batter that he faced. The Bears used four pitchers including starter and loser, Shaine O'Keefe, who did not register an out while giving up two hits, six runs, hitting a batter, and issuing three walks. Three Southwest relievers combined to give up eight runs on seven hits and a walk. The sweep put PRCC within one win of an MACCC title.

Speaking of his team's play, Coach Avalon said:

> They did a really good job of barreling balls up. A lot of credit to them. The big thing was that I didn't see the run total keep going up. I knew we had a chance if we could get going. Thankfully, our guys picked up the slack, and that momentum carried over into game two.

On Friday April 29, PRCC closed out the month by going on the road to play the Northeast Mississippi Community College (NEMCC) Tigers. Good hitting supporting good pitching took the Wildcats to a relatively easy first-game victory. The seven-inning game was run-ruled as Pearl River hitters delivered 11 hits including two doubles and three home runs. Wildcat third baseman Alex Perry and designated hitter Logan Walters led the way. Perry smacked two homers, drove in three runs, and scored three runs. Walters went three-for-four, hit a homer, drove in two runs, and scored two runs. The Cats scored in five innings and put crooked numbers on the scoreboard in four innings. Winning pitcher, Dakota Lee, threw 5 1/3 innings, giving up six hits and three runs while striking out six batters. Landen Payne threw the last 1 2/3 innings and gave up nothing. Northeast batters managed only six hits including two doubles. Starting and losing pitcher, Seth Bagwell, went 3 1/3 innings and gave up six hits and six runs. Davis Oswalt relieved pitching for 3 2/3 innings, giving up seven hits and six runs. Final score, PRCC 12, NEMCC 3.

The victory made the PRCC Wildcats champions of the MACCC for the second consecutive year. It also assured the Wildcats a bye in the playoffs and that they would host the NJCAA Division II Region 23 Tournament. Coach Avalon said:

> We preach in our program that it's bigger than yourself. We've seen a lot of selfless players this year. The most impressive thing about this group is that we haven't been beaten back-to-back all year long. That's special. When we've gotten knocked down, we've gotten back up and responded. I'm just very proud of this

very special group and this very special place.

The second game seemed to be almost an afterthought for the Wildcats. NEMCC got a little revenge as they flipped the script. The Booneville Boys collected 11 hits off eight PRCC pitchers and pushed 11 runs across the plate. Five Tigers had RBIs, and both second baseman Logan Bland and catcher Jackson Owen had three hits and three RBIs. Tiger winning pitcher, Colby Holcombe, threw five innings and gave up four hits and three runs. He was followed by two relievers, who combined to give up two hits and two runs. Sam Hill started for PRCC and pitched an inning, giving up three hits and a run. Losing pitcher, Byrion Robinson, pitched 2/3 of an inning, giving up two hits and three runs. Six other relievers followed Robinson and combined to give up seven hits and seven runs. No PRCC pitcher threw more than an inning. Taylor Woodcock hit a double; Gabe Broadus hit a triple, and D.K. Donaldson hit a home run. Final score, Northeast 11, Pearl River 5.

At the end of April, PRCC stood 34-10 overall and 22-6 in the conference. The Wildcats were ranked #1 in the country and were on the cusp of a promising postseason.

On May 7, PRCC played an out-of-conference doubleheader against Chattahoochee Valley Community College (CVCC) on the Pirates' home field in Phenix City, Alabama. The games proved to be a good warmup for post-season play.

The first game went nine innings, and the Wildcats led from the get-go, scoring a run in the top of the first inning and adding single runs in the second and fourth before the Pirates scored their first run in the bottom of the fourth. The fifth inning was good for both teams as PRCC scored three runs, and CVCC countered with two. PRCC scored another run in the eighth while CVCC failed to score the rest of the game. The Cats managed 11 hits including four doubles. Five Wildcats drove in runs, and three had more than one hit as PRCC cruised to victory. Coach Avalon seemed to be managing his pitching staff as postseason play approached. He sent five pitchers to the mound. Ryan Burt, who entered the game in the fifth inning and threw two innings, giving up two hits, a walk, and no runs, was the winner. Cole Tolbert pitched the last three innings and earned a save. Final score, PRCC

7, CVCC 3.

The second game was a lopsided affair as the Wildcats run-ruled the Pirates 13-0 in five innings. Five PRCC pitchers each threw one inning, giving up no runs on a total of two hits and nothing else. Leif Moore, who pitched the second inning, during which the Wildcats scored six runs, was the winning pitcher. The Cats managed eight hits that included only one extra-base hit, a triple by Ian Montz, but eight PRCC hitters registered RBIs.

Post Season Play

PRCC returned to action May 16-20 as they hosted the double-elimination Region 23 Tournament. The seeding in the six-team tournament field was #1 Pearl River, #2 East Mississippi, #3 LSU Eunice, #4 Hinds, # 5 Jones College and #6 Northwest Mississippi.

PRCC faced familiar foe Northwest Mississippi Community College (NWMCC) Rangers in the first game of the regional. Although Northwest put eight runs on the scoreboard, it really wasn't much of a contest. The Wildcats run-ruled the team from Senatobia 18-8 in five innings. PRCC trailed NWMCC 4-1 going into the fourth inning. Then the Wildcats exploded for 16 runs in the bottom of the inning. Northwest mounted somewhat of a comeback in the top of the fifth by scoring four runs on a grand slam by Peeko Townsend. PRCC scored a single run in the bottom of the fifth to push its lead to 18-8 and trigger the run-rule that ended the game. The box score captures the scoring:

PRCC -
2B: Tate Parker, D.K. Donaldson, Matt Mercer, Logan Walters (2)
HR: Alex Perry
RBI: John Griffin Bell (2), Gabe Broadus, Tate Parker (3), Alex Perry (3), Ian Montz, D.K. Donaldson, Matt Mercer (2), Logan Walters (4)

NWMCC -
2B: Peeko Townsend
HR: Landon Rogers, Ryan Lee, Peeko Townsend
RBI: Landon Rogers, Ryan Lee, Peeko Townsend (6)
Sac Fly: Dawson Griffin

Five Wildcats had multiple RBIs, and the Rangers' Peeko Townsend had

6.

PRCC's winning pitcher, Turner Swistak, registered his sixth win against no losses by throwing 4 2/3 innings and giving up eight hits and six runs. NWNCC's losing pitcher, Zach Willingham, lost his fourth game against six wins by throwing three innings and giving up five hits and six runs. Four pitchers followed Willingham over two innings. They gave up 12 runs on eight hits.

Coach Avalon remarked:
> The hit by D.K. [Donaldson in the fourth] on the hit-and-run gave us some momentum. That's a difference between this team and some of our teams of the past. That's something that we're able to do this year to put some pressure on folks and get us going. We put pressure on them and were able to get around the bases. This is a big win. Getting that first one out of the way is huge for our program and this tournament. I'm very proud of our guys.

Next up on May 17 was another familiar foe, the Hinds Community College (HCC) Eagles, and another five-inning run-rule victory for the Wildcats. The Cats subdued the Eagles 13-3 on 10 hits, only one of which went for extra bases, Alex Perry's double. This time the Cats had two big innings, scoring five runs in the third inning and six in the fifth. Seven Wildcats got hits with runners on base and drove in runs, John Griffin Bell (2), Gabe Broadus, Alex Perry (3), D.K. Donaldson (2), Matt Mercer, Logan Walters, and Taylor Woodcock. Left fielder Broadus sparked the Cats, going two-for-three at the plate, driving in two runs, stealing two bases, and scoring three runs. Perry was two-for-three with three RBIs. Parker and Woodcock each collected two hits. Alex Perry walked off the run-rule win with a sac fly that scored John Griffin Bell with two outs in the fifth inning. Dakota Lee won his fourth game against no losses by pitching four innings, giving up four hits and three runs while striking out three batters. Blake Hooks threw the final inning for PRCC and gave up two hits and no runs. Hinds' starter and loser, Connor Nation, gave up five hits, two walks, and seven runs. Two relievers followed Nation to the hill and combined to give up five hits and six runs over 2 2/3 innings. Clay Benson smacked a two-run homer for the Eagles in the fifth inning.

After the game Coach Avalon said:
> That wasn't easy. Dakota was big-time today. Him putting up zeros early let us get ourselves going. That's so important in post-season baseball. I learned a long time ago that you have to score in postseason baseball, but you have to put up zeros too, and they are hard to come by. I'm proud that we finished this. The message to the guys was let's get ourselves ready to play tomorrow. This win is just one step. Tomorrow will not be easy, but we will get ready tonight.

The Wildcats had run-ruled their opponents in their last three games. That streak came to a halt when they faced a second game against the Hinds Eagles on May 18 in a game that went 12 innings. There were some interesting features to this sloppy game that ended with a 6-5 PRCC victory. In the ninth inning, HCC led 5-4, but PRCC scored a run in the bottom of the inning to force extra innings. Neither team scored in the 10th or 11th innings, and HCC did not score in the 12th. Pearl River finally put an end to the contest in the bottom of the 12th. Catcher Matt Mercer doubled, and designated hitter Preston Soper hit a single up the middle to drive Mercer home and make the Wildcats winners. The loss eliminated Hinds and propelled PRCC to the next round to face LSU Eunice.

In a nine-inning game, PRCC blasted the LSU Eunice Bengals, the reigning national champions, 11-4. The Wildcats scored six runs in the bottom of the first, and the Bengals never threatened. Among the Wildcats' 18 hits were two doubles and four home runs. Perry hit a three-run homer, his third in the last four games. Six Cats had RBIs led by Alex Perry with four and Ian Moore with two. Tate Parker went four-for-five at the plate, scored two runs, and drove in one. Parker's homer was the 34th of his career, making him the Wildcats' all-time leader in home runs. Starting and winning pitcher, Sam Hill, brought his record to 4-2 by throwing six innings. Will Passeau earned a save by pitching the final three innings. Bengal batters managed only eight hits and three RBIs. Starting and losing pitcher, Miles Clark, lasted only 2/3 of an inning, giving up four hits and six runs. Four Bengal pitchers followed Clark to the mound, and combined they gave up 14 hits and five runs over 7 1/3 innings.

The win over LSU Eunice made PRCC Champions of Region 23 and sent them to the NJCAA Division II College World Series in Enid, Oklahoma, that began May 29. The 10-team field was divided into two five-team brackets for the double-elimination tournament. PRCC, the #1 seed, was in bracket 1 along with #8 Florida State College at Jacksonville; #9 Phoenix Community College, Arizona; #4 Frederick Community College, Maryland; and #5 Lansing Community College, Michigan. Bracket 2 included #2 seed Madison Area Community College, Wisconsin; #7 Murray State Community College, Kentucky; # 10 Mercer County Community College, New Jersey; #3 Hartland Community College, Illinois; and #6 Kirkwood Community College, Michigan.

Because the Wildcats were the #1 seed, they drew a bye in the first round of the series. On Sunday, May 29, the Cats played their first game against Florida State College at Jacksonville (FSCJ) at David Allen Memorial Ballpark. PRCC hit and pitched its way to a 10-2, run-ruled seven-inning victory. In six innings, the winning pitcher, Dakota Lee, gave up five hits, a walk, and two runs. Blake Hooks completely shut down FSCJ in the seventh inning. In the six innings they batted, PRCC hitters generated nine hits including a double and three home runs. Shortstop John Griffin Bell went three-for-three at the plate with a home run and two RBIs. Catcher Matt Mercer went two-for-four with a home run and drove in three runs. Center fielder Tate Parker hit a double and a home run, generating two RBIs. The Wildcats scored three runs in the first inning, four in the fourth, and three in the sixth. FSJC scored a run in the second and sixth innings. FSCJ's losing pitcher, Brian Veniard, threw four innings and gave up seven hits and seven runs. Tyler Green pitched the final two innings for the Blue Wave, giving up two hits, two walks, and three runs.

The PRCC website noted:
> [Gabe] Broadus turned in arguably the catch of the year in the top of the third inning. With a runner in scoring position at second base, the left fielder sprinted to his right before leaving his feet to make an incredible catch and put an end to the in-

ning. Broadus turned in another remarkable catch in the top of the fifth inning, mimicking his earlier catch almost identically to prevent a run from scoring.

About his starting pitcher who improved his record to 7-0, Coach Avalon said:

> What more could you ask for from Dakota Lee? The start that he gave us was phenomenal. He made some tough pitches and worked out of some tough situations. I told him how much I appreciated him. When he came out of the game after throwing 100 pitches, he said, "Thanks for trusting me, coach."

PRCC took on the Lansing Community College Lugnuts the next day in the winners' bracket. Run-ruling their opponents was becoming routine with the Wildcats, and they did it again with a 17- 8 victory over the Lugnuts. PRCC bats stayed hot as the Cats stroked 17 hits including two doubles and a home run. Taylor Woodcock with six RBIs and John Griffin Bell with three RBIs led the onslaught as five Cats drove in more than one run. In four of the six innings they batted, the Wildcats put crooked numbers on the scoreboard. PRCC starting pitcher, Turner Swistak, threw four innings, giving up five hits and five runs. Reliever Ryan Burt threw an inning and gave up three hits and three runs but earned a win, his third of the season. Cole Tolbert closed for the Cats, pitching two innings while giving up nothing and striking out four batters. The Lugnuts' second pitcher, Elijah Stark, came into the game in the fourth inning, pitched 2/3 of an inning, gave up five hits and five runs, and was tagged with the loss. LCC batters collected eight hits, which included a double, a triple, and a solo home run.

Coach Avalon praised both teams:

> That's a quality team we played right there. They're strong; they're physical, and they swing the bats well. They were ready to play, credit to them. They squared some balls up. I thought there were some tough calls that didn't go our way tonight, but we didn't let the frustration get the better of us. I'm very proud of our guys for their performance.

Florida State College at Jacksonville won a loser's bracket game and earned the right to play PRCC again. This time around the Blue Wave performed better against the Wildcats but still fell to PRCC 13-11. PRCC hitters remained scalding hot, stroking 18 hits including seven doubles and a home run. Eight Wildcats drove in at least one run, led by Alex Perry with three RBIs, and D.K. Donaldson and Tate Parker with two each. Sam Hill started on the mound for PRCC and threw 4 1/3 innings, giving up five hits and five runs. Winning pitcher, Will Passeau, came in in the fifth inning, threw 2 2/3 innings, and gave up five hits and five runs. Three other pitchers followed Passeau to the Hill including Blake Hooks, who finished the game, throwing 1/3 of an inning, giving up nothing and earning a save. Midway through the seventh inning, the Blue Wave led PRCC 8-6, but the Cats exploded for seven runs in the bottom of the inning. The PRCC website explained what happened in the seventh:

> The seventh inning was one to remember for the Wildcats as they sent 13 batters to the plate and scored a remarkable seven runs. Broadus led things off with an infield single and advanced to second base on a throwing error. He advanced to third and then scored on a passed ball to cut the deficit to 8-7. Perry singled and stole second base, then Ian Montz sent him home with an RBI single. Enter D.K. Donaldson. Donaldson has been tagged as a clutch hitter all year long, and he lived up to that by destroying a 1-1 pitch over the left-field wall to put the Wildcats back in front, 10-8. Mercer didn't let the momentum die there, doubling off the jumbotron in right center field. Walters was hit by a single, and Woodcock drove a single into right field for an RBI. Bell extended the Wildcat lead out to 12-8 with a fielder's choice on the first pitch of his at-bat. Great base running from Broadus followed as he turned a single to the center fielder into a double. The Blue Wave opted to intentionally walk Parker, but Perry drew a bases-loaded walk to give the Wildcats a 13-8 lead.

The Blue Wave put three runs on the scoreboard in the eighth inning to close within two runs of the Cats, but PRCC pitchers Ryan Burt and Blake Hooks put a zero on the board in the ninth to seal the victory and propel PRCC to the championship series.

Located in Madison Wisconsin, Madison Area Technical College came into the championship series with an overall record of 47-9. PRCC stood 42-10. In the first game, played on June 1, PRCC lost for the first time since April 29. The Cats had won 10 games in a row including all seven games they played in postseason tournaments. The Wolves scored three times in the first inning and never trailed in the game. Wolves pitchers held the Wildcats to eight hits and four runs while Madison batters generated 15 hits and 11 runs. Winning pitcher, Luke Hansel, threw six innings and gave up six hits and all four of the Cats' runs. Riley LeTourneau relieved Hansel and pitched an inning without giving up a hit or a run. Chris Byhre closed the game for Madison, throwing two innings, giving up two hits and a walk and earning a save. The Cats' starting and losing pitcher, Leif Moore, lasted only 1 2/3 innings, giving up seven hits, two walks, and five runs. Moore was followed to the mound by four relievers, who combined to give up eight hits and six runs. The only longballs hit in the game were doubles; Madison had five and PRCC two. Final score, Madison 11, Pearl River 4.

Coach Avalon remarked:

> We got beat tonight. That's a quality team. They pitched it well and swung it well. They jumped on us early, and that was the difference. Thankfully, this is a best of three, so it comes down to tomorrow. We need to show up and battle back. It's going to be tough because they're a really good ball club. It'll be up to us to decide that we can do this. I know that they're going to decide to do it. They don't quit. We'll regroup and get ready for tomorrow.

The Wildcats would have to win two straight games from the powerful Wolves, and they began to work on that chore with a vengeance the next day. In the second game, played June 3, Pearl River scored four runs in the top of the first inning. Madison scored one run in the bottom of the first. PRCC went on to score 18 more runs, including seven in the fifth inning, while Madison scored none. Final score, a resounding win for the Wildcats, 19-1. Wildcat batters registered 15 hits including two doubles and two home runs. Center fielder Tate Parker got three hits, drove in a run, and scored three runs. While going three-for-five including a home run, third baseman Alex Perry drove in three runs and scored three runs. First baseman D.K. Donaldson went three-for-four, drove in three runs, and scored two. Meanwhile, after the first inning, Wildcat pitching and fielding stopped every potential scoring threat that the Wolves mounted. Cat pitchers held the Wolves to eight hits, none of which went for extra bases, and Cat fielders turned six double plays. PRCC ace Dakota Lee earned his eighth win against no losses, throwing six innings and giving up six hits, four walks, and one run. Three relievers followed Lee to the hill and in three innings gave up two hits and no runs. Madison sent six pitchers to the mound, and Pearl River scored two or more runs off four of them. Wolf starter, Carson Fluno, threw three innings and gave up four hits and seven runs, all earned. PRCC's resounding victory set up a decisive third game that would decide the 2022 NJCAA Division II College World Series Championship.

Coach Avalon commented:

> It's been a long week, and yesterday was a long day. I thought there was a difference tonight from last night. That difference was our focus and our energy. That's what we have to have. There's nothing I should have to say tomorrow. We get to put on our golds [uniforms] and play for a National Championship. Regardless of what happens, I want these guys to know I am proud of them. I'm going to play free tomorrow knowing that they've accomplished a lot. They've made our college proud. This is every kid's dream to play in a National Championship. I'm thankful that these young men get to do it because they one hundred percent deserve it. I think they'll be ready for it.

The third game in three days against Madison was played on Saturday, June 4, 2022. It turned out to be an historic day for Pearl River Community College Baseball. Despite giving up a two-run homer to Madison third baseman Zach Storbakken in the first inning, PRCC's winning pitcher, Cole Tolbert, was sensational. Madison held a two-run lead through five innings, but PRCC scored three runs in the top of the sixth to take the lead. Tolbert threw seven innings, gave up five hits, a walk, and two runs while striking out 11 batters and earning his third win against one loss. Turner Swistak followed Tolbert to the slab and gave up a hit and nothing else over two innings. Five of the six hits Madison managed were singles. Meanwhile, PRCC hitters managed 10 hits including home runs by Tate Parker and Alex Perry. While PRCC played a clean game in the field, a balk and four errors didn't help Madison's cause. Madison starting and losing pitcher, Jacob Wilde, hurled 5 2/3 innings, giving up six hits and three runs. Three Madison relievers combined to give up four hits and four runs. Final score, Pearl River Community College Wildcats 7, Madison College Wolves 2. PRCC was the 2022 NJCAA Division II College World Series Champion.

Coach Michael Avalon:

> They didn't make it easy for sure. That's the way we wanted it, and that's the way we prepared all year. We were down early, and these guys never quit. That's just not who we are. Man, what a special group. They simply made history today. All day today, I looked out there and thought this is the last time I get to coach Woody (Taylor Woodcock) and J.G. (John Griffin Bell) in the middle. It's the last time I get to call pitches with Matt Mercer. The last time I get to coach Tate Parker, who is the best player that I have ever coached, and he's so humble about it. It's a storybook ending to one of the best chapters of my life. I can't thank all of these guys enough for this because they are a special, special group. All of these guys would tell you this is bigger than us. There have been a lot of really good players and really good teams that weren't blessed enough to be here. This group will live forever, and that's what is special. This is the best program in the country. This is the best community college in the country. I'm just thankful and blessed to be a part of it and be at Pearl River. The last thing that me and my dad talked about before he passed was when he told me to get back here and win the whole thing. We did it. I'm proud of it. I miss him, but I knew he was here before we went out. Before the last inning, "Glory Days" played. That was his favorite song, and it played across the speakers. I knew he was here.

Pearl River Community College President Dr. Adam Breerwood said: "Mission accomplished. This is just a remarkable team and a remarkable coaching staff. I'm in awe of them," he said. "Everything they have done this year has been amazing. Here we stand, and we stand as a family. Hats off to coach Avalon, his staff, and these players. It's incredible. We're so proud of them for bringing home the first National Championship."

Postseason Honors

Coach Michael Avalon's Wildcats captured the baseball program's first NJCAA Division II National Championship. PRCC also won its second straight MACCC Championship along with winning the NJCAA Region 23 Title. The Wildcats finished the year with a 45-11 record. Avalon was named the 2022 MACCC, NJCAA Region 23 and NJCAA National Coach of the Year.

The American Baseball Coaches Association named Wildcat hitting coach and recruiting coordinator, Slater Lott, the 2022 NJCAA DII Assistant Coach of the Year. Head Coach Avalon said:

> What a tremendous and well-deserved honor for Slater. We are very thankful to have Slater and his family. Since day 1, he has been a tireless worker and wanted to do his part in helping this program take the next step. Slater continues to invest in our program, but more importantly, he invests in our student-athletes and helps them reach their potential. I am extremely thankful for all he does for our program, but also very appreciative of his friendship.

From the National Junior College Athletics Association website:

> **Charlotte, NC** – Pearl River's Tate Parker has been named the 2022 NJCAA Division II Baseball Player of the Year after a stellar sophomore season. [Tate's brother Brandon Parker won the same award as a freshman playing for Gulf Coast Community College in 2018.] Parker ended the 2022 campaign batting .450 with 19 home runs (fifth in the nation) and 65 RBI. The sophomore also ranked in the top five in the nation in four statistical categories: hits (90, third); runs (76, third); home runs (19, fifth); total bases (164, fifth).

The ABCA/Rawlings National Player of the Year helped lead Pearl River to a Division II Baseball World Series championship where he continued to shine bright. In six championship games, Parker batted .417 with three home runs and nine RBIs, having gotten at least one hit in each game. His efforts throughout the Wildcats' championship run earned him Offensive Player of the Tournament honors.

"When I look back at Tate's time here, what stands out to me is just the impact he had on our program for two years," PRCC coach Michael Avalon said. "He was the missing piece to take our program to the next level. If you look at all great teams in history, they have a great leader and player at the top, and that was Tate for us the last two years. Tate can just flat out hit. Over the past two years, Tate led one of the toughest conferences in the country in average, home runs, and RBIs. Not only did he excel at the plate, he was elite in all facets of his game; he played phenomenal defense in center field and made an impact running the bases. He's a true five-tool player."

Player Profile
Position: Center Field, Height: 5'11", Class: Sophomore, Hometown: Gulfport, MS
2022 Statistics
55 games played, 200 at-bats, 76 runs, 90 hits, 11 doubles, 19 home runs, 65 RBI, 29 walks, .450 batting average, .531 on-base percentage, .820 slugging percentage
2022 Accomplishments
NJCAA DII Baseball ABCA/Rawlings National Player of the Year, NJCAA DII Baseball ABCA/Rawlings First Team All-America, NJCAA First-Team All-American, MACCC First-Team All-American

Several Wildcats signed with four-year schools on the first day they were eligible to do so. Of those signing then, Coach Avalon said:

As coaches, this is one of the big reasons why we do what we do. Signing day is always a special and humbling time. During the recruiting process with these guys, they told us their dreams and aspirations to play at the four-year level. They also had the dream and goal of helping Pearl River win its first National Championship. Today is for them, their families, and their teammates to celebrate their accomplishments. We are thankful they chose Pearl River and trusted this program to help them along their way. This is an incredibly talented group, and we expect to have more guys join them with their decision to continue their careers at the next level.

Before signing was over, 10 Wildcats had signed to continue their baseball careers at four-year institutions. Southern Miss signed Tate Parker, Gabe Broadus, and Landen Payne; South Alabama inked Cooper Cooksey; Delta State signed Triston Hickman; Louisiana Tech signed Blake Hooks; Mississippi State signed Will Passeau; Tennessee signed Alex Perry; Louisiana-Lafayette took Byrion Robinson, and Cole Tolbert signed with Ole Miss.

In a May 3, 2023, interview, Coach Avalon told the author a great backstory about the three-game championship series. Leif Moore, who started the first game and lasted only 1 1/3 innings was not his normal self. Moore's father who had been struggling with cancer had just died. In fact, Leif was on the bus to Enid with the team when he got a message to come home. He left the team at Little Rock and went home to his father's funeral. Leif rejoined the team before the first game, and he wanted the ball and his teammates thought that he had earned the right to start. It didn't turn out well for Leif, but it proved to be inspiration for the team. Avalon walked through the team hotel for a bed-check the night after the first game loss. He couldn't find a single player, but he soon found a team manager who told him everything was okay. The team leaders had called a players only meeting and they were all in attendance.

On May 3, 2023, I also interviewed three hold-over players from the 2022 team, Logan Walters, Gabe Broadus, and Will Passeau. PRCC would host the MACCC Baseball Tournament beginning the next day with an opportunity to win their way to the NJCAA Region 23 Tournament. It was refreshing to get to talk to those young men. They praised everything PRCC, especially their coaches, teammates, and the journey they had taken together to the national championship. They mentioned what it was like to come to PRCC not knowing their future teammates and within a very short time becoming a band of brothers who would spend almost all their time together and become lifetime friends. They especially praised the sophomore team members, who had accepted them and made them welcome. Logan Walters talked about how great it was to win the championship but said that after a very brief time, his thought was, "When can we play again?" Gabe Broadus mentioned the people he met along the journey, including the host family he stayed with in Enid, Oklahoma. They discussed the players' only meeting after the loss in the first game of the College World Series. My take-away was that the Pearl River Wildcats Baseball Team had no intention of losing again. They told each other they had worked too hard, come too far, and they had too much trust in each other not to play well and win the next two games and a national championship for PRCC.

Coach Avalon uses the acronym S.O.A.P., which he learned from his father William (Billy) Vance Avalon II, a former Marine and a very successful teacher and coach, to motivate PRCC players and to remind them constantly of what it takes to achieve success. Success = Organization, Attitude and Pride. It seems that everything in the PRCC baseball program is built on this. Graham Crawford played for PRCC from 2019-2021. His father, Trey Crawford, wrote the following about his son's experience.

> I didn't realize how much of an impact Coach Avalon and his staff were going to have on Graham when we moved him down to Poplarville. He went from a kid who was trying to figure out how to get out of work all the time to a kid that started picking up trash on the ground wherever he went. S.O.A.P. is a philosophy that my son has ingrained in his mentality, and that's something that he will carry throughout his life, long after his baseball career ends! More than all the team and individual successes he has had while at PRCC, his S.O.A.P. mentality is what I am most proud of.

Billy Avalon believed that picking up trash says a lot about character and success in life. So does his son Michael.

Madison Central High School

CHAPTER 6
Madison Central High School Jaguars – Baseball America's 2021 High School Baseball Team of the Year

Madison County, Mississippi, has experienced tremendous population growth since 1990 when approximately 54,000 people lived in the county. In 2020 the population had increased to approximately 109,000, of which some 28,000 live in the city of Madison. Madison Central High School (MCHS) is one of five high schools in the Madison County School District. MCHS opened in 1991 when it absorbed students from Madison Ridgeland High School and East Flora High School. In recent years the Madison County School District has achieved an "A" rating based on the statewide accountability model, which contains several measurables.

Madison Central has a well-earned reputation for both academic and athletic excellence. The Jaguars won state championships in football in 1999 and 2021; in boys golf in 2013, 2014, 2015, and 2016; in boys soccer in 2013, 2014, 2015, 2016, and 2021; girls soccer in 2014, 2015, and 2016; girls swimming 2021 and 2022; boys swimming 2021and 2022; and girls tennis 2022. Madison Central also won state championships in baseball in 2016 and 2021.

This is the story of head coach Patrick Robey's highly decorated 2021 Madison Central High School Jaguars Baseball Team.

The first game of the 2021 season featured the Madison Central (MC) Jaguars and the perennial power, Oak Grove Warriors. The game was played February 22 in Oak Grove, and Madison Central run-ruled the Warriors 21-5 in six innings. Winning pitcher Austin Tommasini threw 3 1/3 innings and gave up one hit and no runs while striking out six batters. First baseman Hunter Hines went two-for-four at the plate, hit two homers, drove in four runs, and scored four runs. Connor Nation went two-for-four, drove in six runs, and scored four. Relief pitcher Austin Tommasini threw 3 1/3 innings and gave up a hit, two walks, and no runs while striking out six batters.

MC played North Pike in the Mid-Mississippi Classic on February 26 in Madison. The Jags gave up no hits and no runs while run-ruling the Pike County Jaguars 10-0 in five innings. Winning pitcher, Ranard Grace, threw four innings, and Brendon Minor threw the fifth inning. Ross Highfill hit a homer and drove in three runs while going two-for-four at the plate. Beau Bryans went one-for-three, hit a double, and drove in two runs.

Next up was a home game against the Tuscaloosa County (Alabama) Wildcats. MC registered its second straight no-hit shutout and its third straight run-rule victory, handling the Wildcats 11-0 in five innings. MC batters managed nine hits including three doubles, as three Jags, Ross Highfill, Connor Chisolm, and Jake Cook, each drove two runs. Winning pitcher, Beau Bryans, threw three innings, giving up no hits, no walks, and no runs while striking out seven hitters. Braden Montgomery threw two innings, giving up a walk and no runs while striking out five batters.

Shutouts, no hitters, and run-ruling opponents came to a halt on March 4 when MC played Taylorsville High School at Columbia, Mississippi. Nevertheless, the Jags stayed undefeated by edging the Tartars 2-1. MC managed only seven hits. Connor Chisolm went three-for-three at the plate, and Hunter Hines went two-for-three. The only extra-base hit was struck by Connor Nation, who went one-for-three and drove in both of MC's runs with a home run. MC pitchers showed out again as Connor Nation, who threw 2 1/3 innings, and winning pitcher, Austin Tommasini, who threw 4 2/3 innings, limited the Tartars to three singles and one run.

The second game of the March 4, doubleheader was played against Columbia High School. The Jags' hitters and pitchers were back to their dominating ways as they prevailed over the Wildcats, 15-1. The run-rule didn't come into play because the Jags led 9-1 going into the top of the seventh inning, in which they scored six runs. MC hitters collected 13 hits, including three doubles, a triple, and a home run while driving in 14 runs. Both Braden Montgomery and Hunter Hinds produced three hits and three RBIs. Eric Gibbs started on the mound for the Jags. He gave up three hits and one run over four innings. Winning pitcher, Brendon Minor, came in and gave up one hit and four walks while striking out six hitters over the last three innings. The Wildcats sent five pitchers to the hill, and they combined to give up 13 earned runs.

After five games the Jags had outscored their opponents 59-7, and they had committed only two errors! A great season was a possibility!

March 6 found MC playing West Jones in Laurel. It was another run-rule affair as the Jags outscored the Mustangs 11-0 in six innings. The Jags as a team batted .500 for the game while connecting for 16 hits including three doubles and a triple. Hunter Hines went two-for-four and drove in three runs. Ross Highfill went two-for-five and drove in two runs. Beau Bryans threw four innings, giving up no runs and striking out 10 batters. Braden Montgomery threw the last two innings and gave up nothing while striking out four batters.

MC visited Northwest Rankin High School in Brandon on March 9 and left with a 20-2 five-inning run-rule victory. MC scored four runs in the top of the first inning, and Northwest Rankin countered with two in the bottom of the inning. After that it was all MC as the Jags scored seven runs in the second, three in the third, and six in the fifth. Launching a hitting barrage that included 13 hits, three doubles and a home run, MC hitters posted 15 RBIs and a team batting average of .481. Ross Highfill hit a double in four at-bats and drove in four runs. Jake Cook went two-for-two at the dish and drove in three runs. In three at-bats Hunter Hines's only hit was a solo home run. Three other Jags had two RBIs. MC base runners swiped five bases. In an unusual occurrence, the Jags made two errors in the field. Winning pitcher, Ranard Grace, threw all five innings and gave up two runs on two hits while striking out eight batters and walking none.

MC visited in-county rival Germantown at the Mavericks' home field on March 12. The visitors imposed their will by administering a 16-0 five-inning, run-rule loss on the home team. Jaguar batters registered 14 hits including two doubles and a triple. Hunter Hines went four-for-four at the plate, hit a double, and drove in five runs. Braden Montgomery went one-for-four and drove in three runs. Winning pitcher, Montgomery, threw three innings and gave up no hits and no runs while walking a batter and striking out eight. Reliever Connor Nation pitched the last two innings, giving up the Mavericks' only hit while striking out three batters. The Montgomery/Nation combination would soon dominate several games. Germantown pitchers gave up nine bases on balls, and their fielders made four errors. It wasn't pretty.

Neshoba Central High School from Philadelphia, Mississippi, visited MC on March 13. Beau Bryans and Brendon Minor combined to throw a no-hitter at the Rockets. Bryans started and gave up a walk and struck out three batters over two innings. Minor threw five innings and gave up a walk while striking out seven batters. Philadelphia pitchers cooled off MC bats somewhat. The Jags registered eight hits including three doubles and produced six runs against two Rocket pitchers. Both Connor Chisolm and Hunter Hines went two-for-three at the plate; both hit a double, and both drove in two runs. MC stole three bases and committed no errors in the field.

On March 13, another Madison County neighbor, Ridgeland High School, visited MC and left disappointed. The Jags scored two runs in the bottom of the first inning, and the Titans countered with a run in the top of the second. MC would go on to score four runs in the third and one in the fourth, while the Titans did not score after the second. The Jags collected nine hits. Hunter Hines hit a home run in his only official at-bat and drove in two runs, and Ross Highfill hit a solo homer. Eric Gibbs started for the Jags, threw three innings, and gave up two hits and a walk and struck out two batters. Winning pitcher, Austin Tommasini, threw the last four innings, giving up four hits, two walks, and a run while striking out three batters. MC stole eight bases and committed one error. Final score, Madison Central, 8 Ridgeland 1.

MC had won 10 consecutive games to start the season. The three most important facets of the game--pitching, fielding, and hitting--had simply been outstanding.

MC welcomed the North Pike Jaguars to Madison on March 18 for their second encounter of the season. MC had won the first game 10-0, and this game would turn out to be similar as the Madison Jags won 12-3. North Pike scored a run in the first inning and two in the sixth while MC scored in four innings including three runs in the second inning and six in the fifth. MC hitters stroked 14 hits including two home runs. Gatlin Sanders went four-for-four batting, drove in five runs, and scored two. Connor Nation went three-for-four, drove in three runs, and scored one. Four other Jags drove in one run each. MC runners stole five bases, and North Pike runners stole four. Uncharacteristically, MC fielders committed four fielding errors while North Pike committed three. Two MC pitchers combined to throw a one-hitter. Starting and winning pitcher, Braden Montgomery, gave up two runs, a hit, and two walks while striking out four batters over four innings. Connor Nation pitched the last three innings and surrendered a run while giving up a walk and striking out five batters.

March 19 found the Jags in Philadelphia facing the Newton County Cougars in the first game of a doubleheader. MC run-ruled the Cougars 13-1 in five innings. It was a very unusual game, as each team managed only four hits. Nothing went well for the Cougars as walks and errors determined the outcome of the game. Seven Newton pitchers walked nine Jags, and MC pitcher Ranard Grace walked none. MC didn't make an error; the Cougars made three. Grace pitched five innings and gave up four hits and one run while striking out nine batters.

In the second game, MC faced Neshoba Central and defeated the Rockets 15-3. The Jags were ahead 10-3 going into the top half of the seventh inning when they scored five runs to put the game away. MC managed 15 hits, including three doubles, as they accumulated 14 RBIs. Creek Robertson hit a double while going two-for-four at the plate and driving in three runs. Braden Montgomery went two-for-four and drove in two runs while Hunter Hines went three-for-four, stroked a double, and drove in four runs. MC batters combined to hit .469 off six NC pitchers. The Rockets connected for only four hits, all singles. MC stole four bases, and NC stole one. Three MC pitchers, Eric, Gibbs, Brendon Minor, and winning pitcher, Austin Tommasini, gave up one hit each. Minor gave up two runs and Tommasini one.

MC returned home to face Northwest Rankin again on March 22. The Jags' ace pitcher, Braden Montgomery, threw a jewel of a two-hit shutout at the Cougars as MC won 9-0. Montgomery's teammates supported him by stroking 10 hits, stealing three bases, and playing errorless ball in the field. The Jags led 3-0 going into the sixth inning when they exploded for six runs. Hunter Hines went two-for-four at the dish, homered, and drove in four runs. Creek Robertson went three-for-three, hit a double, and drove in two runs.

St. Joseph Catholic High School is located less than two miles from MC in the city of Madison. The St. Jo Bruins faced the Jaguars on March 29 at Madison Central. Braden Montgomery was back on the hill for the Jags, and he was outstanding again. Montgomery threw four innings, giving up two walks and a run while striking out seven batters as the Jags downed the Bruins 9-1. Montgomery helped his own cause by hitting a double that drove in three runs. Montgomery is human; he made MC's only error. Connor Nation pitched an inning, and Austin Tommasini pitched two and closed out the game. Neither Nation nor Tommasini gave up a run. Hunter Hines hit three doubles and scored three runs. Jag batters managed a total of nine hits. Losing pitcher, Cooper Chaplain, started for the Bruins and threw five innings, giving up eight hits, six walks, and eight runs while striking out two Jags. Hudson Sandifer threw an inning for the Bruins, giving up a hit and a run while striking out two batters.

At this point in the 2021 season Madison Central had won 15 games and lost none. The Jags were about to play their first district opponent.

The Jags went to nearby Jackson to play the Murrah Mustangs on April 1 in the first of a three-game series. MC got off to a great start in district competition by throttling Murrah 18-1 in a game ended by the mercy rule after five innings. The Mustangs managed only one hit and one run as MC's Ranard Grace spun a gem of a game. Seventeen Jags batters produced 11 hits and worked Mustang pitchers for 11 bases on balls, while Jag base runners stole 11 bases, and Mustang fielders committed four errors.

The next day Murrah and MC played a doubleheader in Madison. The first game turned out to be the same song, second verse, only worse. MC won 23-0. The Jags scored 23 runs in the bottom of the first inning, and the game ended after Murrah didn't score in the top of the second. Sixteen MC batters produced 23 hits, and MC base runners stole five bases. Brendon Minor pitched two perfect innings and struck out five Mustangs. Murrah sent two pitchers to the mound; the first one didn't register an out.

The second game of the doubleheader was just another verse to the same song. MC won 13-1 in four innings. Winning pitcher, Eric Gibbs, pitched all four innings for the Jags and gave up a hit and a run while striking out nine batters. Eleven MC batters produced 10 hits. Rashard Grace went two-for-three at the plate and drove in three runs. MC base runners stole five bases. While several starters were sitting this one out, MC fielders made three errors.

MC stood 3-0 in the district, having run-ruled Murrah three times by a combined score of 54-2. The Jags would next take on district rivals, the Warren Central Vikings, in a three-game set.

The first game was played in Vicksburg on April 6, and the visitors topped the home-standing Vikings 6-0 behind the one-hit shutout pitching of Braden Montgomery and Connor Nation. Montgomery threw six innings and gave up no hits and struck out 16 batters. Nation threw the last inning and gave up a hit and struck out three batters. Winning pitcher, Montgomery, helped his cause by getting two hits and driving in a run. Hunter Hines hit a homer and drove in three runs. Three Vikings pitchers combined to give up 10 hits and four walks while registering only one strikeout. Both teams fielded well; the Vikings committed one error and the Jags none.

The second game was also played in Vicksburg on Saturday, April 10. This time the home team got run-ruled 16-3. Beau Bryans and Austin Tommasini combined to give up five hits and three runs over five innings. Madison Central hitters struck 17 hits including home runs by Braden Montgomery and Hunter Hines. Gatlin Sanders drove in four runs, and both Hines and Jeff Cook drove in three. This was the Jaguars' 20th game of the season, and they had yet to lose.

The third game of the series was played at MC, and the Jags prevailed again, run-ruling the Vikings 13-2 in five innings. Ranard Grace threw all five innings for the Jags, giving up two runs on five hits and two walks while striking out nine batters. Meanwhile, MC's bats were hot as the Jags totaled 12 hits off three WC pitchers. Braden Montgomery drove in two runs, and Connor Chisolm and Connor Nation drove in three each. The Jags were 6-0 in the district with another district rival, Clinton, next on the schedule.

On April 13 the Jaguars and the Clinton High School Arrows squared off on the Arrows' home field in the first game of a three-game series. The Jaguars dispatched the Arrows 11-3. The Montgomery-Nation pitching combination clicked again. Montgomery, who pitched four innings, and Nation, who threw three, combined to give up only three hits and three runs. Montgomery went three-for-four at the plate and drove in three runs, but again he proved to be human; he gave up a home run to Grant Holmes. Hunter Hines went one-for-three at the plate and drove in three runs. Arrow fielders committed six errors behind four Clinton pitchers, who gave up 11 hits and five walks.

Madison Central hosted Clinton in the second and third games of the series on April 16 and 17. In the first game, the Jags scored five runs in the second inning and five in the sixth to run-rule the Arrows 10-0. Ranard Grace was developing a habit of throwing complete games. He shutout the Arrows, scattering five singles and a double while walking two batters and striking out four. Ross Highfill hit a homer and drove in four runs for the Jags. MC didn't make an error, while Clinton made two.

The third game was a different kind of affair. The Arrows led 3-2 going into the bottom of the third inning when MC scored two runs to take the lead. In the bottom of the fourth the Jags added another run. Final score, Jags 5, Arrows 3. Beau Bryans started for the Jags, threw 1/3 of an inning and gave up a hit and two runs while walking four batters. Connor Nation relieved and gave up a hit and four walks over two innings. Winning pitcher, Austin Tommasini, threw the final 4 2/3 innings and gave up a walk and a run. Gatlin Sanders went three-for-four at the plate, hit a double, and drove in two runs. With this victory, MC won the district championship with a 9-0 record.

The Jags would play three non-conference games, two against Brandon and one against Oxford before the state playoffs began.

The visiting Brandon High School Bulldogs shocked the Jags on April 23 as they handed MC its first loss of the season. MC enjoyed the lead only once, 2-1 after three innings. For once the Montgomery-Nation combination didn't succeed. Montgomery gave up four hits, four walks, and a run in three innings of work. The Bulldogs scored four runs in the fourth inning and two more in the sixth off Nation. Final score, Bulldogs 7, Jags 6. The Dogs collected nine hits as K.K. Clark went three-for-five, scored a run, and drove in two runs. Two other Bulldogs each drove in a run, and seven Bulldogs scored single runs. MC managed only seven hits off three Brandon pitchers. Andrew Jones started for the Dogs, pitched 1/3 of an inning, and gave up a hit. Winning pitcher, Josh Sullivan, relieved Jones and threw six innings, giving up six hits and six runs while walking four batters and striking out five. Will Martin pitched the last 2/3 of an inning and gave up nothing. Hunter Hines went three-for-four at the plate, hit a double, and drove in three runs. Both teams made three errors. With the loss, the Jags stood 24-1.

On May 26 the Jags retaliated against the Bulldogs, blasting them 15-4 in Brandon. The Jags brought their big bats, this time registering 13 hits including two doubles and three homers. Ross Highfill, who was heating as the playoffs approached, went three-for-four at the plate, hitting two home runs and driving in five runs. Creek Robertson chipped in, hitting a double and a home run and driving in five runs. Winning pitcher, the reliable Ranard Grace, threw six innings, giving up five hits and four runs while striking out 11 batters. Eric Gibbs threw the final inning for the Jags and gave up a hit while striking out a batter. Brandon sent five pitchers to the mound. Drew Tucker, who came in with one out in the first inning and threw 2 1/3 innings, giving up three hits, four walks, and four runs, was charged with the loss. Brandon batters registered eight hits including three doubles and a home run. Jonah Katsaboulas led Brandon at the plate, going two-for-four, hitting a double and a homer, and driving in two runs.

The Lafayette County High School Commodores out of Oxford faced MC in the final game before the playoffs began. The Jags shutout the Commodores 10-0 on April 27. Braden Montgomery, Brendon Minor, and Austin Tommasini combined to give up six hits and four walks while striking out nine and giving up no runs. Minor, who threw three innings, was the winning pitcher. Braden Montgomery hit two homers and drove in five runs. Lafayette threw five pitchers. Losing pitcher, Sam Larson, went two innings and gave up four runs on three hits and a walk.

Madison Central ended the regular season 26-1 overall and 9-0 in their district. There were high expectations for the state playoffs. In each round of the playoffs, the teams play a best two-of-three series.

In the 6A tournament MC drew a first-round bye and then played the South Panola Tigers, who had defeated Southaven in the first round two games to none. On May 6, MC played the Tigers in Madison. The Jags run-ruled the Tigers 26-5 in five innings. Ross Highfill went four-for-four at the plate, hit a double, drove in six runs, and scored a run. Braden Montgomery went three-for-four, hit two doubles, and knocked in three runs. Five Jags got two or more hits, and 10 Jags drove in at least one run. Montgomery was the winning pitcher, going four innings, giving up four hits, two runs, and striking out seven batters. Eric Gibbs threw the last inning, giving up three hits and three runs. South Panola used three pitchers who combined to give up 16 hits, 11 walks, and 26 runs. Five errors did not help the Tigers' cause.

The next day the two teams played in Batesville. The home-field advantage didn't kick in for the Tigers as the Jags run-ruled them again 11-0 in five innings. Ranard Grace and Austin Tommasini combined for the shutout. Grace gave up the Tigers' only hit, a single. Ross Highfill hit a home run and drove in three runs. Montgomery hit a double and drove in a run, and Gatlin Sanders went three-for-four, drove in a run, and scored three runs.

MC advanced to the third round against Starkville. The Starkville Yellowjackets had defeated both Hernando and Lewisburg two games to none to advance to the third round.

There was little drama in the first game as the Jags throttled the Jackets 14-1 in a game ended by the mercy rule after 4 ½ innings. On May 13, playing on their home field, the Montgomery-Nation combination clicked again. The Jackets' only hit was a run-scoring double by Ethan Pulliam. Montgomery threw four innings, giving up a hit, four walks, and the only run. Nation threw an inning, striking out three batters and giving up nothing. Meanwhile, the Jags' bats were hot. Leadoff hitter, Gatlin Sanders, went three-for-four, drove in a run, and scored three runs. Second-place hitter, Ross Highfill, went three-for-four, hit a homer, and knocked in three runs. Nation went two-for-four, hit a homer, and drove in four runs. Five Jags stole a base. MC made one error, while Starkville committed five.

In the second game played in Starkville, May 14, the Jackets cooled the Jags and saddled them with their second loss of the season, 3-2. The Jackets' winning pitcher, Ethan Pulliam, pitched six innings, scattering five hits, all singles, while allowing four walks and two runs and striking out seven batters. Jackson Owen threw the final inning for the Jackets, walking two batters and striking out two. MC's starting pitcher, Ranard Grace, had another good game. He threw 4 1/3 innings giving up three hits, four walks, and two runs while striking out seven batters and hitting two. Losing pitcher, Austin Tommasini, finished for the Jags, striking out four batters while giving up two hits, two walks, and the winning run.

The next day the Jaguars were back in Madison, playing for their season. Despite having a 29-2 record, another loss to Starkville would end their season without a state championship. The resilient Jags showed up and showed out for their fans. In a game stopped after 4 ½ innings by the mercy rule, the Jags subdued the Jackets, 19-1. In an unusual occurrence, Connor Nation started on the mound for the Jags. He threw one inning, faced four batters, gave up a hit, and struck out three hitters. Brendon Minor threw the final four innings, giving up a hit, three walks, and a run while striking out seven batters. After leaving the mound, Nation played the rest of the game in the field, going three-for-three at the plate, hitting three doubles and driving in three runs and scoring two. The Jags' 17 hits included five doubles, a triple, and a home run. Six players drove in two or more runs. Starkville used seven pitchers, none of whom lasted more than an inning.

On May 24 and 25, MC played the Tupelo High School Golden Wave in a home and away series. Coming into the matchup the Wave boasted a 27-8 record including a 6-3 district mark. MC was 30-2 including a 9-0 district mark.

The first game was a thriller as two of the state's best pitchers, Braden Montogomery and Hunter Elliott, faced off in a classic pitchers' duel. Montgomery won the battle, shutting out the Wave on two hits and two walks while striking out 12 batters. Elliott gave up seven hits and one walk while striking out 10 batters. MC won 2-0 off solo homers by Connor Nation and Braden Montgomery in the first and sixth innings. Both Montgomery and Elliott would earn Freshman All-American honors in 2022, Montgomery at Stanford and Elliott at Ole Miss.

The second game played in Tupelo proved to be another barnburner. Trailing by four runs going into the bottom of the seventh inning, the Wave put three runs on the scoreboard, and MC escaped with a 10-9 victory. Winning pitcher, Ranard Grace, threw five-plus innings, giving up eight hits, a walk, and six runs while striking out six hitters. Austin Tommasini followed Grace and gave up three runs on two hits and three walks while striking out one batter. Mason Morris went two-for-four at the plate for the Wave, hit a double and a triple, drove in five runs, and scored two. The first two hitters in the Jags' lineup, Gatlin Sanders and Ross Highfill, combined to get three hits, drove in two runs, and scored three. Connor Nation went two-for-four, including a double, and drove in three runs. Tupelo's cause was hurt by five errors and MC's five stolen bases.

With the sweep of Tupelo, Madison Central was 32-2. They then faced the Northwest Rankin Cougars 27-7 in a best two-of-three matchup at Trustmark Park in Pearl for the 6A state championship. On June 4, the Cougars encountered MC's daunting pitching combination of Braden Montgomery and Connor Nation. Northwest used a combination of three pitchers, Nick Monistere, Blake Summerlin and Powell Ingram, who made the Jags' 3-2 victory an instant classic. The two teams' pitchers gave up a total of four hits, two for each team. The Jags' Hunter Hines hit a double, and Nations hit a triple. Brady Thomas and Brice Ainsworth hit singles for the Cougars. Montgomery and Nation faced 27 batters and struck out 17. Cougar pitchers faced 31 batters and struck out four. The Cougars led 1-0 going into the top of the sixth inning when MC scored two runs. In the bottom of the inning, Northwest scored a run to tie the game. In the top of the seventh, MC scored a run, and the Cougars failed to score in the bottom of the inning. The Jags had a chance to win the championship the next day.

The Jags run-ruled the Cougars 11-1 in the June 5 championship game. MC scored in all five innings and put crooked numbers on the scoreboard in three. Northwest scored its only run in the first inning. Winning pitcher, Ranard Grace, threw all five innings, giving up five hits and two walks while striking out three batters and allowing a run. MC batters managed 12 hits and eight walks while MC base runners stole five bases off four Cougar pitchers. Five different batters hit a total of five singles for the Cougars.

In July 2021 the Madison Central High School Jaguars were named Baseball America's High School Team of the Year. Baseball America's high school team rankings are produced by a poll of representatives from the National High School Baseball Coaches Association.

Led by Head Coach Patrick Robey, the Jags finished the season with a 34-2 record, which was good enough to win Mississippi's classification 6A State Championship. MC went undefeated in district play and outscored opposing teams 422-64. Coach Robey said the following about this team and their school.

> We were very talented, and you've got to be to finish No. 1 and win a state championship. But it goes a lot further than that. We had a group of very selfless kids who loved each other and didn't care who got the credit. They just wanted to win. You take a talented team with a team-first attitude and families who care about the team, that culminates into a very successful year.
>
> Offensively, we had some guys who could hit for power, some

guys who could run, a lot of senior leaders who had a lot of at-bats under their belts and were all tough outs. There were three or four juniors in that group who were very key contributors. We had a group of guys who really enjoyed playing the game; they enjoyed being around each other; they didn't like to lose, whether it was checkers, ping pong, or baseball, so that was a pretty good combination.

They loved each other; they truly did. I really believe God rewards faith, sacrifice and obedience, and those guys were not afraid to sacrifice for each other. They knew their roles, and they accepted their roles. They knew they couldn't all be starting shortstop; they couldn't all hit third. But those guys have played baseball together for a long time, and whether it was ping pong or baseball, they wanted to compete hard.

We have a winning culture and a successful school. They want to win in the classroom, on the athletic field, on the basketball court, so the competitive nature is in our kids. Are we going to win a state championship every single year? Absolutely not. But our kids know they have to work hard to maintain the level of success we've had at Madison Central. We've got some really talented players coming back, (and) we'll have a chance to make a good run next year too.

The quality of school baseball starts with Mississippi high schools. When I talked with Coach Michael Avalon of Pearl River Community College, he said that in his opinion, based on population, Mississippi has the best high school baseball in the country. On June 15, 2023, I interviewed Coach Patrick Robey about his 2021 team and asked him what he thought about the overall quality of high school baseball in the state. He said it was good and getting better. He noted that several baseball programs in metropolitan centers have been excellent for years and that less-populated areas are now producing excellent teams. Baseball coaching talent is now widely spread in the state, and there is good community support for baseball at the high school level as well as the community college and four-year college levels. When I asked him what he thought about travel ball, he said it is a mixed blessing. It provides some good coaching and helps to develop talent. However, it is costly and may cause some players to experience burnout at an early age. Overall, it is good for high school baseball.

In discussing the 2021 championship season, Coach Robey had many good things to say about the team and the support it received from Madison Central High School and the Madison community. The school's administrators, teachers, staff and students were solidly behind the coaches and the players as was the community. The baseball facilities were excellent, and the coaches had everything they needed to create an environment that was conducive to a baseball championship. Good facilities help team members take pride in their school. The players were simply super they loved each other and put the team and winning above themselves. They enjoyed the game, accepted coaching and had loads of talent.

Coach Robey said that team leadership was of tremendous importance, and this team had an abundance of it. Three team leaders were especially impressive: Braden Montgomery, Hunter Hines, and Ross Highfill. He noted that Montgomery and Hinds were very different, personality-wise, but they had great work ethics and were excellent teammates. Montgomery was exuberant and as demonstrative as a kid enjoying himself. But he was also very disciplined and had a plan for improvement that he stuck to. Hines was more laid back, but he also worked to be the best he could be. Highfill was a catcher and, as catchers tend to be, a good leader.

There was never a turning point in the season when greatness emerged. Coach Robey said the team simply took things day-by-day without highs or lows. He gave an example, saying after their first loss of the season to Brandon 7-6, they were not down and showed their resilience by defeating the Bulldogs 15-4 the next day.

When asked what the biggest challenge to high school baseball was, Coach Robey answered: team chemistry. That is, maintaining good team chemistry, which can so easily be affected by social media. It doesn't help a team when it loses a game and a particular player who had played well is highlighted on social media. Any loss is a team loss, and therefore a loss even to a player who had a good game.

I asked Coach Robey if he thought his 2021 team was the best Mississippi high school baseball team ever. He said that a good argument could be made that they were, but there have been many excellent Mississippi high school baseball teams over the years. If you look at the statistics, the writer agrees that a good argument could be made that they were indeed the best.

In 2023 several of the 2021 Jags continued their baseball careers at the college level.

Braden Montgomery pitched and played outfield for the Jags. He was named First-Team All-American in 2021 by Baseball America. As a pitcher, Montgomery posted a .74 ERA, won nine games, and lost none. He also batted .479, hit seven doubles, five triples, seven home runs, and drove in 50 runs. In June of 2023, Montgomery pitched and played outfield for Stanford. He was named PAC 12 Freshman of the Year in 2022 and Freshman All-American by Collegiate Baseball, Perfect Game and NCBWA. Stanford made it to the NCAA Division I College World Series in both 2022 and 2023. Braden Montgomery is a big reason why. Montgomery transferred to Texas A&M for the 2024 season. He batted .322, posted a .454 on base percentage and a .733 slugging percentage while hitting 27 home runs and driving in 85 runs for the Aggies. Texas A&M finished second in the Men's College World Series. Unfortunately, Mongomery did not get to play in the MCWS. He suffered an ankle injury in the first game of a Super Regional against Oregon and did not play in the MCWS. Montgomery was drafted by #12 in the first round of the 2024 Major League Baseball Draft.

First baseman Hunter Hines batted .465, hit 12 doubles, and seven home runs while driving in 55 runs. Hines signed with Mississippi State University, where he was named All-SEC and Freshman All-American in 2022. During the 2023 season Hines led the Bulldogs with 22 home runs and drove in 61 runs. He was named a Ferriss Trophy finalist (most outstanding college baseball player in Mississippi) and First-Team All-SEC.

The Jags' Ranard and Rashard Grace are twins. Ranard pitched, and Rashard was a role player at third base and as a catcher. Ranard Grace won 10 games and lost none as a pitcher while posting a 1.55 ERA. The twins signed with Southern University, and Ranard was redshirted during the 2022 season. Reshard saw limited duty as a catcher for Southern during the 2022 and 2023 seasons. He batted .364 in 13 games in 2023. In 14 appearances in relief, Ranard posted a record of no wins, no losses, and one save.

Connor Nation pitched and played in the outfield for the Jags. He batted .342, hit four home runs, and drove in 42 runs during the 2021 campaign. After playing two years for Hinds Community College, Nation announced in May 2023 that he had signed to continue his baseball career at Louisiana Tech.

Catcher Ross Highfill hit .400 and drove in 45 runs for the 2021 Jags. He saw limited actions during both the 2023 and 2024 seasons for the Mississippi State Bulldogs.

Infielder Connor Chisolm, who played the 2022 and 2023 seasons at Hinds Community College, committed to Ole Miss in the spring of 2023. Chisolm batted .316 in 2022 and .419 in 2023. During the 2023 season Chisolm hit well and with power; he generated an excellent 1.237 on-base plus slugging (OPS) statistic.

Shortstop Creek Robertson signed with Southern Mississippi and was redshirted in the 2022 season. In 2023 he appeared in 19 games.

APPENDIX

Mississippi State University 2021 Baseball Statistics
Ole Miss 2022 Baseball Statistics
Pearl River Community College 2022 Baseball Statistics
Madison Central High School 2021 Baseball Statistics

JAMES R. CROCKETT

2021 Mississippi State Baseball
Overall Statistics for Mississippi State (as of Jun 30, 2021)
(All games Sorted by Batting avg)

Record: 50-18 Home: 30-9 Away: 12-4 Neutral: 8-5 SEC: 20-10

Player	avg	gp-gs	ab	r	h	2b	3b	hr	rbi	tb	slg%	bb	hp	so	gdp	ob%	sf	sh	sb-att	po	a	e	fld%
5 Allen, Tanner	.383	67-67	261	72	100	19	5	11	66	162	.621	23	16	35	5	.456	5	0	11-14	90	5	1	.990
4 Jordan, Rowdey	.323	68-68	269	74	87	22	4	10	45	147	.546	29	17	43	3	.417	4	0	9-10	123	2	2	.984
19 Tanner, Logan	.287	67-66	244	45	70	13	0	15	53	128	.525	39	0	48	11	.382	2	0	0-1	700	30	4	.995
3 Dubrule, Scotty	.278	67-61	223	42	62	6	0	0	31	68	.305	38	1	29	6	.384	1	4	6-11	105	123	3	.987
6 James, Kamren	.264	67-67	250	50	66	12	0	12	61	114	.456	31	7	60	2	.354	6	0	20-23	35	80	14	.891
20 Hancock, Luke	.262	68-68	233	40	61	4	0	10	63	95	.408	47	8	17	7	.393	7	0	3-3	262	20	1	.996
25 McDonald, Kyte	.389	12-1	18	5	7	4	0	1	6	14	.778	1	0	2	0	.421	0	0	0-0	0	0	0	.000
33 Cumbest, Brad	.306	49-33	121	23	37	9	2	5	21	65	.537	9	5	33	2	.372	2	0	2-2	39	2	2	.953
50 Pimentel, Brandon	.286	10-1	14	3	4	0	0	1	6	7	.500	3	0	6	1	.412	0	0	0-0	19	2	0	1.000
9 Jordan, Landon	.281	12-9	32	2	9	2	0	0	5	11	.344	6	1	8	1	.410	0	1	2-2	3	13	0	1.000
12 Meche, Davis	.250	10-0	12	4	3	1	0	0	1	4	.333	2	1	4	0	.400	0	0	0-0	2	7	0	1.000
11 Clark, Kellum	.237	33-26	93	22	22	7	1	5	16	46	.495	14	3	29	1	.355	0	0	1-1	10	1	1	.917
31 Leggett, Tanner	.235	42-19	81	18	19	4	0	1	10	26	.321	10	3	25	3	.337	1	4	5-7	24	36	7	.896
43 Forsythe, Lane	.231	59-58	186	30	43	5	0	1	21	51	.274	23	3	56	3	.321	3	3	1-1	55	119	13	.930
8 McGowan, Drew	.212	24-8	33	6	7	2	0	0	7	9	.273	8	1	3	1	.364	2	0	2-3	12	1	0	1.000
36 Skinner, Brayland	.205	50-21	83	19	17	3	1	1	10	25	.301	12	4	23	1	.333	0	5	6-7	43	1	0	1.000
10 Hatcher, Josh	.189	58-39	148	17	28	8	0	2	12	42	.284	8	3	31	3	.245	0	1	6-7	241	25	3	.989
44 Garner, Kace	.154	11-0	13	4	2	1	0	0	3	3	.231	3	0	3	0	.313	0	0	0-0	19	0	0	1.000
Totals	.276	68	2314	476	644	122	13	75	437	1017	.439	306	73	455	50	.375	33	13	74-92	1811	515	60	.975
Opponents	.220	68	2247	304	494	77	7	72	280	801	.356	266	49	817	32	.314	13	22	37-56	1737	645	89	.964

LOB - Team (528), Opp (482). DPs turned - Team (45), Opp (57). CI - Team (0), Opp (2). IBB - Team (8), Allen 3, James 1, Clark 1, Tanner 1, Hatcher 1, Hancock 1, Opp (8). Picked off - Jordan, R. 1.

(All games Sorted by Earned run avg)

Player	era	w-l	app	gs	cg	sho	sv	ip	h	r	er	bb	so	2b	3b	hr	b/avg	wp	hp	bk	sfa	sha
24 Bednar, Will	3.12	9-1	19	16	0	0/4	0	92.1	72	35	32	26	139	14	1	12	.214	2	8	1	3	2
28 MacLeod, Christian	5.23	6-6	19	19	0	0/2	0	82.2	79	55	48	33	113	9	0	16	.248	8	6	0	1	5
38 Alford, Kole	0.00	0-0	1	0	0	0/0	0	0.1	1	0	0	1	1	0	0	0	.500	0	0	0	0	0
51 Carmouche, Dylan	1.23	0-0	9	0	0	0/1	0	7.1	6	2	1	3	11	1	0	0	.222	1	1	0	1	0
23 Sims, Landon	1.44	5-0	25	0	0	0/4	13	56.1	29	9	9	15	100	6	0	2	.149	3	1	0	0	2
15 Smith, Cade	2.40	3-0	10	1	0	0/0	0	15.0	6	5	4	10	20	1	0	0	.115	0	1	0	0	0
32 Stinnett, Parker	2.41	1-0	17	1	0	0/2	1	18.2	8	5	5	16	31	2	0	1	.125	7	4	1	0	0
18 Patrick, Chase	2.57	0-0	19	0	0	0/0	0	14.0	14	5	4	6	10	1	0	3	.286	4	1	0	0	1
48 Harding, Houston	3.05	7-2	21	8	0	0/1	0	62.0	50	25	21	21	67	8	0	8	.218	4	2	1	1	3
35 Johnson, Preston	3.82	4-0	22	0	0	0/3	0	33.0	25	16	14	14	50	3	1	4	.212	0	4	0	1	1
7 Smith, Brandon	4.12	4-4	21	2	0	0/2	1	39.1	36	23	18	12	43	6	1	5	.235	5	1	0	1	3
29 Koestler, Carlisle	4.12	3-0	11	2	0	0/0	0	19.2	20	9	9	7	23	3	0	2	.260	3	3	0	1	1
2 Hunt, KC	4.80	0-0	14	0	0	0/2	0	15.0	15	10	8	8	14	2	0	1	.268	8	2	0	1	1
17 Simmons, Stone	4.81	1-1	19	0	0	0/0	2	24.1	22	15	13	8	29	4	0	1	.234	2	1	0	0	1
39 Tepper, Mikey	5.25	2-0	11	2	0	0/1	0	12.0	8	8	7	9	14	2	0	1	.174	6	0	2	0	0
14 Self, Riley	5.40	0-0	7	0	0	0/2	0	5.0	9	4	3	4	7	1	0	0	.375	0	0	0	0	0
27 Fristoe, Jackson	5.69	3-3	16	13	0	0/1	0	49.0	41	32	31	37	68	4	3	9	.223	5	4	1	0	1
37 Cerantola, Eric	5.71	0-1	10	4	0	0/0	0	17.1	13	11	11	11	24	0	1	2	.206	4	6	0	0	0
40 Forrester, Jaxen	6.00	0-0	3	0	0	0/1	0	3.0	2	2	2	2	1	1	0	0	.200	2	0	0	1	0
26 Lovett, Xavier	6.75	0-0	6	0	0	0/1	0	4.0	3	4	3	2	1	2	0	0	.188	1	1	0	0	0
45 Tullar, Cam	6.86	0-0	23	0	0	0/1	1	19.2	23	15	15	11	25	5	0	1	.291	2	1	0	2	1
55 Price, Spencer	7.36	1-0	9	0	0	0/1	0	7.1	5	6	6	5	13	0	0	2	.179	2	1	0	0	0
47 Talley, Drew	9.00	0-0	4	0	0	0/1	0	3.0	4	3	3	1	7	2	0	0	.357	0	0	0	0	0
13 Rokose, Davis	10.80	0-0	4	0	0	0/0	0	3.1	2	4	4	4	6	0	0	1	.167	0	1	0	0	0
Totals	4.04	50-18	68	68	0	8/6	18	603.2	494	304	271	266	817	77	7	72	.220	69	49	6	13	22
Opponents	6.50	18-50	68	68	3	1/0	4	579.0	644	476	418	306	455	122	13	75	.278	69	73	6	33	13

PB - Team (5), Tanner 4, Hancock 1, Opp (8). Pickoffs - Team (2), Harding 1, Patrick 1, Opp (1). SBA/ATT - Tanner (31-42), MacLeod (7-13), Bednar (9-11), Hancock (6-7), Harding (6-7), Patrick (0-4), Tepper (3-3), Fristoe (1-3), Johnson (2-2), Cerantola (2-2), Stinnett (2-2), Talley (0-1), Tullar (0-1), Smith, C. (1-1), Hunt (0-1), Carmouche (1-1), Sims (1-1), Simmons (1-1), Self (0-1), Price (1-1).

WHEN MISSISSIPPI SCHOOLED AMERICA IN BASEBALL

2022 Ole Miss Baseball
Overall Statistics for Ole Miss (as of Jun 26, 2022)
(All games Sorted by Batting avg)

Record: 42-23 Home: 19-12 Away: 15-8 Neutral: 8-3 SEC: 14-16

Player	avg	gp-gs	ab	r	h	2b	3b	hr	rbi	tb	slg%	bb	hp	so	gdp	ob%	sf	sh	sb-att	po	a	e	fld%
20 Calvin Harris	.336	43-29	110	26	37	7	1	3	21	55	.500	15	1	31	0	.417	1	0	2-3	162	10	2	.989
35 Kevin Graham	.335	47-47	194	32	65	11	0	11	51	109	.562	9	4	47	3	.371	3	0	1-2	78	1	0	1.000
8 Justin Bench	.316	65-65	256	62	81	17	1	4	42	112	.438	25	17	43	6	.409	3	1	4-9	94	44	4	.972
25 Tim Elko	.300	65-65	240	63	72	10	0	24	75	154	.642	43	1	84	7	.407	1	0	2-2	413	32	2	.996
12 Kemp Alderman	.286	61-58	203	41	58	15	0	11	45	106	.522	29	6	58	2	.388	2	0	2-3	10	0	3	.769
7 Jacob Gonzalez	.273	65-65	242	67	66	9	3	18	52	135	.558	50	5	32	7	.405	2	1	4-6	70	137	14	.937
6 Reagan Burford	.260	38-30	104	24	27	8	0	3	19	44	.423	11	1	30	3	.322	5	0	2-3	21	33	11	.831
9 Hayden Leatherwood	.250	51-38	132	24	33	7	1	5	17	57	.432	10	3	43	2	.317	0	0	0-0	60	3	4	.940
1 Peyton Chatagnier	.248	62-61	230	47	57	12	2	11	45	106	.461	18	8	63	3	.317	6	1	6-9	91	106	3	.985
16 TJ McCants	.236	60-54	178	34	42	5	1	8	31	73	.410	22	3	65	1	.324	4	2	10-14	104	0	0	1.000
13 Hayden Dunhurst	.231	56-54	169	30	39	8	0	6	30	65	.385	36	3	69	3	.370	3	0	0-0	517	35	8	.986
54 Tywone Malone	.444	7-0	9	3	4	0	0	2	4	10	1.111	1	0	3	0	.500	0	0	0-0	3	1	0	1.000
33 Ben Van Cleve	.302	35-9	43	10	13	5	0	0	4	18	.419	8	1	8	2	.415	1	0	0-0	0	0	0	.000
28 Banks Tolley	.267	26-0	15	5	4	2	0	0	3	6	.400	2	0	5	0	.353	0	0	1-2	11	0	0	1.000
4 Knox Loposer	.222	9-1	9	3	2	1	0	0	4	3	.333	1	2	3	0	.417	0	0	0-0	25	1	0	1.000
17 John Kramer	.214	12-2	14	3	3	0	0	2	2	9	.643	3	1	6	0	.389	0	0	0-0	0	0	0	.000
3 Hudson Sapp	.200	9-1	10	3	2	1	0	0	2	3	.300	2	1	2	0	.385	0	0	0-0	2	0	0	1.000
40 Garrett Wood	.152	28-6	33	5	5	2	0	0	1	7	.212	10	0	14	0	.349	0	0	0-0	3	12	2	.882
2 Derek Diamond	.000	2-0	0	1	0	0	0	0	0	0	.000	0	0	0	0	.000	0	0	0-0	8	7	0	1.000
Totals	.278	65	2191	483	610	120	9	108	448	1072	.489	295	57	606	39	.374	31	5	34-53	1693	464	61	.972
Opponents	.236	65	2157	295	510	97	7	72	275	837	.388	234	54	682	22	.325	12	15	38-55	1654	495	61	.972

LOB - Team (442), Opp (486). DPs turned - Team (26), Opp (49). CI - Team (2), C. Harris 1, H. Dunhurst 1.

(All games Sorted by Earned run avg)

Player	era	w-l	app	gs	cg	sho	sv	ip	h	r	er	bb	so	2b	3b	hr	b/avg	wp	hp	bk	sfa	sha
43 Cole Baker	0.00	1-0	2	0	0	0/0	0	1.1	0	0	0	1	2	0	0	0	.000	0	0	0	0	0
23 Josh Mallitz	1.45	1-0	17	0	0	0/1	2	31.0	19	6	5	12	48	3	0	3	.171	2	1	1	0	0
26 Hunter Elliott	2.70	5-3	20	12	0	0/1	0	80.0	57	29	24	34	102	10	0	4	.201	6	10	0	1	4
45 Mason Nichols	2.84	1-0	21	0	0	0/0	0	31.2	22	12	10	12	41	4	0	4	.193	1	3	1	1	0
56 Jack Washburn	3.35	5-2	15	9	0	0/0	0	40.1	33	20	15	23	42	10	0	4	.220	5	9	2	1	1
18 Mitch Murrell	3.52	0-0	9	0	0	0/0	0	7.2	8	4	3	5	11	2	0	1	.276	4	2	0	0	1
44 Dylan DeLucia	3.68	8-2	21	12	2	1/1	1	95.1	87	44	39	26	105	13	1	14	.238	3	9	0	3	1
24 Jackson Kimbrell	4.00	1-0	8	0	0	0/0	0	9.0	3	4	4	4	12	0	0	0	.103	0	3	0	1	0
27 John Gaddis	4.20	4-2	17	7	0	0/0	1	49.1	50	24	23	19	49	9	1	7	.260	1	2	0	1	1
37 Brandon Johnson	4.32	1-3	24	0	0	0/0	12	41.2	31	21	20	21	71	3	0	8	.199	4	2	1	0	0
19 Matt Parenteau	4.76	0-0	8	0	0	0/0	0	5.2	7	4	3	4	7	0	0	2	.280	0	1	1	0	0
39 Jack Dougherty	4.91	4-3	17	4	0	0/1	2	44.0	48	24	24	16	61	11	0	4	.273	3	4	0	1	3
34 Riley Maddox	5.24	2-1	14	0	0	0/0	0	22.1	26	13	13	9	16	7	1	1	.289	2	2	0	0	0
21 Drew McDaniel	6.06	5-3	15	7	0	0/0	0	32.2	32	28	22	23	45	5	1	5	.244	4	2	0	1	2
2 Derek Diamond	6.89	4-4	16	14	0	0/0	0	65.1	81	53	50	13	57	18	3	14	.292	3	3	1	1	2
38 Logan Savell	9.00	0-0	2	0	0	0/0	0	2.0	2	2	2	1	4	0	0	0	.250	1	1	0	0	0
22 Max Cioffi	10.12	0-0	4	0	0	0/0	0	2.2	3	3	3	3	4	2	0	0	.333	1	0	0	1	0
55 Wes Burton	15.43	0-0	5	0	0	0/0	0	2.1	1	4	4	8	5	0	0	1	.143	0	0	0	0	0
Totals	4.21	42-23	65	65	2	3/2	18	564.1	510	295	264	234	682	97	7	72	.236	40	54	7	12	15
Opponents	7.08	23-42	65	65	0	1/1	8	551.1	610	483	434	295	606	120	9	108	.278	76	57	5	31	5

PB - Team (6), H. Dunhurst 5, K. Alderman 1, Opp (15). Pickoffs - Team (11), H. Elliott 4, H. Dunhurst 3, D. Diamond 2, J. Washburn 1, B. Johnson 1, Opp (1).

2021-22 Baseball Statistics - Pearl River Community College

Record: 45-11   Home: 20-4   Away: 15-5   Neutral: 10-2   Conf: 22-6

No.	Player	AVG	GP	GS	AB	R	H	2B	3B	HR	RBI	TB	SLG%	BB	HBP	SO	GDP	OB%	SF	SH	SB	CS	PO	A	E	FLD%
13	Tate Parker	.450	55	49	200	76	90	11	3	19	65	164	.820	29	11	30	1	.531	5	0	18	0	110	3	2	.983
17	Alex Perry	.385	56	48	187	69	72	6	1	17	62	131	.701	35	13	39	2	.506	2	0	22	2	31	62	9	.912
5	Gabe Broadus	.382	56	50	220	66	84	11	1	3	40	106	.482	33	5	38	2	.467	3	2	39	5	69	44	3	.974
23	D.K. Donaldson	.365	56	49	170	49	62	12	0	7	52	95	.559	29	20	11	0	.493	6	0	7	3	371	65	7	.984
14	Blake Hooks	.357	26	6	14	4	5	1	0	0	3	6	.429	2	0	3	0	.438	0	0	2	0	0	1	0	1.000
20	Will Passeau	.333	14	4	3	0	1	0	0	0	0	1	.333	0	0	1	0	.333	0	0	0	0	0	2	2	.500
12	Logan Walters	.322	47	39	146	45	47	13	0	9	46	87	.596	7	13	33	2	.396	3	0	8	2	19	1	0	1.000
21	Ian Montz	.310	55	48	168	52	52	9	2	13	50	104	.619	35	16	56	0	.464	3	1	21	5	60	3	2	.969
2	John Griffin Bell	.291	34	30	127	40	37	2	0	3	24	48	.378	16	13	12	2	.423	0	2	11	3	35	83	8	.937
3	Taylor Woodcock	.276	55	48	170	38	47	12	0	2	35	65	.382	34	6	31	4	.410	2	0	6	0	75	94	6	.966
4	Matt Mercer	.272	53	46	184	47	50	15	0	8	42	89	.484	17	17	46	4	.380	3	0	11	1	387	37	3	.993
7	Preston Soper	.269	41	23	108	25	29	10	0	4	29	51	.472	12	2	33	3	.344	3	0	7	2	13	9	0	1.000
11	Triston Hickman	.211	17	8	19	5	4	0	0	0	2	4	.211	3	6	8	0	.464	0	0	1	0	60	4	4	.941
22	Ryan Burt	.188	25	6	16	3	3	1	0	0	2	4	.250	3	4	8	0	.435	0	0	0	2	0	3	0	1.000
10	Mason Smith	.000	9	0	1	0	0	-	-	-	0	0	.000	-	-	-	-	.000	-	-	-	-	0	0	0	-
9	Cole Tolbert	.000	20	3	1	0	0	0	0	0	0	0	.000	0	0	1	0	.000	0	0	0	0	2	6	1	.889
	Total	.336	56	56	1734	519	583	103	7	85	452	955	.551	255	126	350	20	.449	30	5	153	25	1248	471	58	.967
	Opponents	.253	56	56	1540	259	390	60	4	40	220	578	.375	201	55	446	17	.357	14	19	69	15	1154	343	86	.946

No.	Player	ERA	W	L	APP	GS	CG	SHO	SV	IP	H	R	ER	BB	SO	2B	3B	HR	AB	B/AVG	WP	HBP	BK	SFA	SHA
33	Parker Harrington	0.00	0	0	5	0	-	-	0	1.2	2	1	-	1	1	-	-	-	7	.286	-	-	-	-	-
9	Cole Tolbert	2.40	3	1	18	3	0	0	3	45.0	30	14	12	23	60	0	0	3	190	.158	8	4	0	0	0
18	Landen Payne	2.88	4	3	15	0	0	0	0	25.0	11	11	8	9	37	0	0	1	96	.115	2	3	0	0	0
22	Ryan Burt	3.43	3	0	13	0	0	0	0	21.0	19	8	8	7	15	2	0	2	77	.247	3	1	0	0	0
14	Blake Hooks	3.57	2	0	16	0	0	0	1	17.2	13	9	7	6	17	1	0	0	61	.213	2	2	0	0	1
15	Turner Swistak	4.15	6	0	16	11	-	-	0	60.2	69	34	28	11	58	2	1	8	185	.373	2	7	2	1	1
25	Dakota Lee	4.43	8	0	16	12	0	0	0	65.0	63	32	32	21	45	3	0	5	238	.265	7	8	0	1	0
15	Leif Moore	4.53	6	3	14	13	2	1	0	45.2	47	32	23	22	42	4	-	6	178	.264	4	4	0	1	2
.	Byrion Robinson	4.85	1	1	14	0	0	0	0	13.0	10	9	7	15	18	1	0	0	46	.217	4	1	0	0	0
3	Sam Hill	4.87	4	2	13	13	2	1	0	40.2	43	27	22	22	50	1	0	6	158	.272	3	3	0	0	2
10	Will Passeau	5.86	0	0	11	4	-	-	1	27.2	27	23	18	18	33	1	-	3	121	.223	5	6	-	-	-
6	Bobby Magee	6.05	1	0	15	0	0	0	0	19.1	22	15	13	15	30	1	0	2	76	.289	3	1	0	0	0
0	Mason Smith	6.75	0	0	6	0	-	-	0	4.0	10	4	3	2	6	-	-	-	17	.588	-	2	-	-	-
19	Harper Jordan	6.91	0	1	13	0	0	0	0	14.1	16	14	11	15	19	2	0	0	98	.163	4	1	0	0	0
14	Dawson Strong	7.36	0	0	5	0	-	-	0	3.2	0	4	3	6	4	-	-	-	10	.000	1	-	-	-	-
18	Jordan Belsome	15.43	0	0	7	0	0	0	0	4.2	9	8	8	6	7	0	0	2	22	.409	0	1	0	0	0
	Total	4.47	42	11	56	56	4	5	5	409.0	391	245	203	199	442	18	1	38	1580	.247	48	44	2	3	6
	Opponents	9.43	9	39	56	56	1	0	3	395.0	548	500	414	242	344	28	2	79	1734	.365	62	122	3	8	1

WHEN MISSISSIPPI SCHOOLED AMERICA IN BASEBALL

Jaguars
Madison, MS · Prep Baseball

Spring 2021

34-2

Scores Live · Active

Batting | Pitching | Fielding | Quality At-Bat Differential

Batting Stats

Standard | Patience, Speed & Power | QABs & Team Impact

Show stats for: Qualifying Games (?)
Filter by date range: Feb 22 vs Oak Grove to Jun 5 vs Northwest Rankin

#	Roster	GP	PA	AB	H	1B	2B	3B	HR	RBI	R	HBP	ROE	FC	CI	BB	SO	AVG	OBP	SLG	OPS
36	Austin Tommasini	2	3	1	0	0	0	0	0	0	0	0	0	0	0	2	1	.000	.667	.000	.667
2	Beau Bryans	23	75	65	17	16	1	0	0	14	17	1	3	1	0	4	14	.262	.293	.277	.570
6	Braden Montgomery	35	134	96	46	27	7	5	7	50	30	2	4	2	0	31	18	.479	.590	.875	1.465
29	Brendon Minor	2	0	0	0	0	0	0	0	0	0	0	0	0	0	0	0	.000	.000	.000	.000
33	Caleb Thompson	2	1	1	1	1	0	0	0	2	2	0	0	0	0	0	0	1.000	1.000	1.000	2.000
8	Connor Chisolm	35	119	93	40	30	8	1	1	26	36	5	6	1	0	19	12	.430	.542	.570	1.112
11	Connor Nation	35	120	102	39	16	16	3	4	42	35	4	4	4	0	13	14	.382	.471	.716	1.186
4	Creek Robertson	33	114	80	26	18	7	0	1	29	31	4	2	2	0	26	16	.325	.496	.450	.946
5	Dillan Smith	7	10	8	4	2	2	0	0	1	4	2	0	0	0	0	3	.500	.600	.750	1.350
1	Gatlin Sanders	35	145	104	45	37	7	1	0	29	65	8	9	4	0	28	7	.433	.570	.519	1.090
18	Hunter Hines	35	131	99	46	27	12	0	7	55	38	9	6	2	0	21	13	.465	.580	.798	1.378
23	Jackson Mize	22	47	36	8	7	1	0	0	12	11	1	0	0	0	10	9	.222	.404	.250	.654
26	Jake Cook	34	111	86	41	35	3	3	0	27	42	1	2	0	0	24	10	.477	.595	.581	1.176
16	Jake Norris	1	1	1	0	0	0	0	0	0	1	0	1	0	0	0	0	.000	.000	.000	.000
38	John Nolan Pajak	18	10	8	4	4	0	0	0	3	16	1	0	0	0	0	0	.500	.500	.500	1.000
13	Mason Winans	1	3	3	2	1	1	0	0	1	2	0	1	0	0	0	0	.667	.667	1.000	1.667
20	Matthew Reed	7	6	4	2	1	1	0	0	2	3	2	0	0	0	0	1	.500	.667	.750	1.417
19	Renard Grace	1	1	1	0	0	0	0	0	0	0	0	0	0	0	0	0	.000	.000	.000	.000
24	Rashard Grace	13	18	9	5	2	3	0	0	8	3	1	0	0	0	7	2	.556	.722	.889	1.611
	Totals	38	1265	966	388	264	81	16	27	366	421	54	49	22	0	216	153	.402	.523	.602	1.125

ttps://gc.com/t/spring-2021/jaguars-5fc656acf74a8fdc1541bc32/stats

JAMES R. CROCKETT

Jaguars
Madison, MS · Prep Baseball

Spring 2021
34-2
Scores Live · Active

Batting | **Pitching** | Fielding | Quality At-Bat Differential

Pitching Stats

Standard | Efficiency | Command | Batter Results | Runs & Running Game | Pitch Breakdown

Show stats for: Qualifying Games

Filter by date range: Feb 22 vs Oak Grove to Jun 5 vs Northwest Rankin

#	Roster	IP	GP	GS	W	L	SV	SVO	BS	SV%	H	R	ER	BB	SO	HBP
36	Austin Tommasini	32.1	11	3	6	1	1	1	0	1.000	19	10	8	17	42	9
2	Beau Bryans	11.1	5	5	2	0	0	0	0	.000	4	3	3	8	23	1
6	Braden Montgomery	56.2	15	11	9	0	0	0	0	.000	17	11	6	27	116	9
29	Brendon Minor	21.1	8	4	5	0	0	0	0	.000	5	3	0	16	31	1
11	Connor Nation	22.0	13	1	2	1	3	3	0	1.000	17	13	7	14	37	5
21	Eric Gibbs	15.0	6	1	1	0	0	0	0	.000	11	5	2	1	18	5
26	Jake Cook	0.0	1	0	0	0	0	0	0	.000	0	0	0	0	0	0
19	Renard Grace	54.1	11	11	10	0	0	0	0	.000	40	19	13	17	77	14
Totals		213.0	36	36	34	2	4	4	0	1.000	113	64	39	100	344	44

IP: Innings Pitched
GP: Games pitched
GS: Games started as the pitcher
W: Wins
L: Losses

SV: Saves
SVO: Save opportunities
BS: Blown saves
SV%: Save percentage
H: Hits allowed

R: Runs allowed
ER: Earned runs allowed
BB: Base on balls (walks)
SO: Strikeouts
HBP: Hit batters

ERA: Earned run average (season)
WHIP: Walks plus hits per innings pitch

Export Season Stats (.csv) All stats can be edited from the game. Visit Schedule to adjust stats for a specific game.

GC CLASSIC
Download the App
Create Your Team
Find Teams
Pricing

CONNECT
Help
Product Blog
Tech Blog

ACKNOWLEDGEMENTS

I would like to thank my wife, Dorothy Crockett, my most loyal supporter and, as always, my first reader. I am also grateful to my son, Clint Crockett, my second reader and a huge baseball fan. I owe a debt of gratitude to Frank Montgomery, my friend and an All-American pitcher at MSU, who was a great help on my last two books. Finally, I would like to acknowledge the professional staff at the Nautilus Publishing for their support and assistance.

SOURCES

Books
Dawg Pile
– By Steve Robertson, Crain Publishing Group, LLC (2021)
Resilient Rebels
– Written and published by Chase Parham (2022)

Newspapers
Clarion Ledger
Daily Journal
Enid News Eagle
Hattiesburg American
Northside Sun
Oxford Eagle

Websites
247sports.com/college/ole-miss/
clarionledger.com
clarionledger.newspapers.com
djournal.com
en.wikipedia.org/wiki/College World_Series
espncdn.com
facj.edu
hailstate.com
lcc.edu
madisoncollege.edu
madison-schools.com
maxpreps.com/ms/madison/madison-central-jaguars/baseball
mcbigblue.com
misstate.edu
misshsaa.com

ncaa.com/sports/baseball/d1
ncaa.com/championships/baseball/d1
njcaa.org
olemiss.edu
olemisssports.com
prccathletics.com
prcc.edu
secsports.com
starkvilledailynews.com
wikipedia

Interviews
Michael Avalon
Mike Bianco
Gabe Broadus
Chris Lemonis
Will Passeau
Patrick Robey
Ron Polk
Landon Sims
Logan Walters

Other
Ole Miss Alumni Review, Summer 2022
Pearl River Community College Baseball 2022 Brochure

About the Author

Jim Crockett is Professor Emeritus of Accountancy at the University of Southern Mississippi (USM). He earned degrees from both Ole Miss and Mississippi State And he has held faculty positions at the University of West Florida, Ole Miss, and the University of Southern Mississippi. Crockett retired as a Lt. Colonel from the U.S. Air Force Reserve. Crockett's previous books include *Operation Pretense, Hands in the Till, Power Greed Hubris* and *Rulers of the SEC* (all published by University Press of Mississippi). He is married to the former Dorothy Douglas and they have two grown sons, four grandchildren, and a great grandchild. He is a life-long sports fan.

www.ingramcontent.com/pod-product-compliance
Lightning Source LLC
Chambersburg PA
CBHW020051170426
43199CB00009B/242